40 MOST-STREAMED Disney SONGS

ISBN 978-1-5400-5656-6

For all works contained herein:

Visit Hal Leonard Online at
www.halleonard.com

Contact us:
Hal Leonard
7777 West Bluemound Road
Milwaukee, WI 53213
Email: info@halleonard.com

In Europe, contact:
Hal Leonard Europe Limited
42 Wigmore Street
Marylebone, London, W1U 2RN
Email: info@halleonardeurope.com

In Australia, contact:
Hal Leonard Australia Pty. Ltd.
4 Lentara Court
Cheltenham, Victoria, 3192 Australia
Email: info@halleonard.com.au

CONTENTS

BEAUTY AND THE BEAST

from BEAUTY AND THE BEAST

Music by ALAN MENKEN
Lyrics by HOWARD ASHMAN

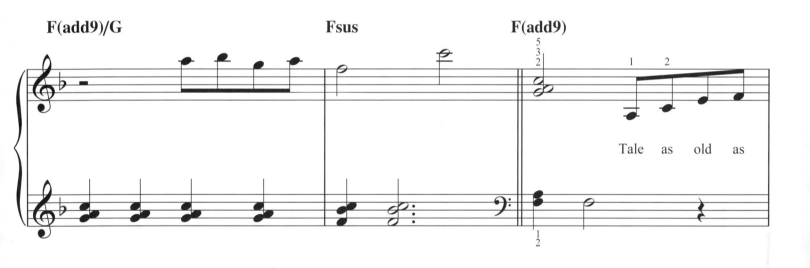

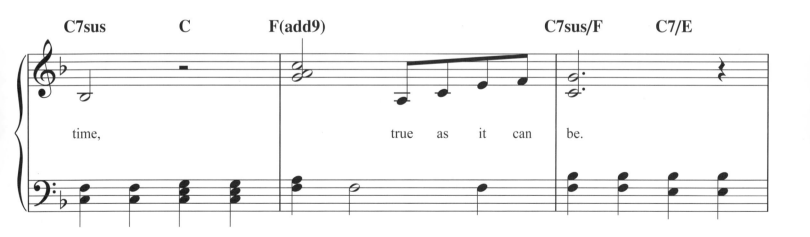

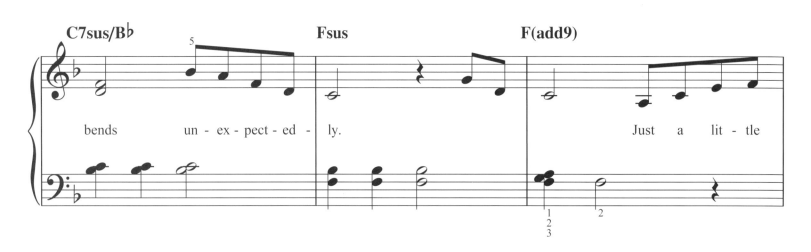

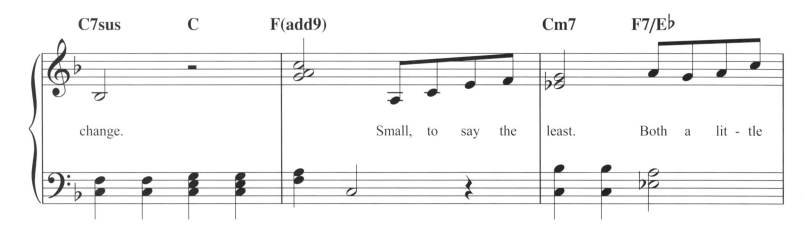

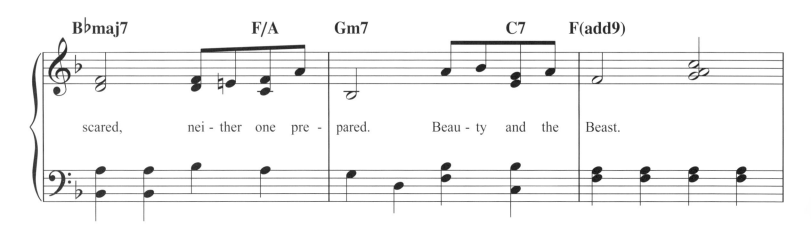

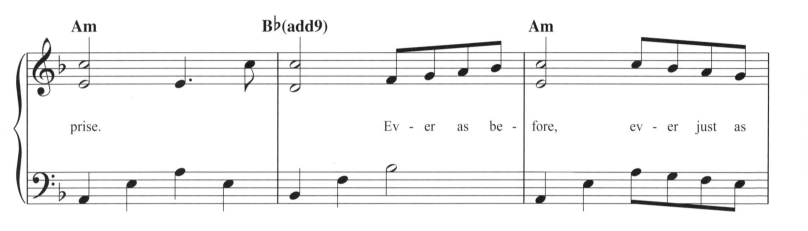

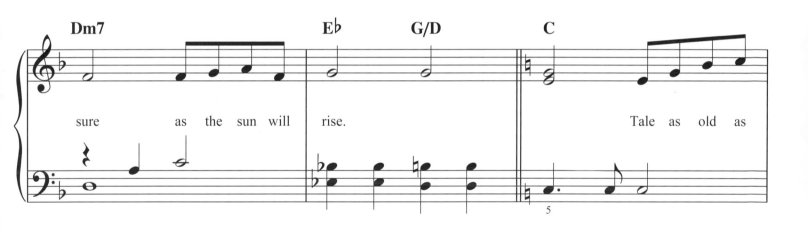

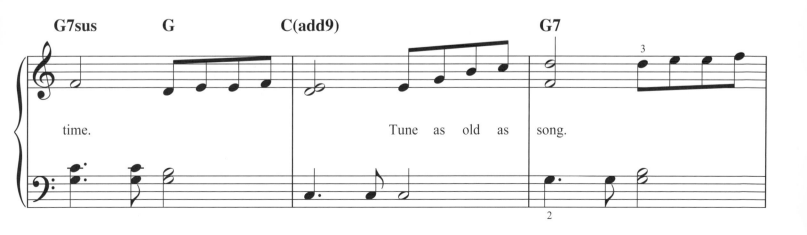

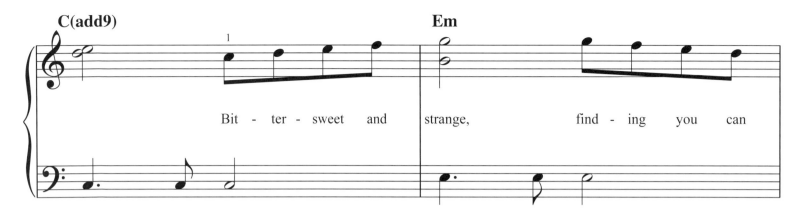

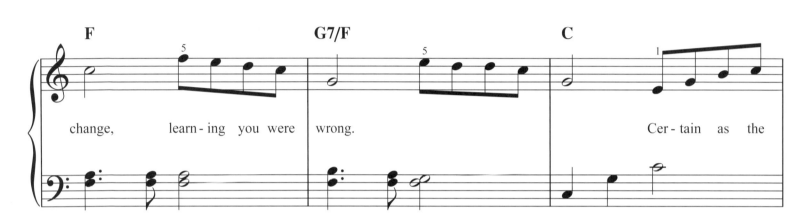

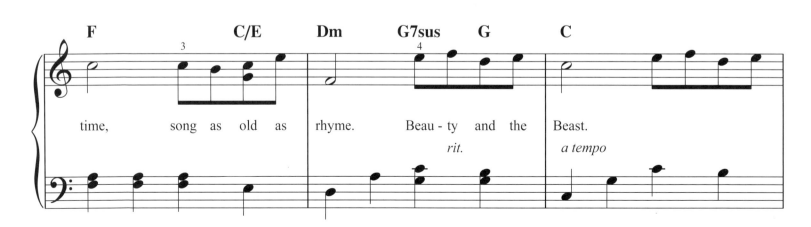

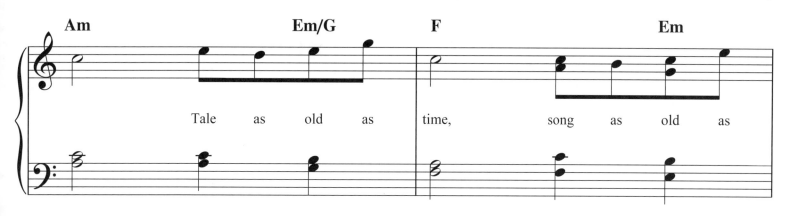

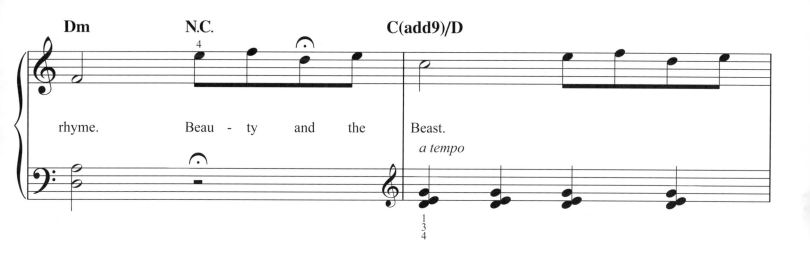

ALMOST THERE

from THE PRINCESS AND THE FROG

Music and Lyrics by
RANDY NEWMAN

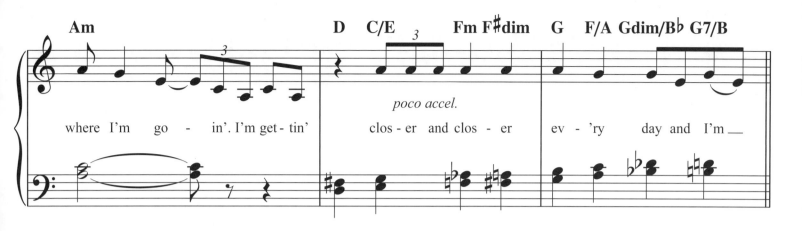

where I'm go - in'. I'm get-tin' / clos - er and clos - er / ev - 'ry day and I'm ___

poco accel.

Moderately fast, steady (in 2)

al - most there, / I'm al - most there. ___

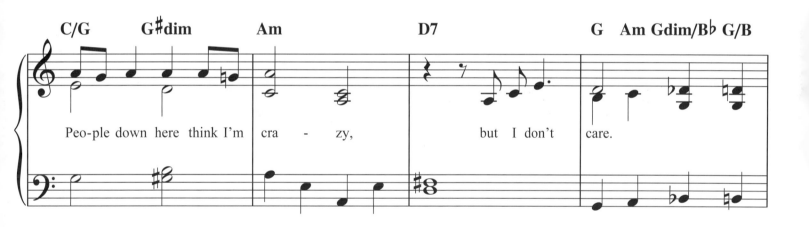

Peo-ple down here think I'm cra - zy, / but I don't care.

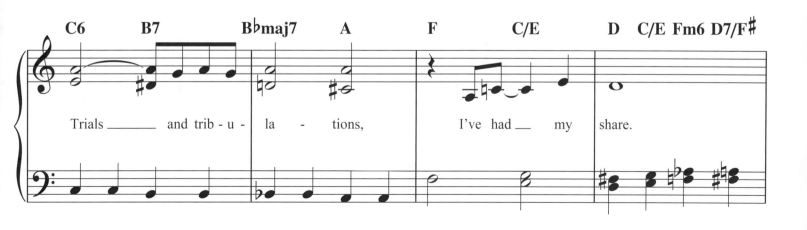

Trials ___ and trib - u - la - tions, / I've had ___ my share.

10

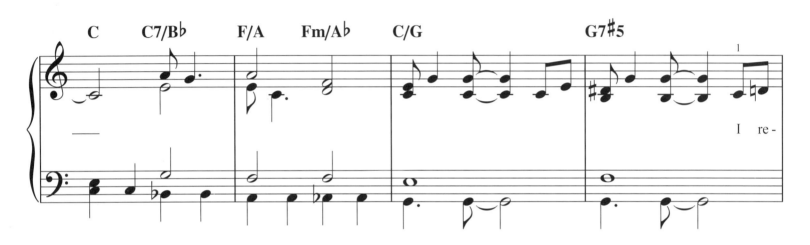

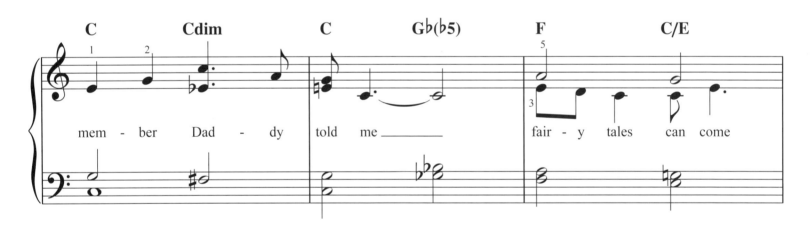

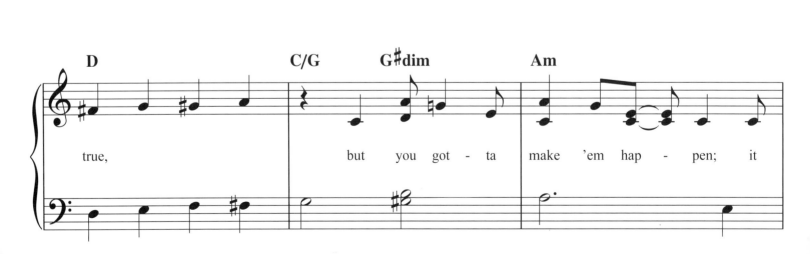

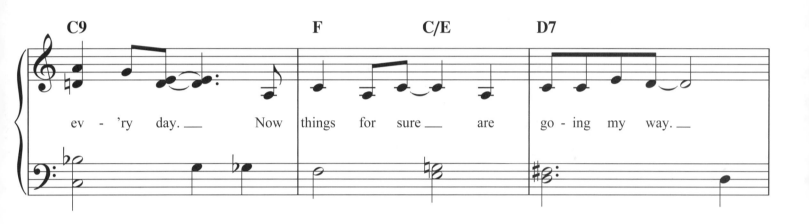

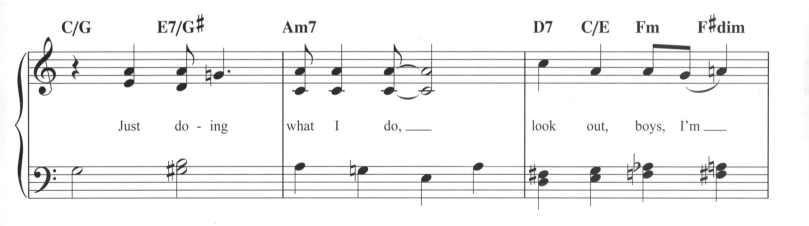

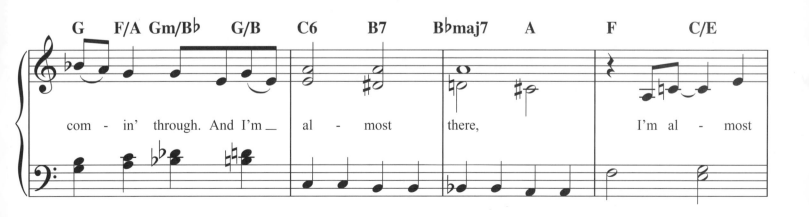

D   C/E   Fm6 D7/F♯   C/E   G♯dim   Am

there.   Peo - ple gon - na come here from   ev - 'ry - where, ___ and I'm

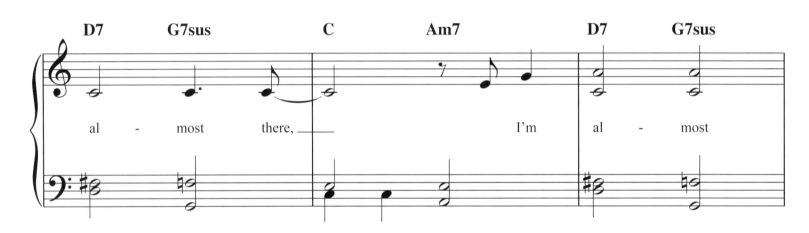

D7   G7sus   C   Am7   D7   G7sus

al - most   there, ___   I'm   al - most

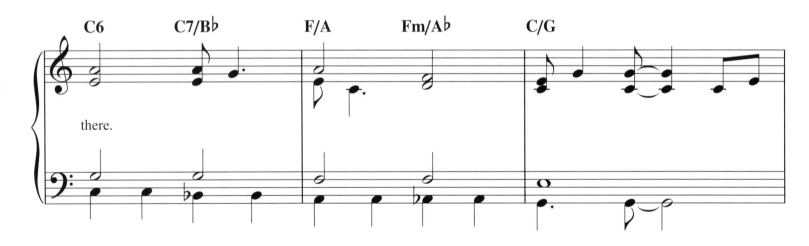

C6   C7/B♭   F/A   Fm/A♭   C/G

there.

Slower

G7♯5   D9/F♯   G7♯5/F   C7sus/F   C7

There've been trials   and   trib - u - la - tions.

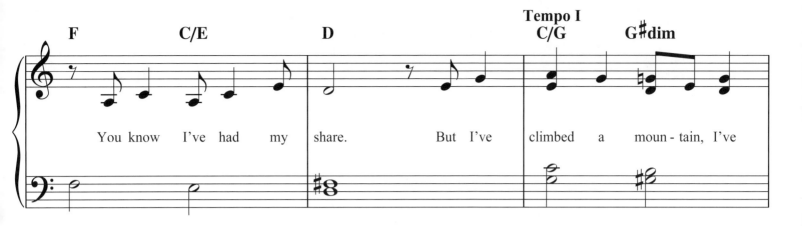

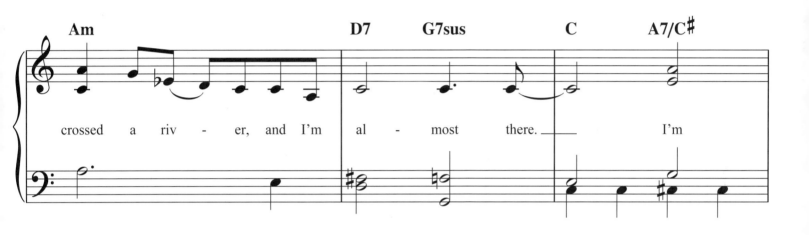

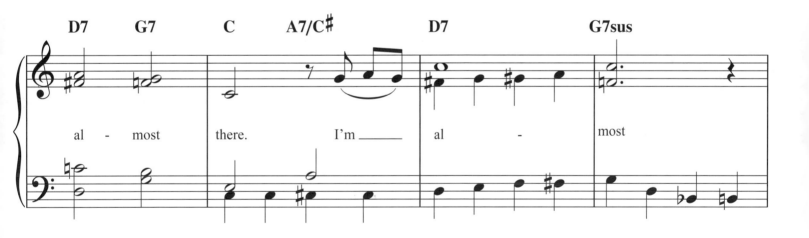

BE OUR GUEST

from BEAUTY AND THE BEAST (2017)

Music by ALAN MENKEN
Lyrics by HOWARD ASHMAN

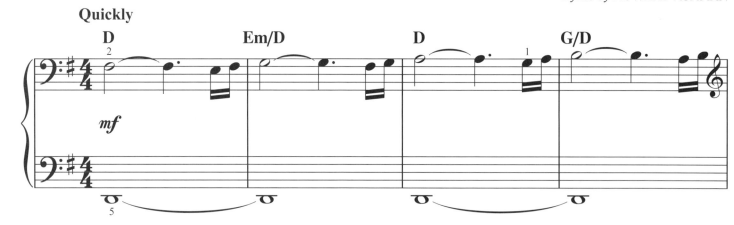

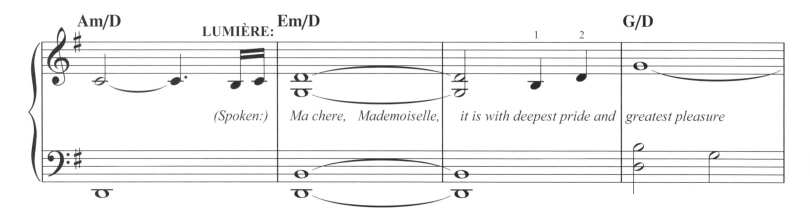

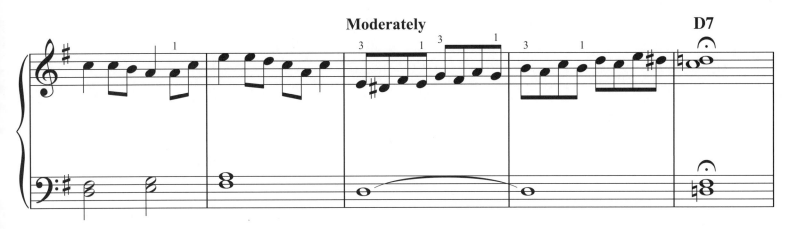

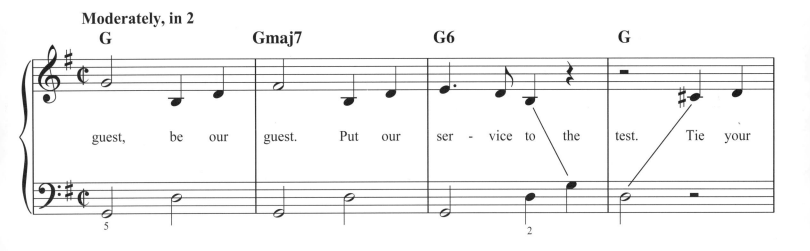

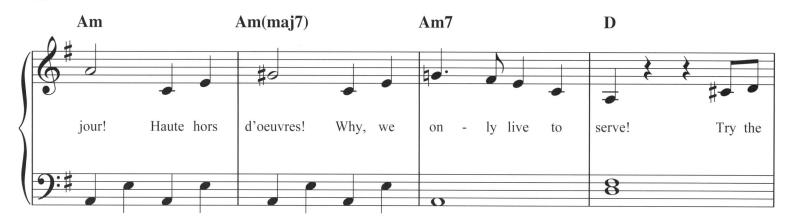

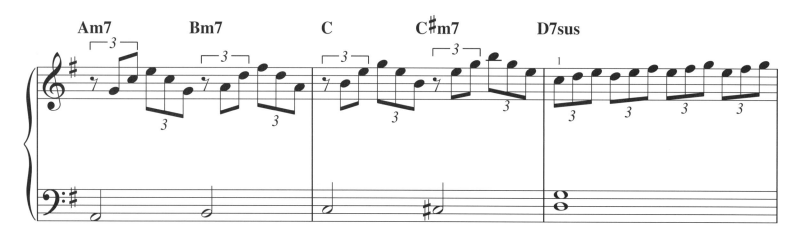

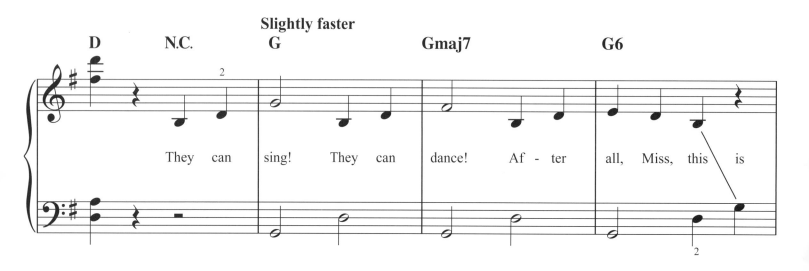

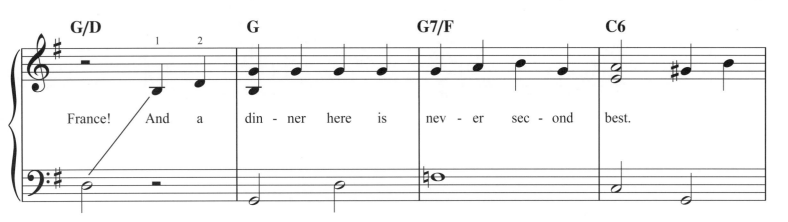

France! And a din-ner here is nev-er sec-ond best.

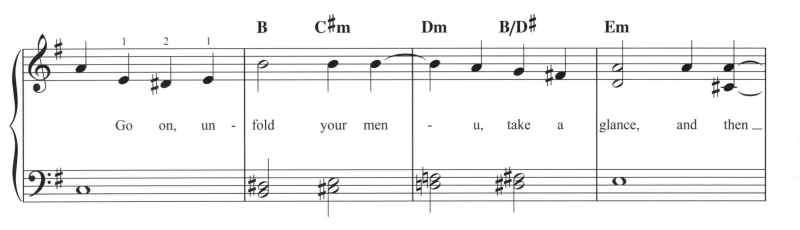

Go on, un-fold your men - u, take a glance, and then __

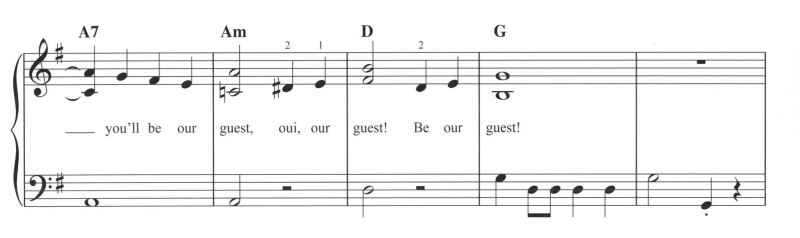

__ you'll be our guest, oui, our guest! Be our guest!

Beef ra -

Slightly faster

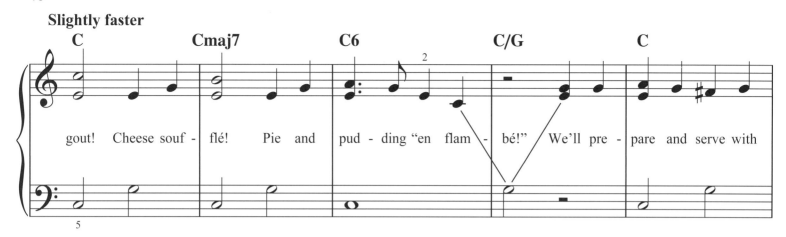

gout! Cheese souf - flé! Pie and pud - ding "en flam - bé!" We'll pre - pare and serve with

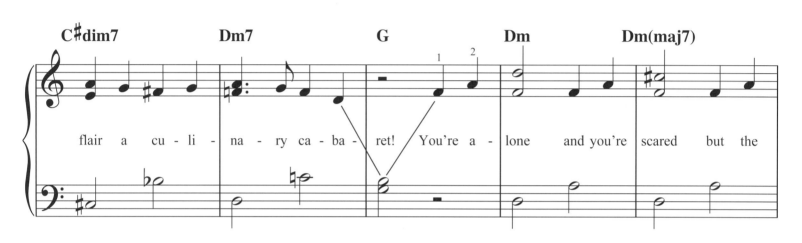

flair a cu - li - na - ry ca - ba - ret! You're a - lone and you're scared but the

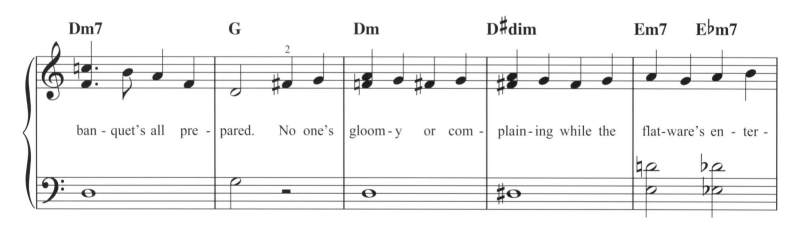

ban - quet's all pre - pared. No one's gloom - y or com - plain - ing while the flat - ware's en - ter -

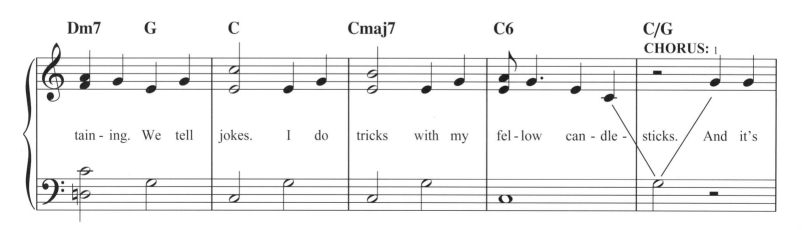

tain - ing. We tell jokes. I do tricks with my fel - low can - dle - sticks. And it's

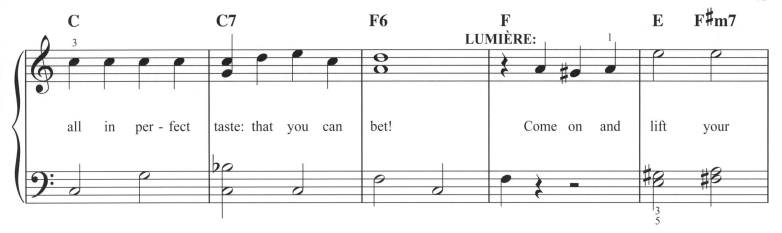

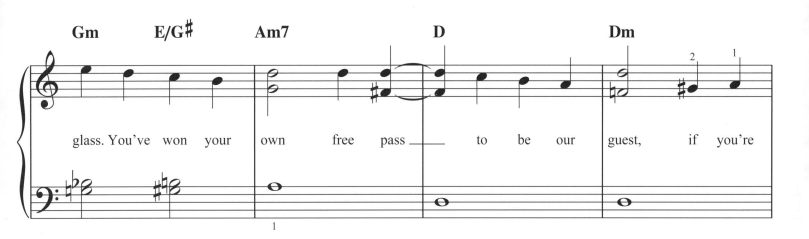

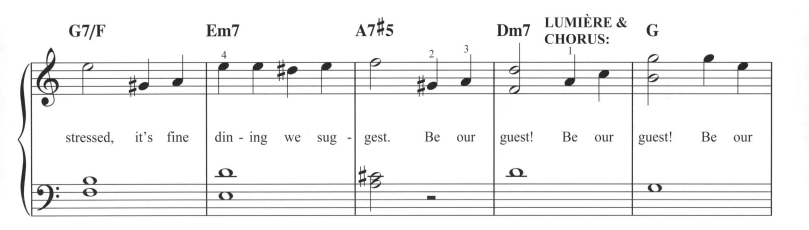

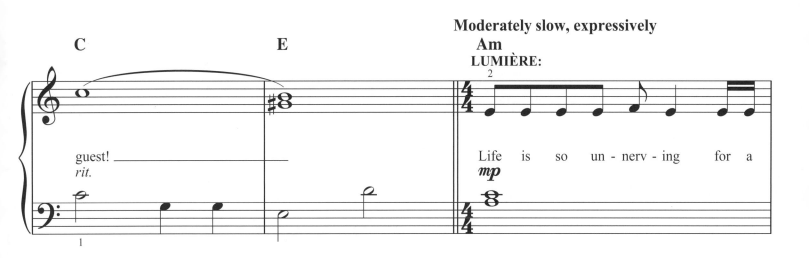

20

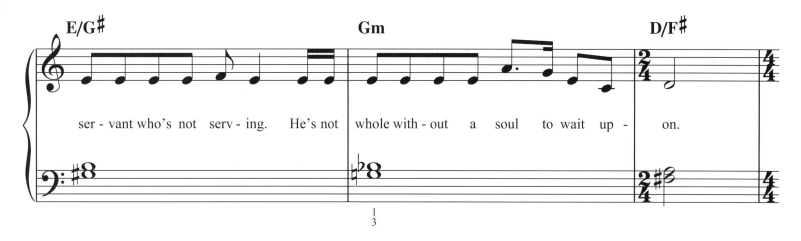

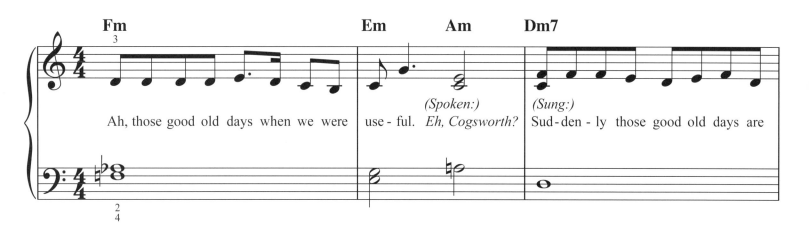

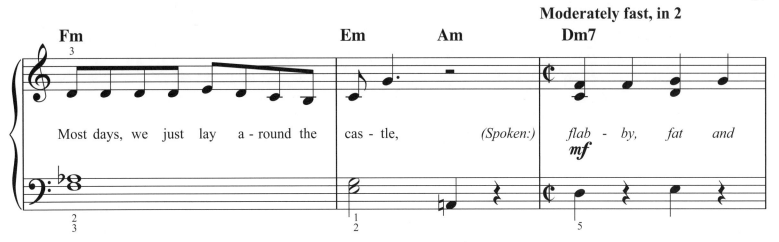

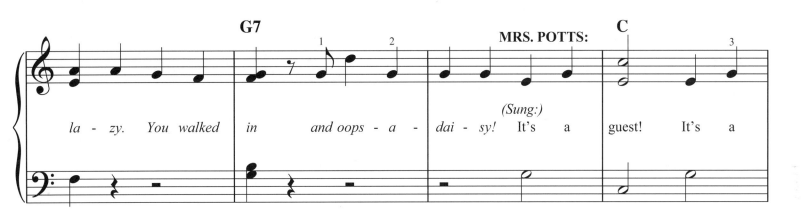

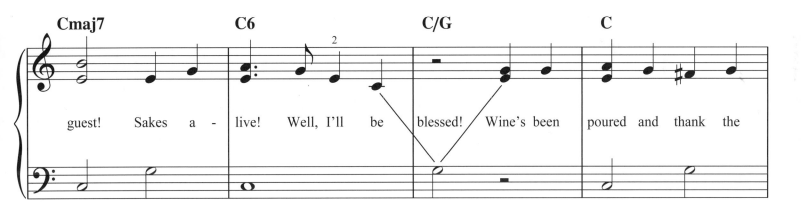

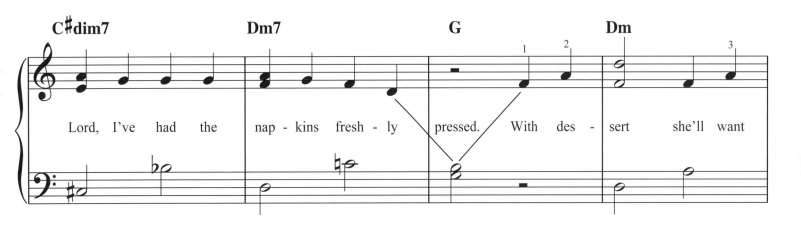

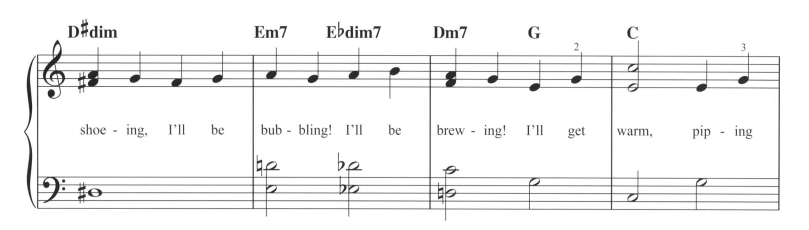

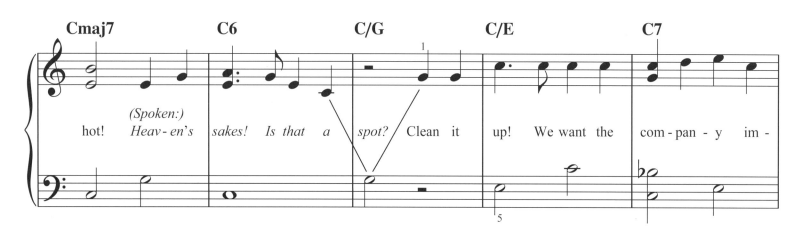

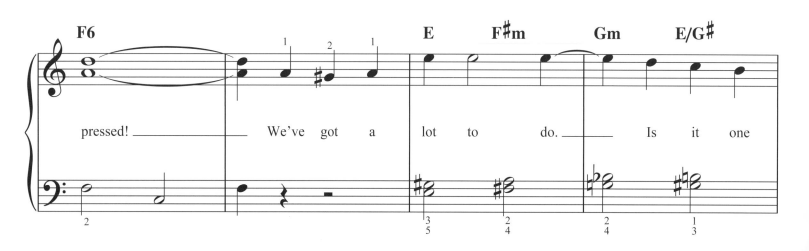

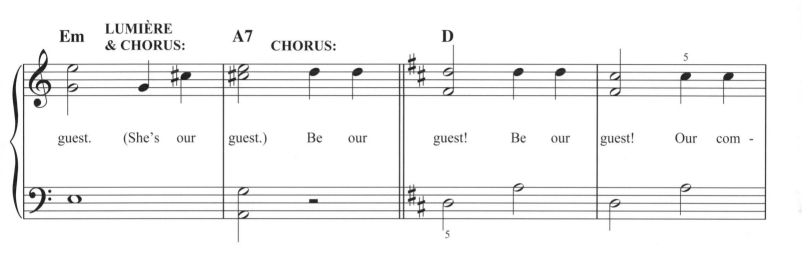

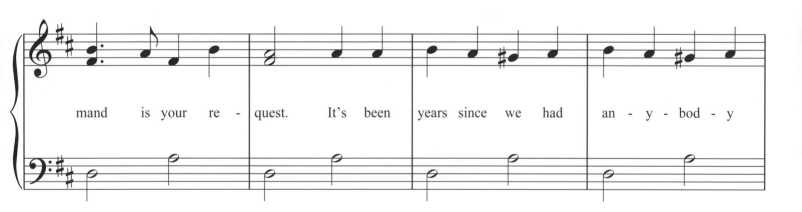

24

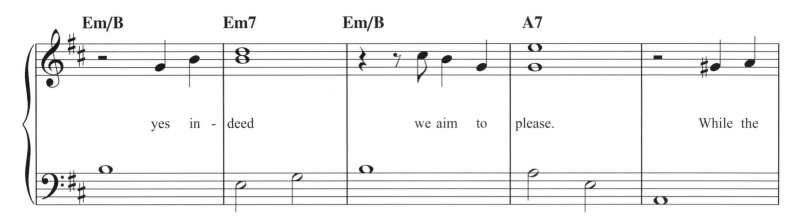

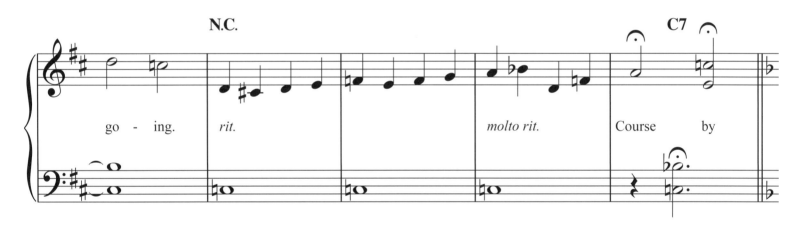

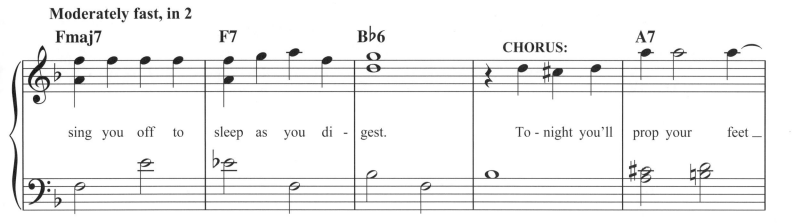

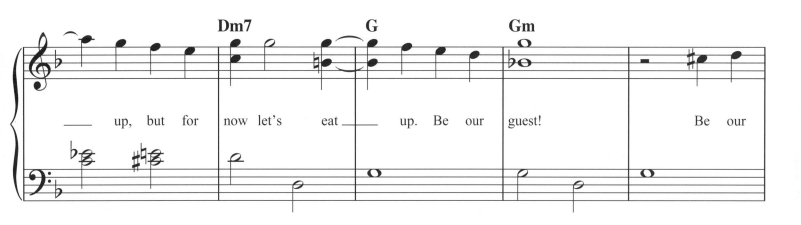

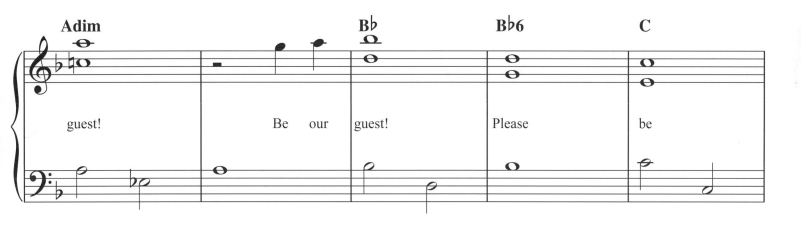

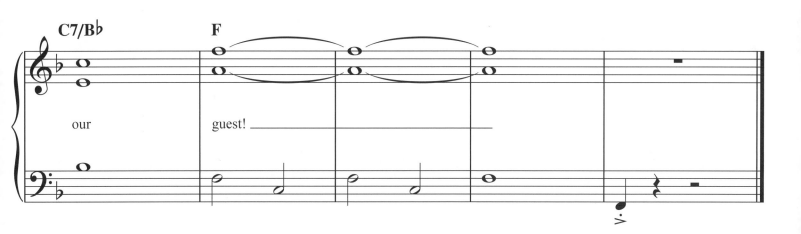

BELLE
from BEAUTY AND THE BEAST (2017)

Music by ALAN MENKEN
Lyrics by HOWARD ASHMAN

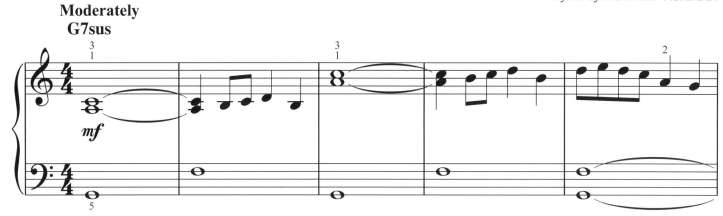

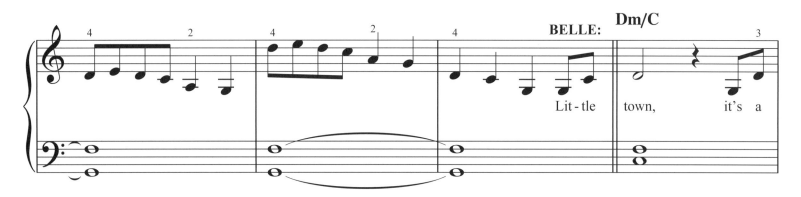

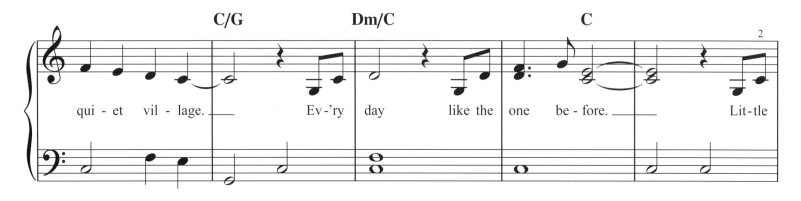

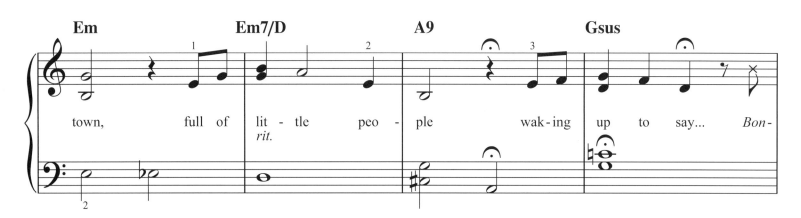

Moderately fast, in 2

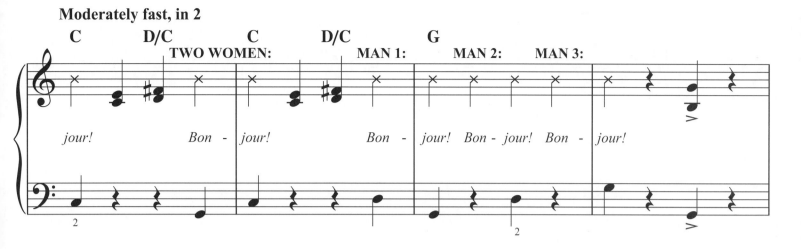

TWO WOMEN: **MAN 1:** **MAN 2:** **MAN 3:**

jour! Bon - jour! Bon - jour! Bon - jour! Bon - jour!

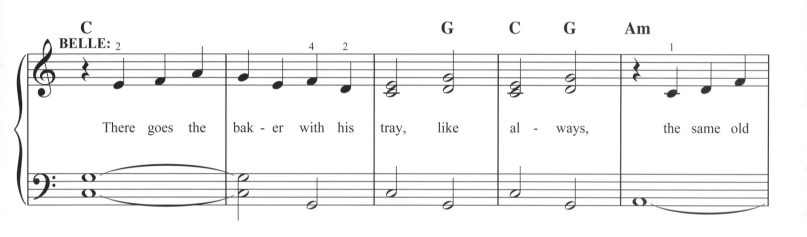

BELLE:

There goes the bak - er with his tray, like al - ways, the same old

bread and rolls to sell. Ev - 'ry morn - ing just the

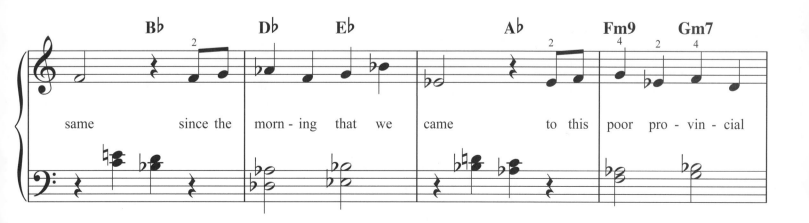

same since the morn - ing that we came to this poor pro - vin - cial

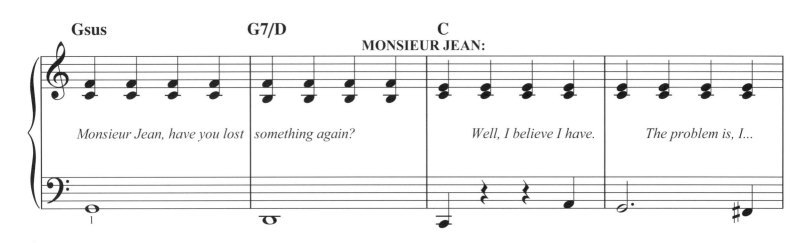

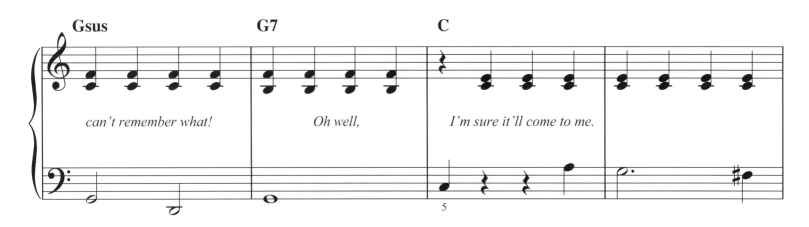

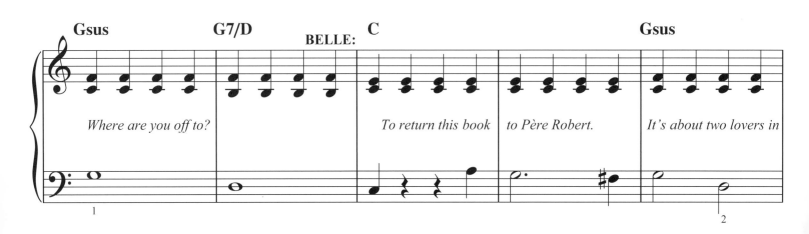

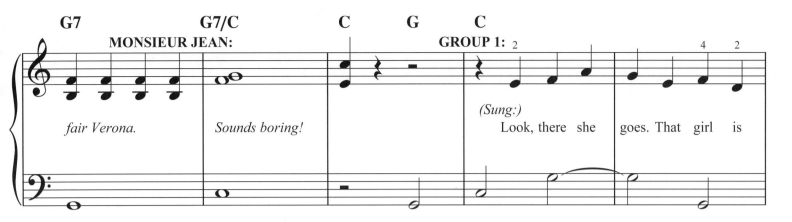

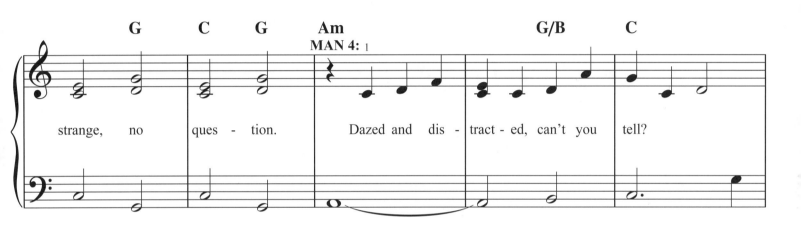

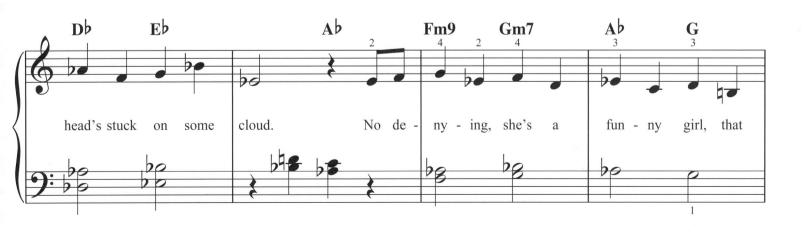

30

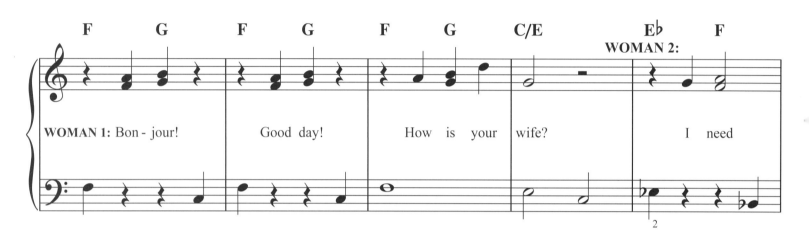

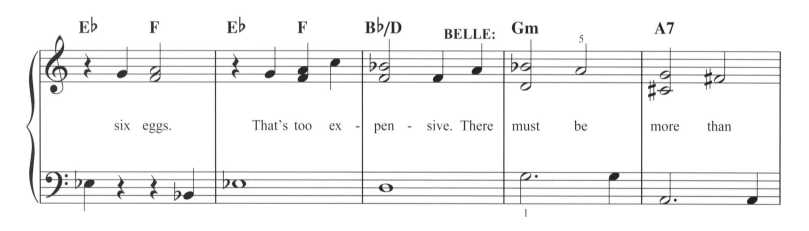

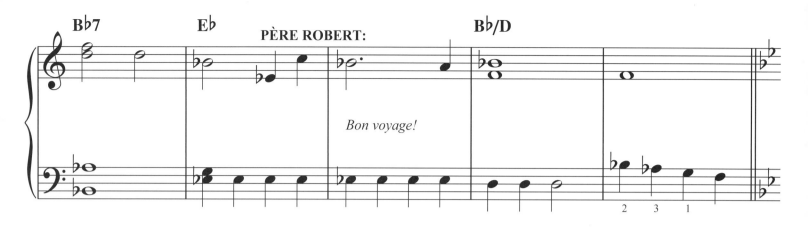

PÈRE ROBERT:

Bon voyage!

MEN:

Look, there she goes. The girl is so pe-

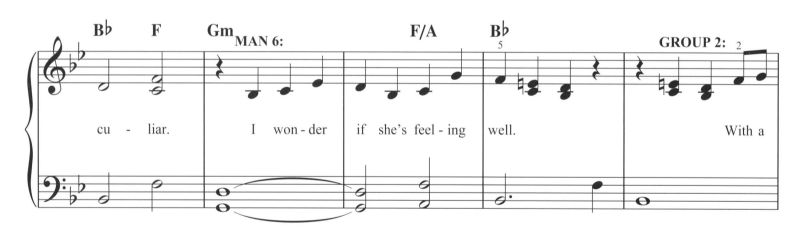

MAN 6:

cu - liar. I won-der if she's feel-ing well.

GROUP 2:

With a

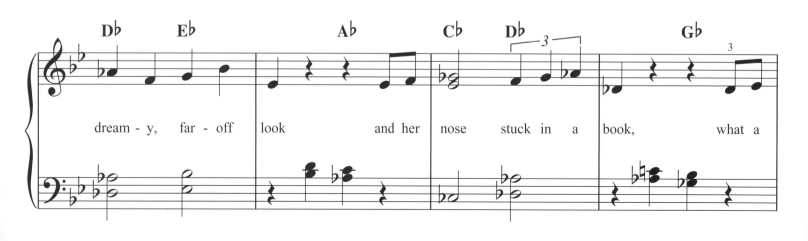

dream - y, far - off look and her nose stuck in a book, what a

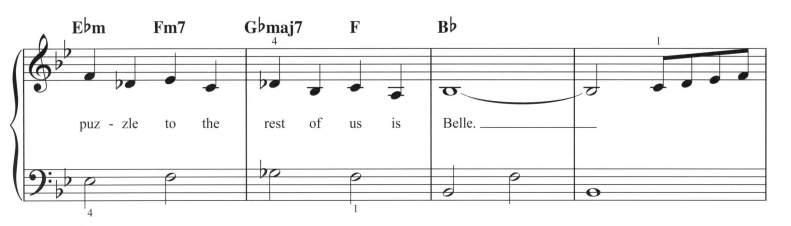

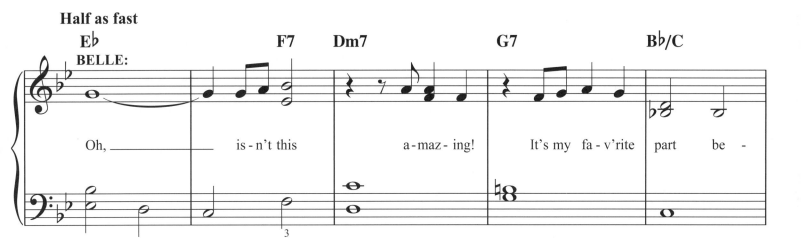

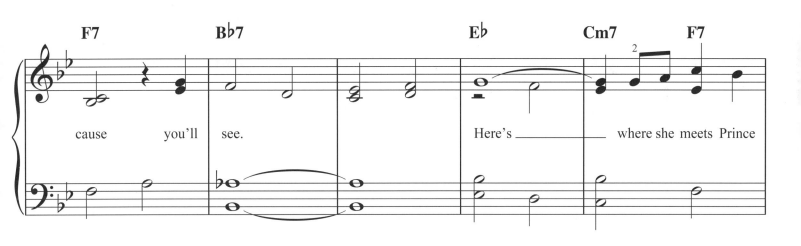

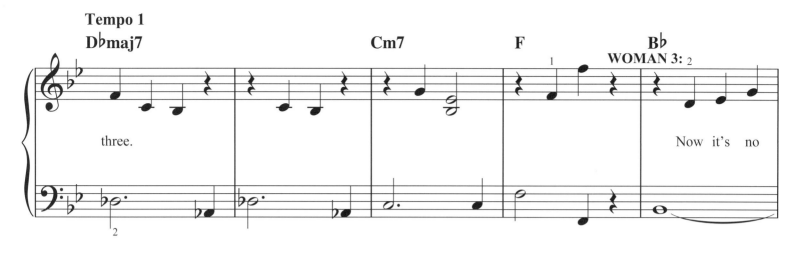

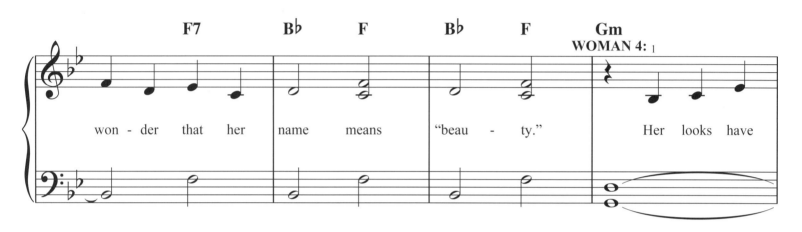

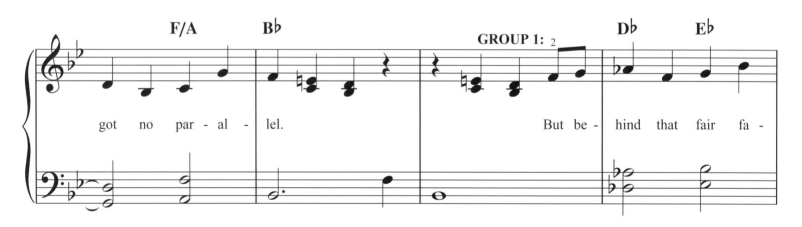

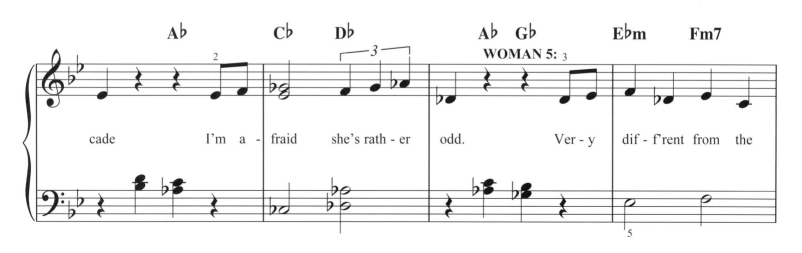

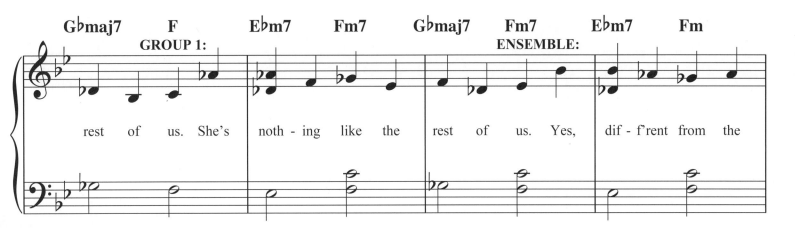

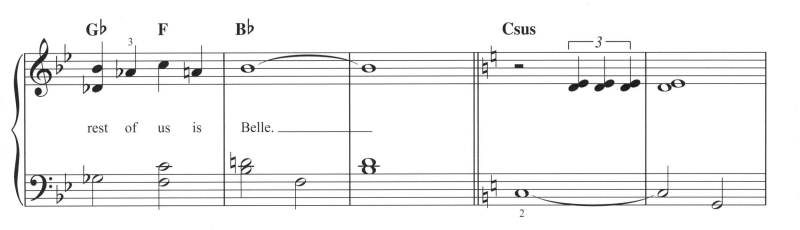

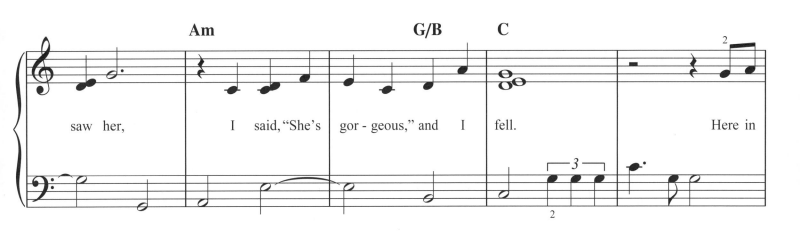

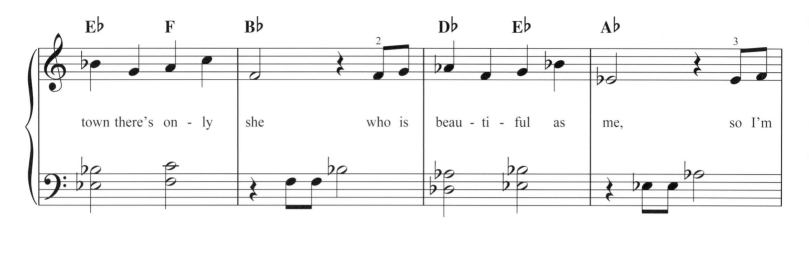

town there's on - ly she who is beau - ti - ful as me, so I'm

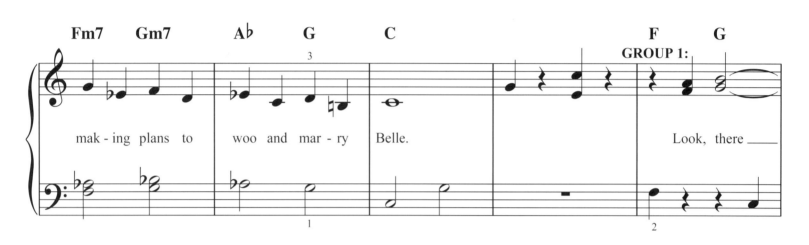

mak - ing plans to woo and mar - ry Belle.

GROUP 1:

Look, there ____

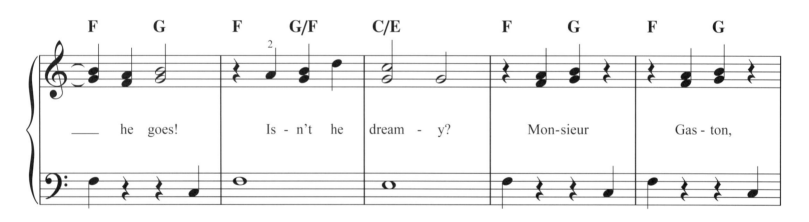

____ he goes! Is - n't he dream - y? Mon - sieur Gas - ton,

oh, he's so cute. Be still ____ my heart! I'm hard - ly

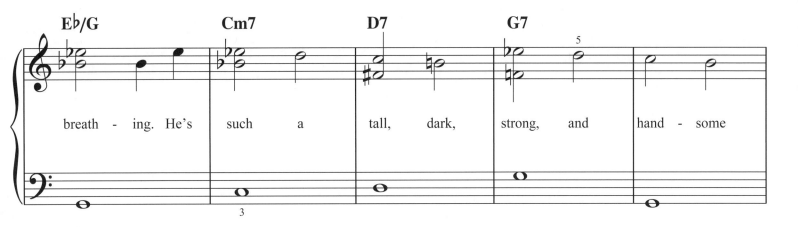

E♭/G   **Cm7**   **D7**   **G7**

breath - ing. He's such a tall, dark, strong, and hand - some

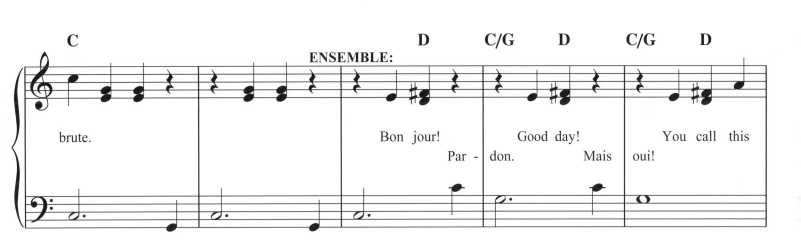

C   **D**   **C/G**   **D**   **C/G**   **D**

ENSEMBLE:

brute.   Bon jour!   Good day!   You call this

Par - don.   Mais oui!

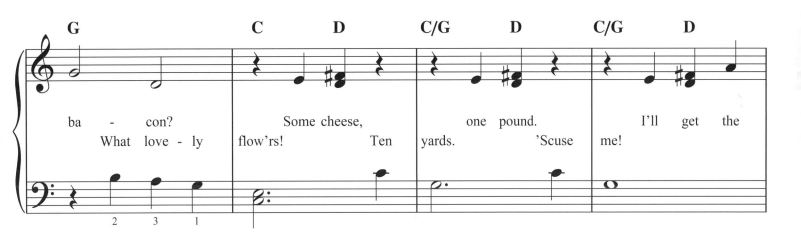

G   **C**   **D**   **C/G**   **D**   **C/G**   **D**

ba - con?   Some cheese,   one pound.   I'll get the

What love - ly flow'rs!   Ten yards.   'Scuse me!

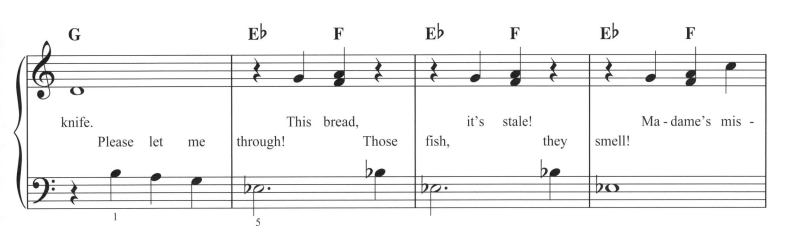

G   **E♭**   **F**   **E♭**   **F**   **E♭**   **F**

knife.   This bread,   it's stale!   Ma - dame's mis -

Please let me through!   Those fish, they smell!

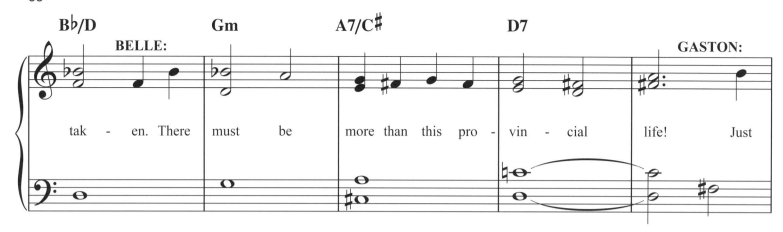

BELLE: tak - en. There must be more than this pro - vin - cial life! **GASTON:** Just

watch! I'm go - ing to make Belle my wife.

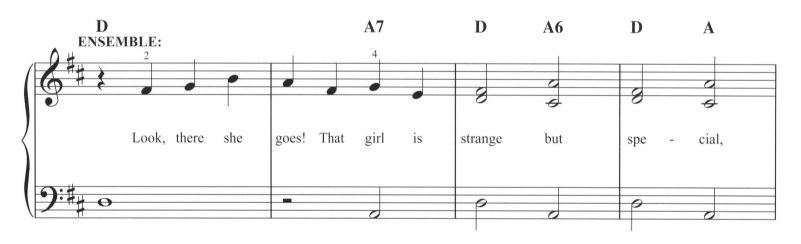

ENSEMBLE: Look, there she goes! That girl is strange but spe - cial,

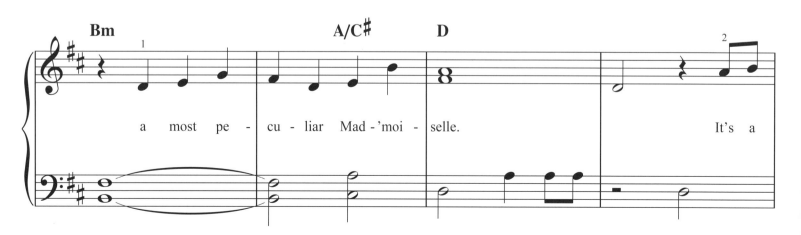

a most pe - cu - liar Mad -'moi - selle. It's a

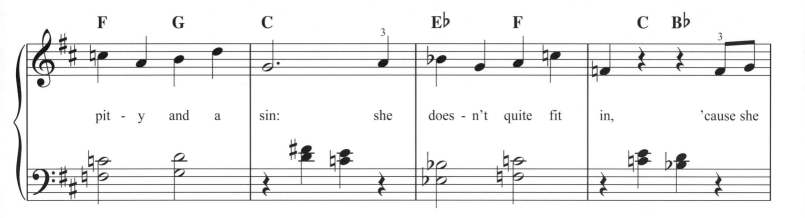

pit - y and a sin: she does - n't quite fit in, 'cause she

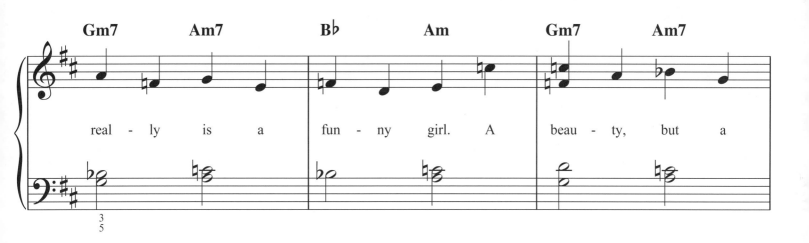

real - ly is a fun - ny girl. A beau - ty, but a

fun - ny girl. She real - ly is a fun - ny girl, ___

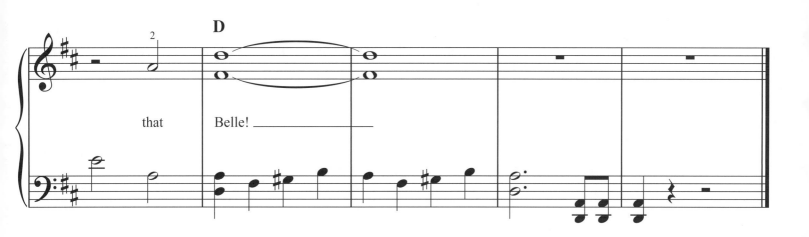

that Belle! ___

CAN YOU FEEL THE LOVE TONIGHT
from THE LION KING 2019

Music by ELTON JOHN
Lyrics by TIM RICE

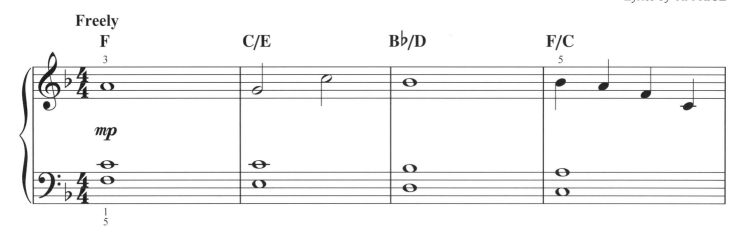

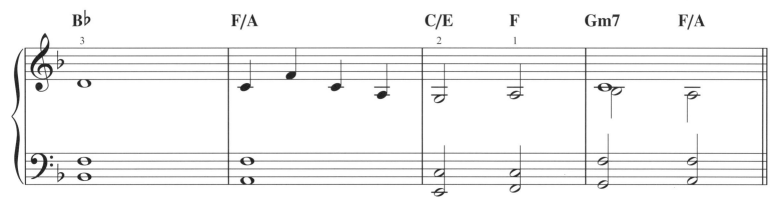

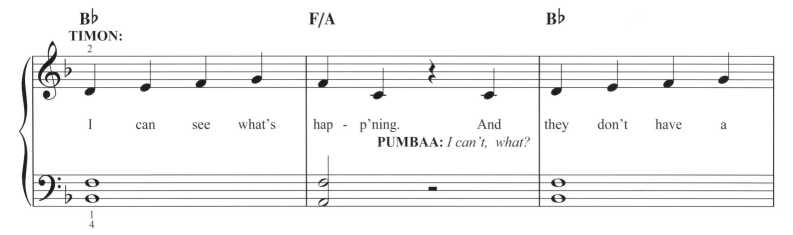

I can see what's hap-p'ning. And they don't have a

PUMBAA: *I can't, what?*

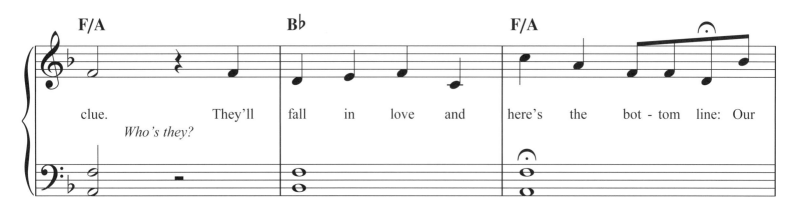

clue. They'll fall in love and here's the bot-tom line: Our

Who's they?

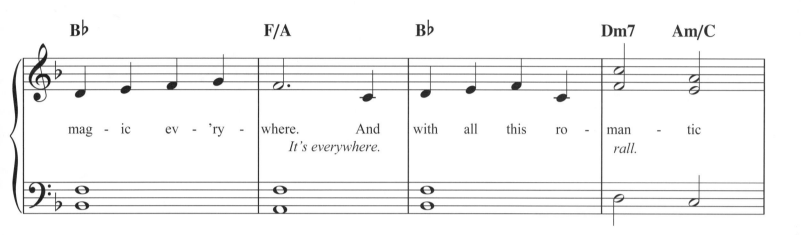

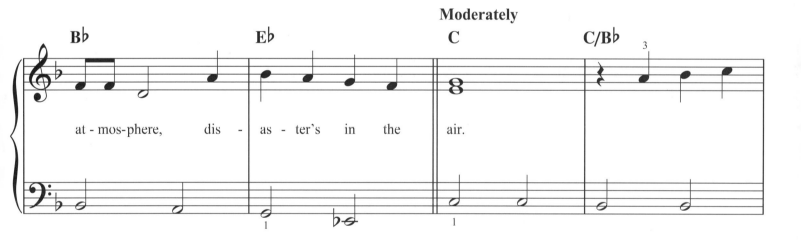

42

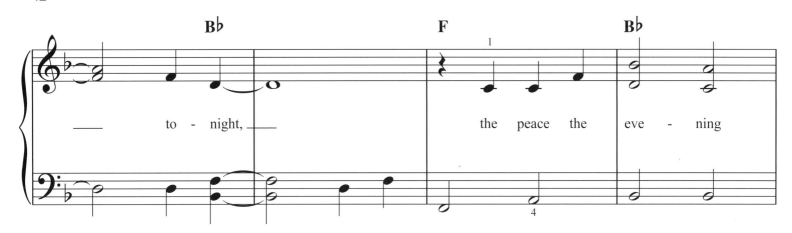

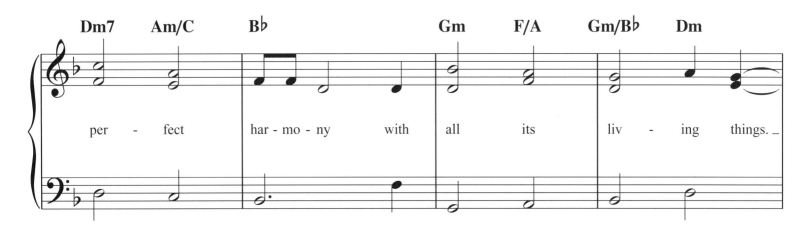

43

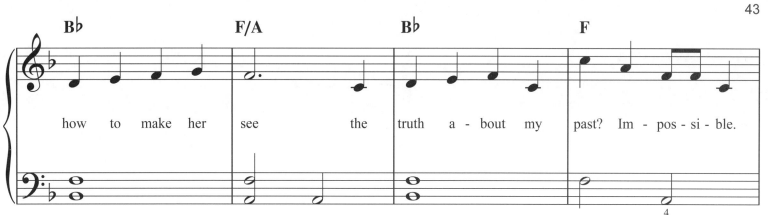

how to make her see the truth a-bout my past? Im-pos-si-ble.

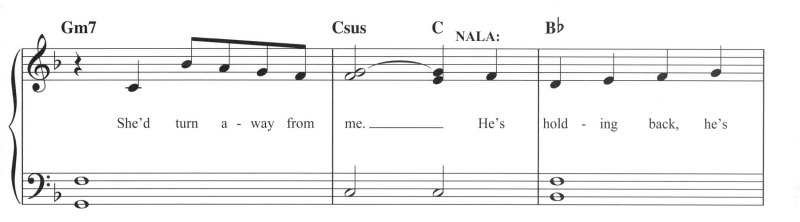

She'd turn a-way from me. _____ He's hold-ing back, he's

NALA:

hid-ing. But what? I can't de-cide. Why won't he be the

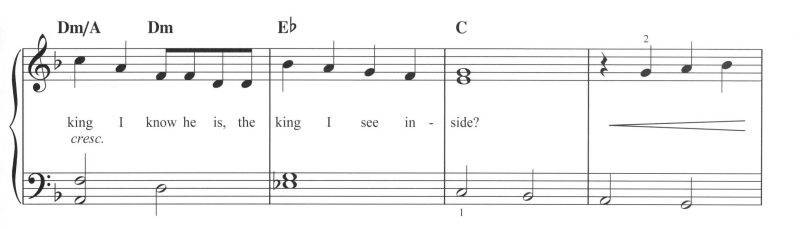

king I know he is, the king I see in-side?

cresc.

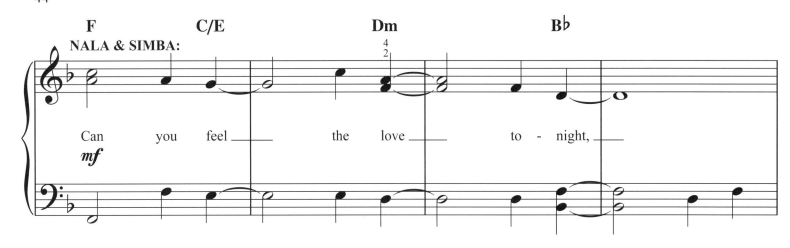

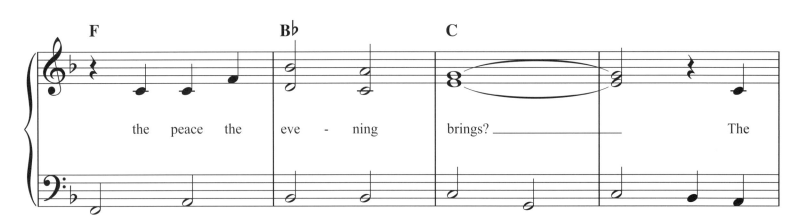

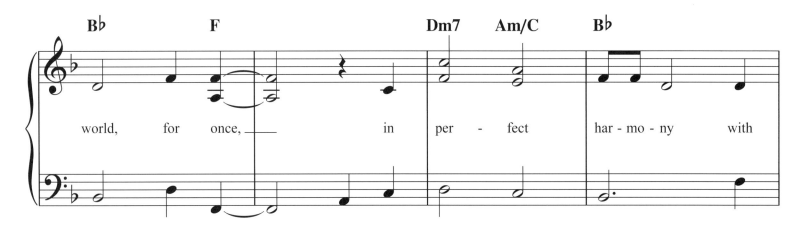

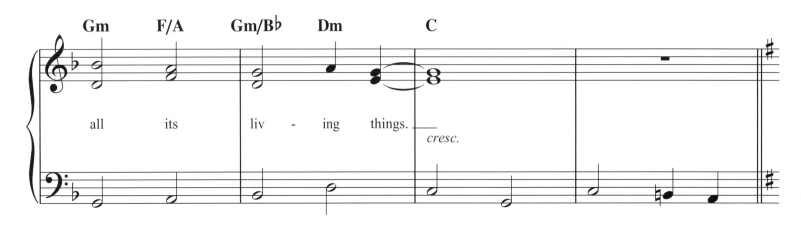

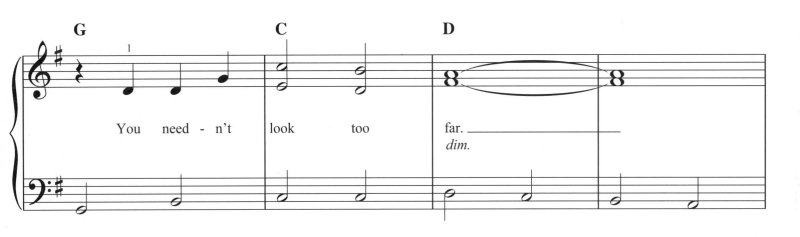

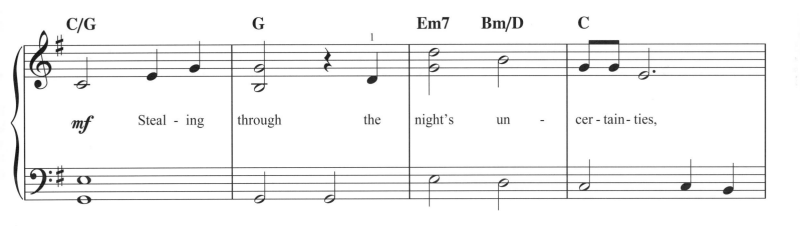

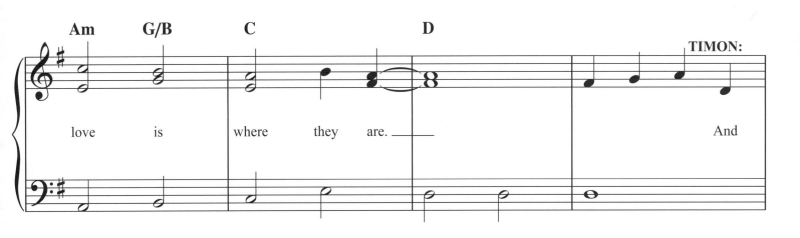

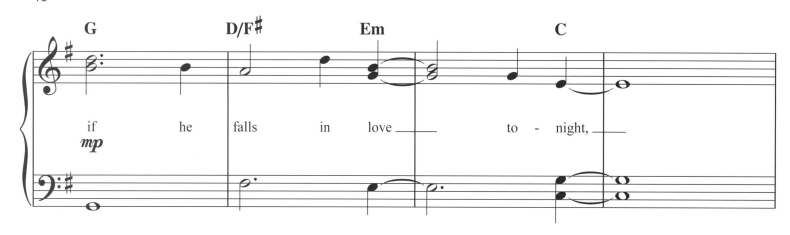

if he falls in love _____ to - night, _____

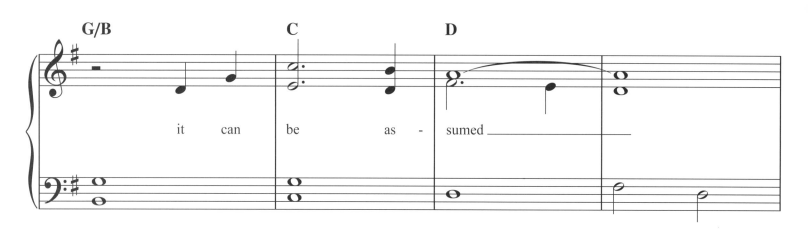

it can be as - sumed _____

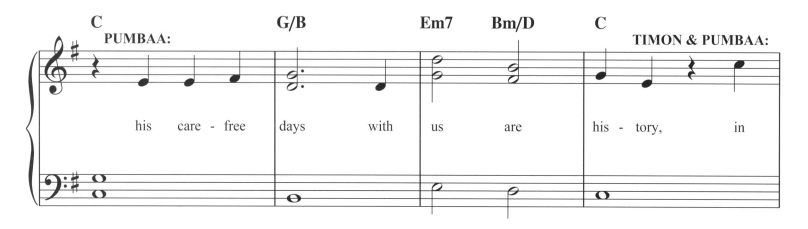

PUMBAA:

TIMON & PUMBAA:

his care - free days with us are his - tory, in

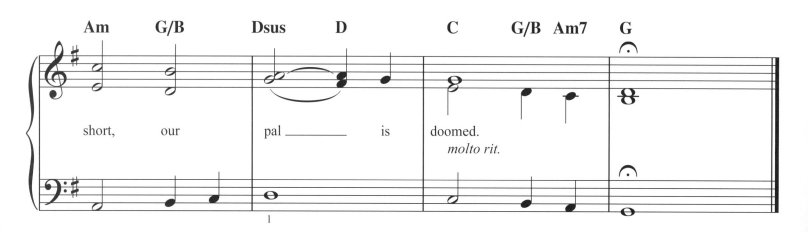

short, our pal _____ is doomed.

molto rit.

1

CIRCLE OF LIFE/NANTS' INGONYAMA

from THE LION KING (2019)

Moderately, with an African beat
NANTS' INGONYAMA

Music and Lyrics by LEBOHANG MORAKE and HANS ZIMMER

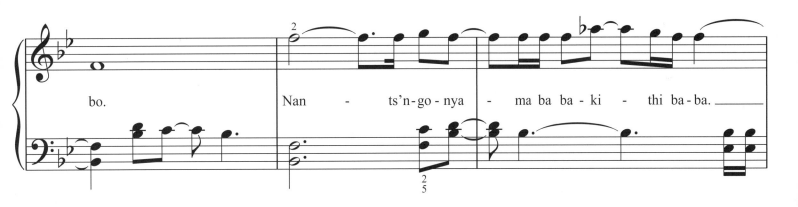

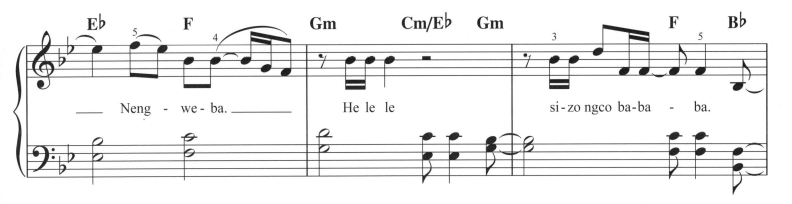

Same tempo, gently rhythmic

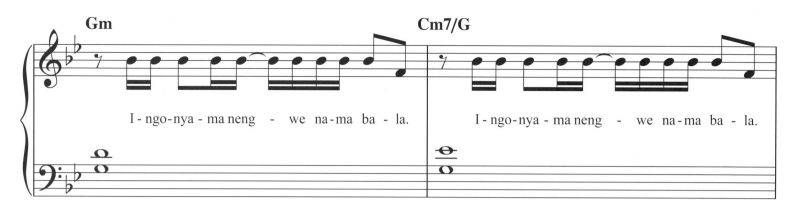

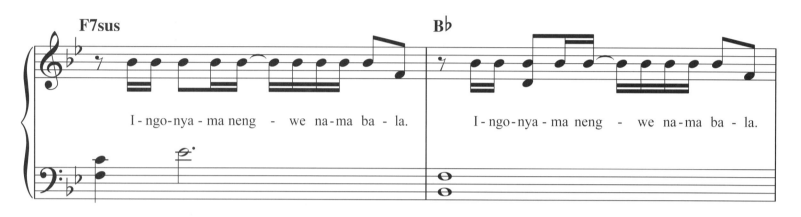

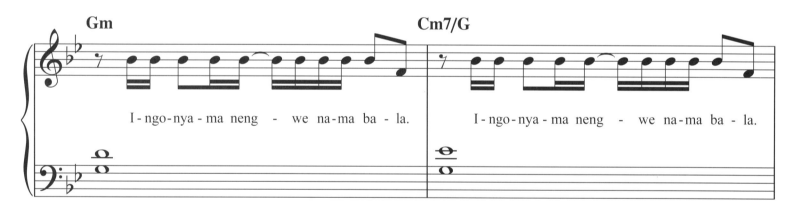

CIRCLE OF LIFE
Music by ELTON JOHN
Lyrics by TIM RICE

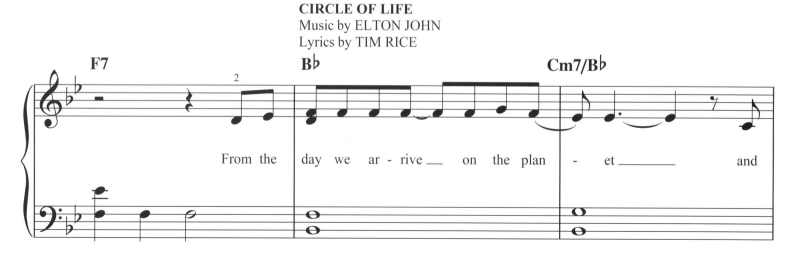

blink-ing, step in - to ___ the sun, ___ there's more to see ___ than can

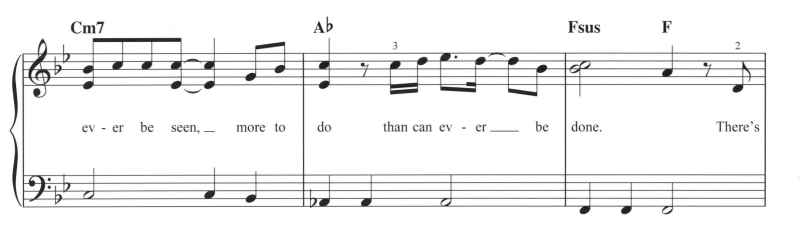

ev - er be seen, ___ more to do than can ev - er ___ be done. There's

far too much ___ to take in ___ here, ___ more to find than can ev - er be

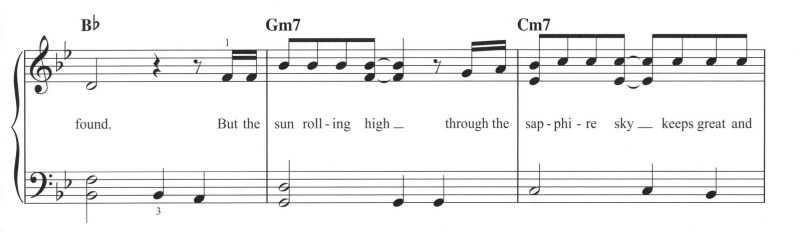

found. But the sun roll - ing high ___ through the sap - phi - re sky ___ keeps great and

50

small on the end - less round. _____ It's the cir - cle _____ of life,

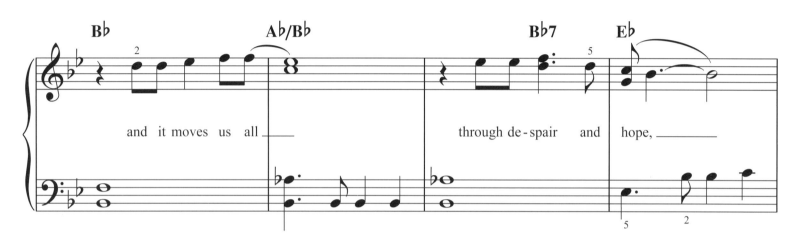

and it moves us all _____ through de-spair and hope, _____

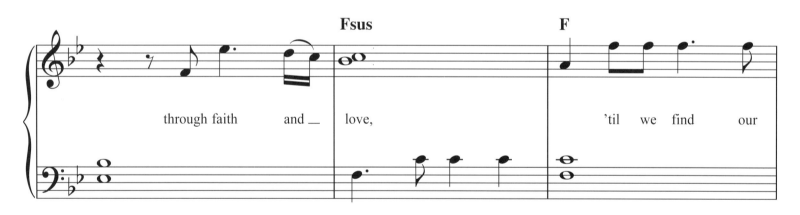

through faith and _ love, _____ 'til we find our

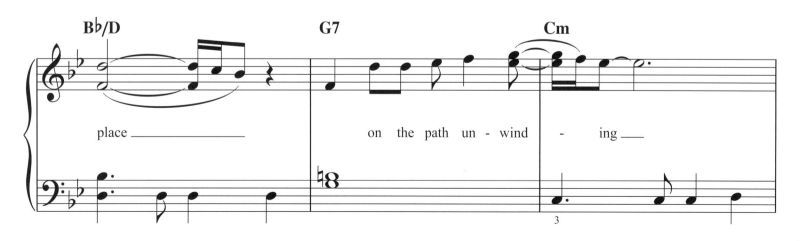

place _____ on the path un - wind - ing _____

in the cir - cle, _____ the cir - cle ___

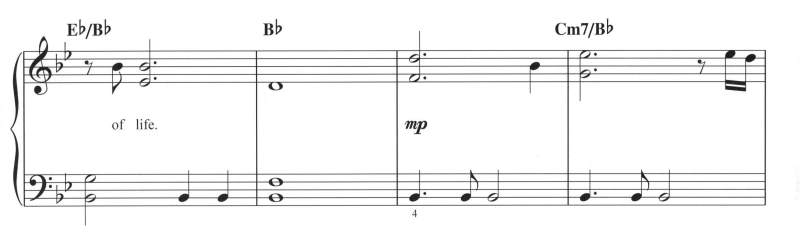

of life. *mp*

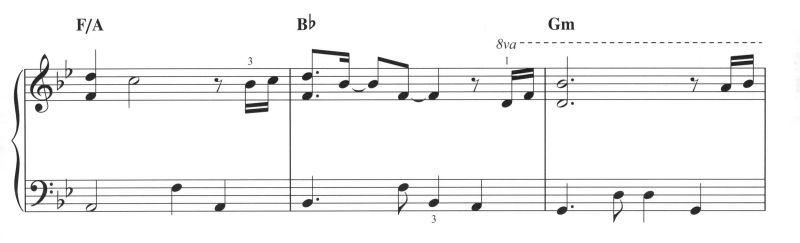

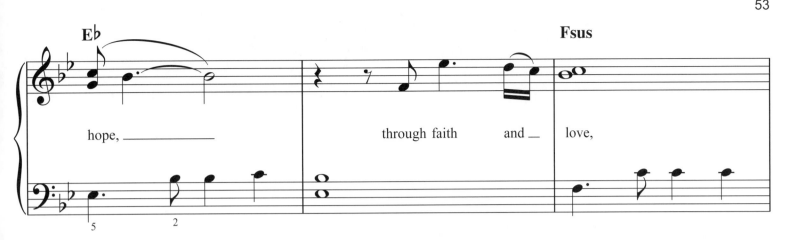

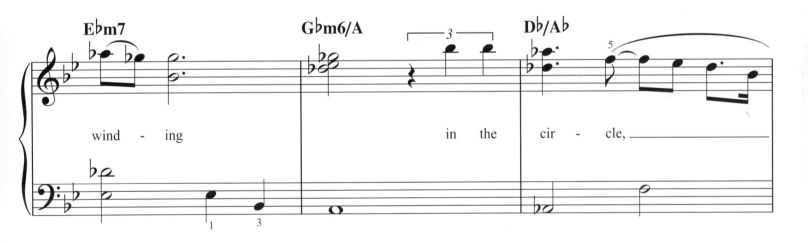

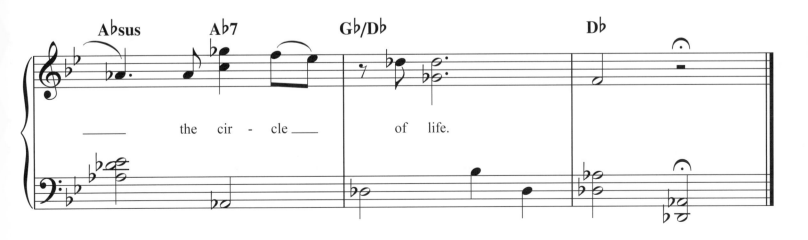

COLORS OF THE WIND
from POCAHONTAS

Music by ALAN MENKEN
Lyrics by STEPHEN SCHWARTZ

You

think you own what-ev-er land you
think the on-ly peo-ple who are

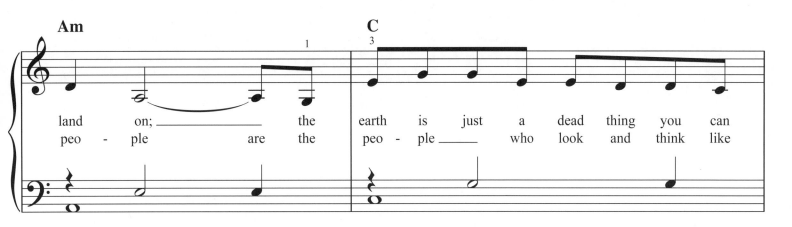

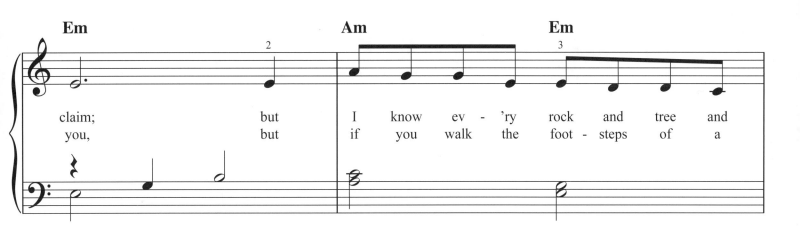

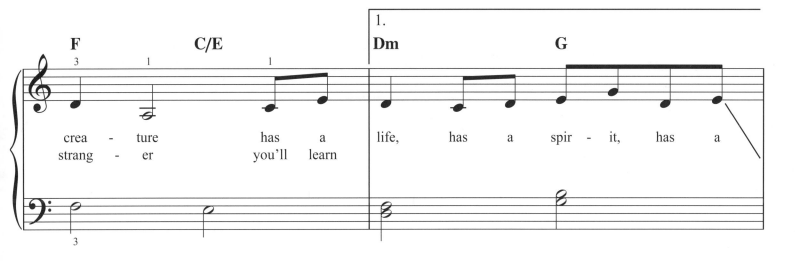

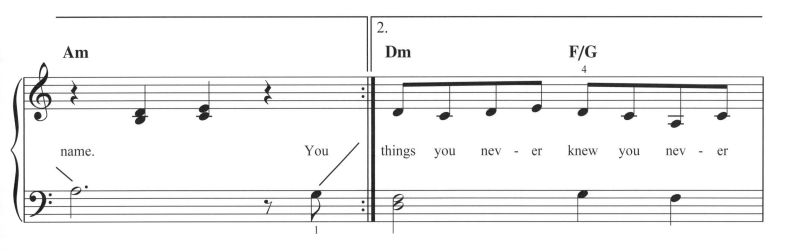

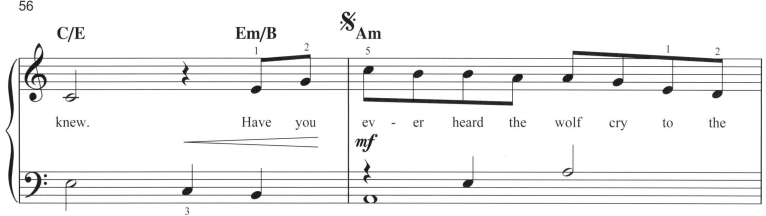

C/E   Em/B   𝄋 Am

knew.   Have you   ev - er heard the wolf cry to the

mf

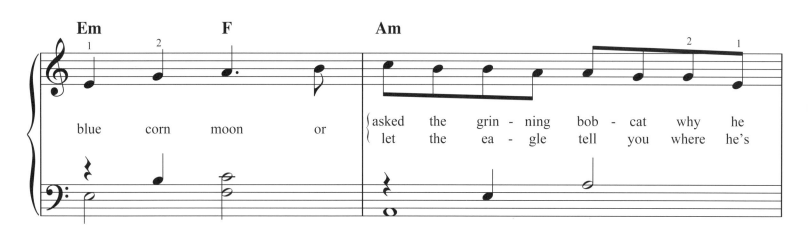

Em   F   Am

blue corn moon or   { asked the grin - ning bob - cat why he
                            { let the ea - gle tell you where he's

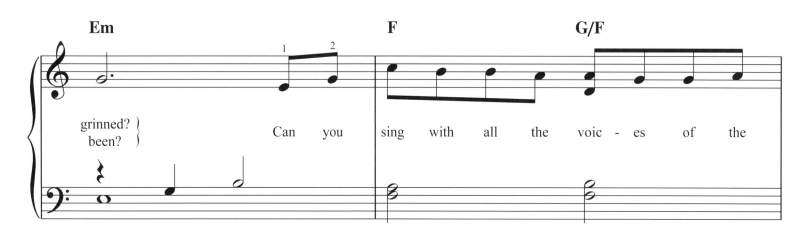

Em   F   G/F

grinned? }
been? }   Can you   sing with all the voic - es of the

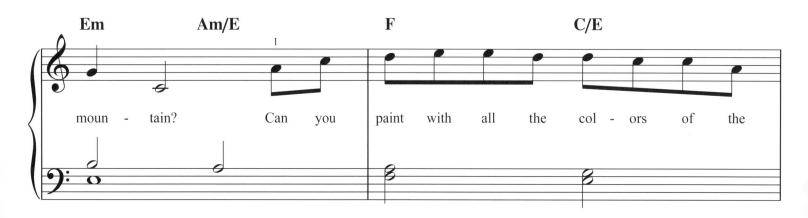

Em   Am/E   F   C/E

moun - tain?   Can you   paint with all the col - ors of the

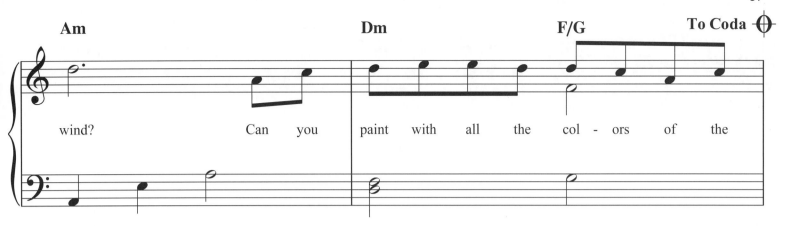

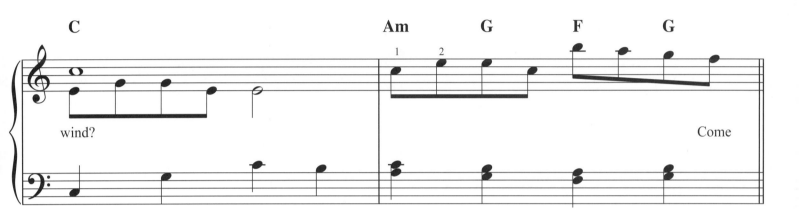

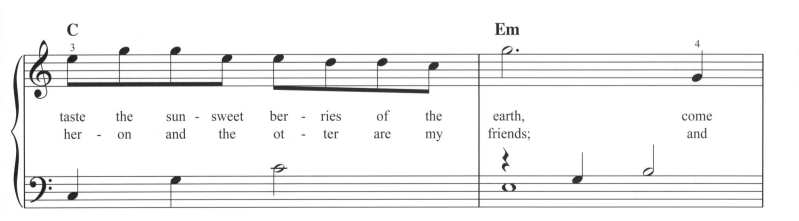

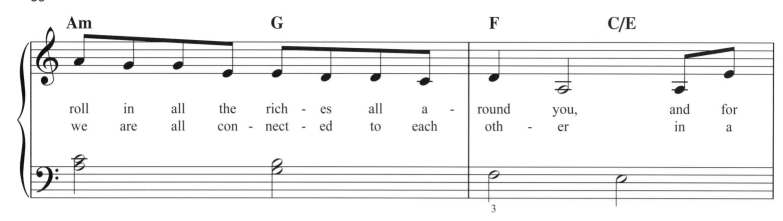

roll in all the rich - es all a - round you, and for
we are all con - nect - ed to each oth - er in a

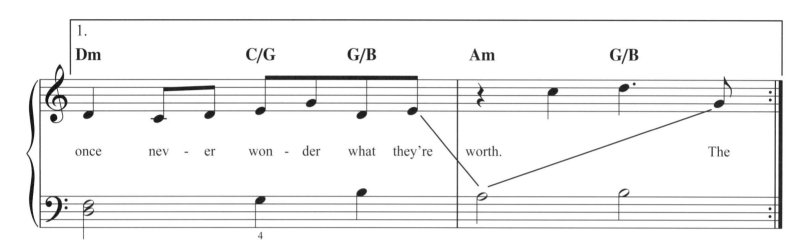

1.

once nev - er won - der what they're worth. The

2.
D.S. al Coda

cir - cle, in a hoop that nev - er ___ ends. ___ Have you

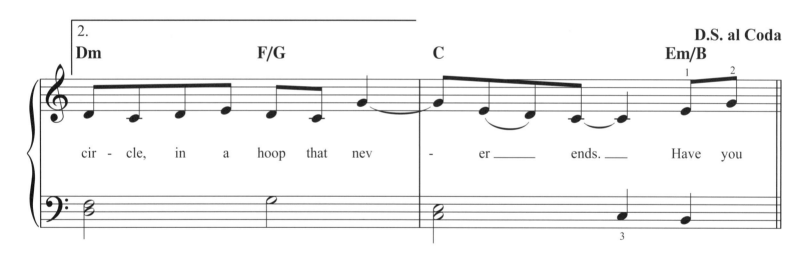

CODA

wind? How high does the

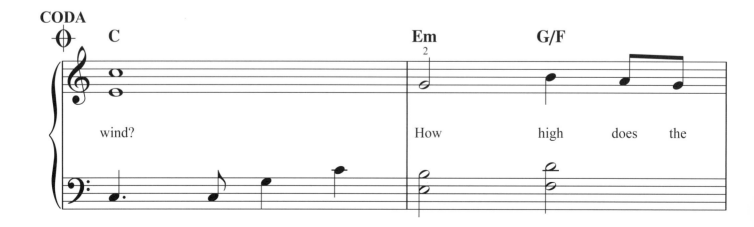

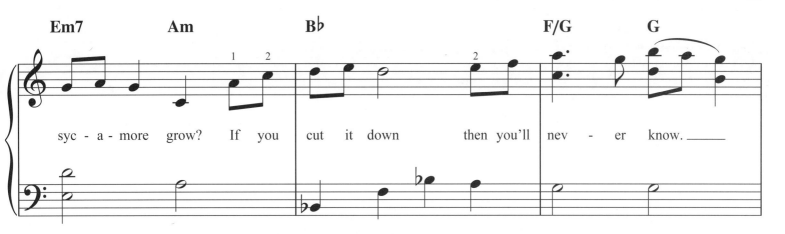

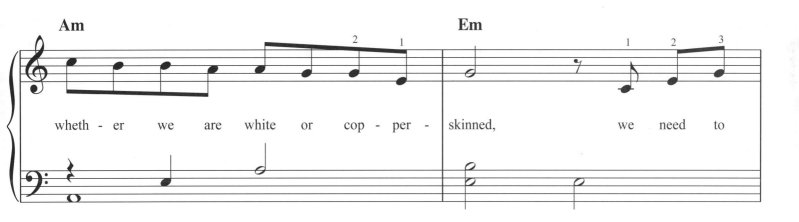

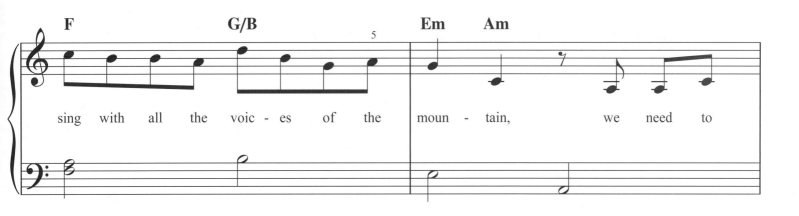

60

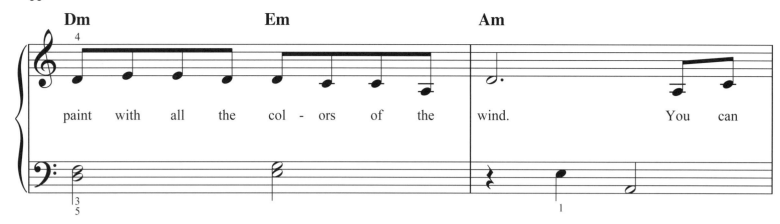

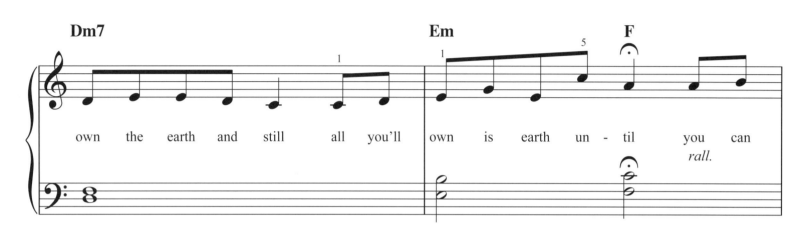

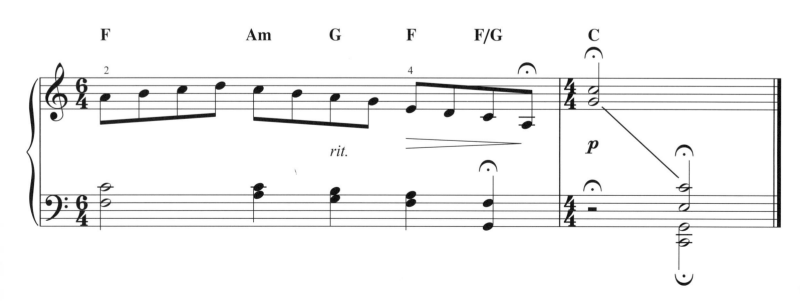

DO YOU WANT TO BUILD A SNOWMAN?

from FROZEN

Music and Lyrics by KRISTEN ANDERSON-LOPEZ
and ROBERT LOPEZ

Moderately fast

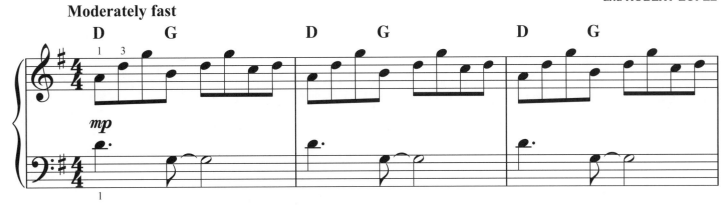

LITTLE ANNA: *(Spoken:)* Elsa? (knocks)   *(Sung:)* Do you want to build a   snow - man?

Come on, let's go and   play!   I nev - er see you

an - y - more.   Come out the   door!   It's like you've gone a - way.

62

We used to be best bud-dies, and now we're not. ___ I

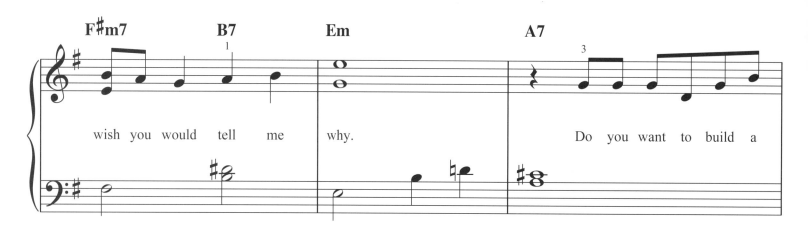

wish you would tell me why. Do you want to build a

snow - man? It does-n't have to be a snow - man.

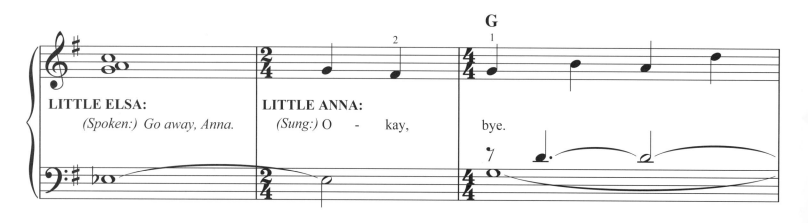

LITTLE ELSA:
(Spoken:) Go away, Anna.

LITTLE ANNA:
(Sung:) O - kay, bye.

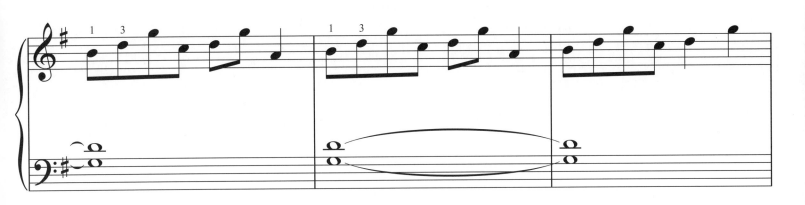
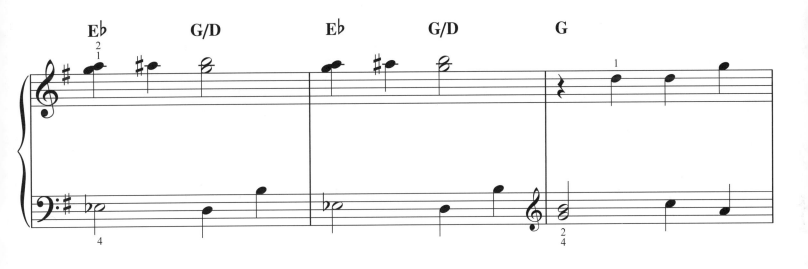
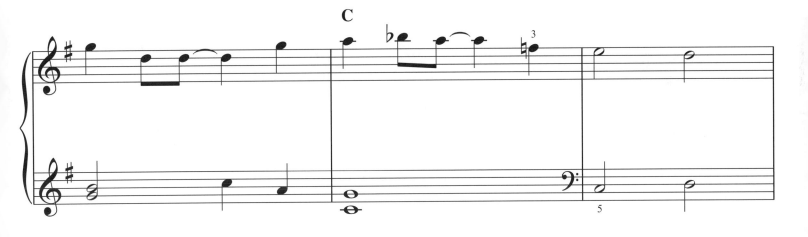

64

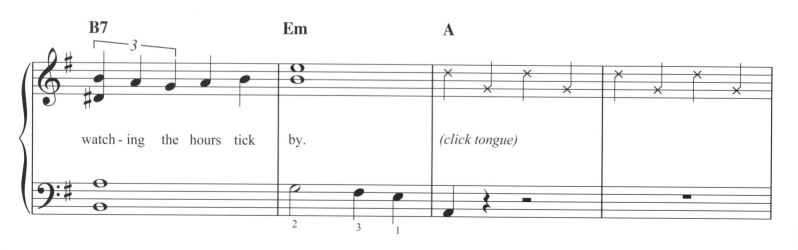

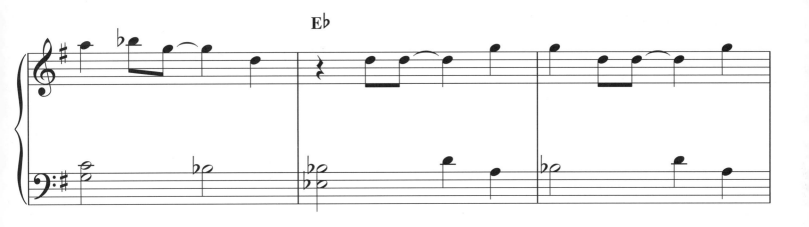

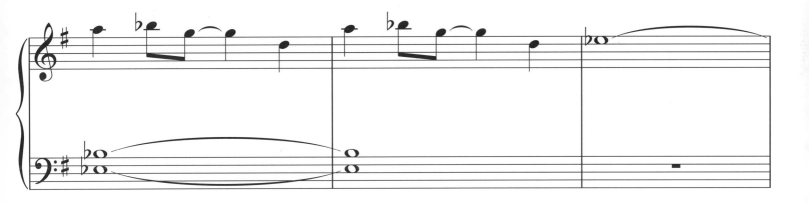

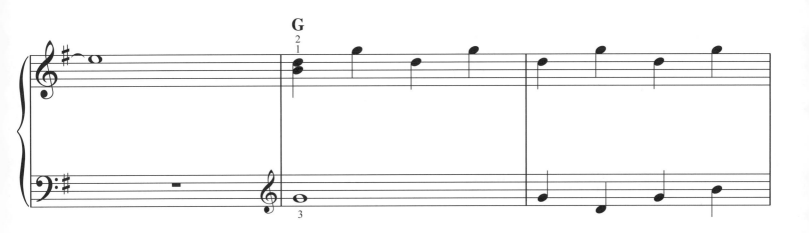

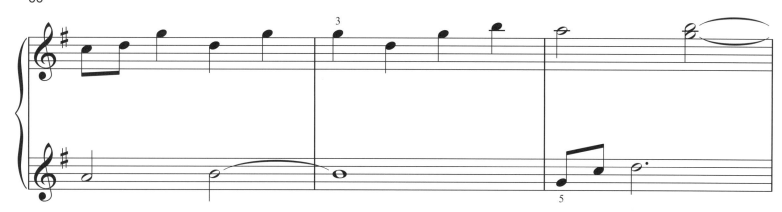

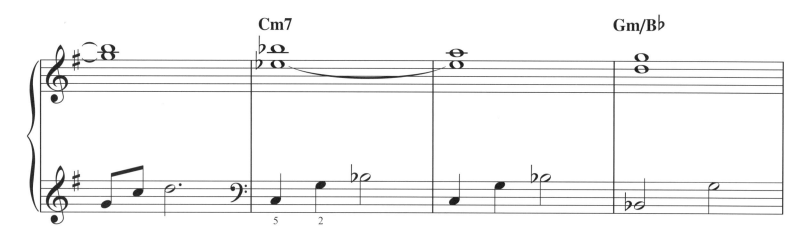

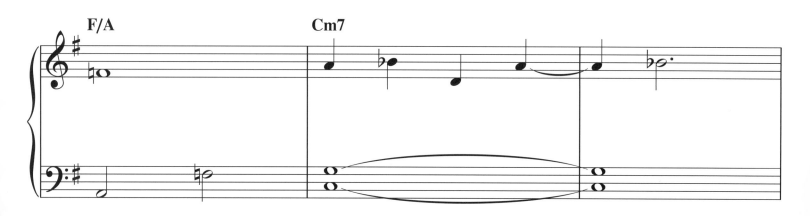

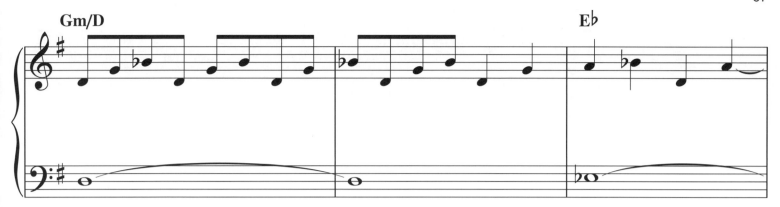

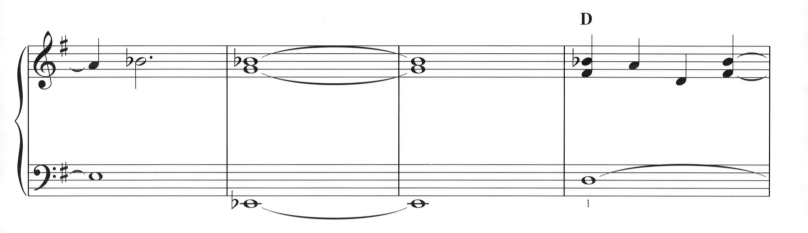

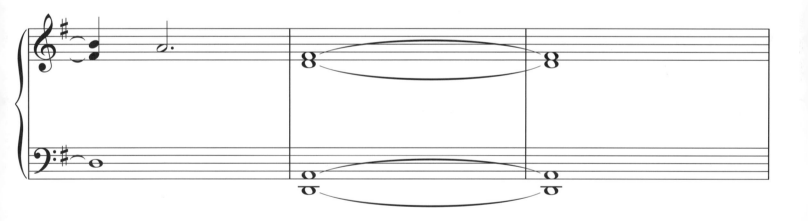

Slower, tenderly

(knocking) *(Spoken:)* Elsa? *(Sung:)* Please, I know you're in there.

68

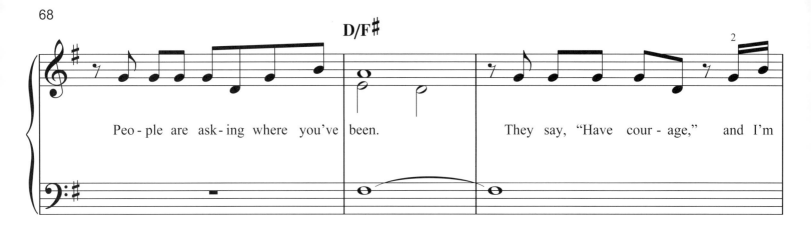

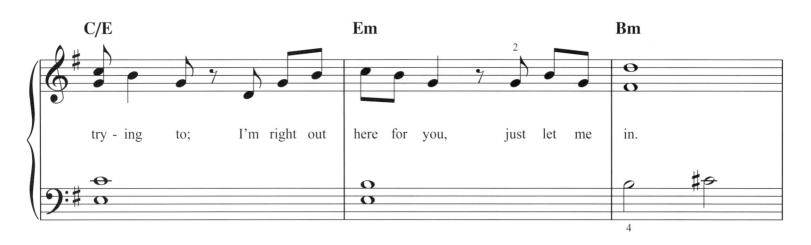

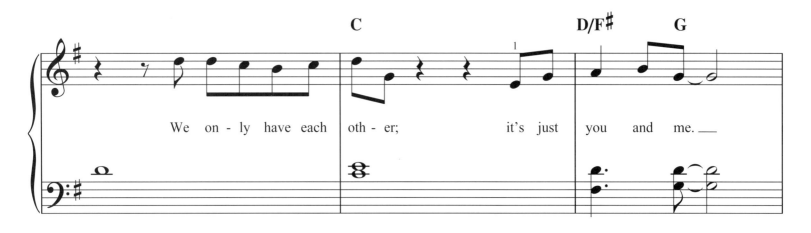

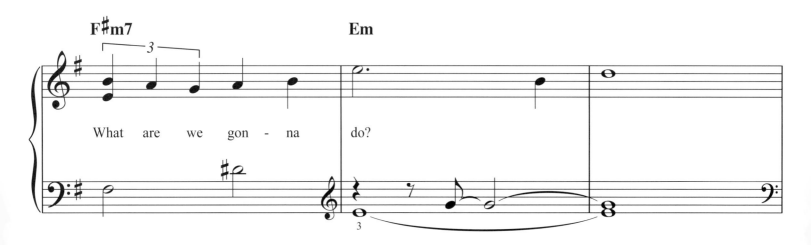

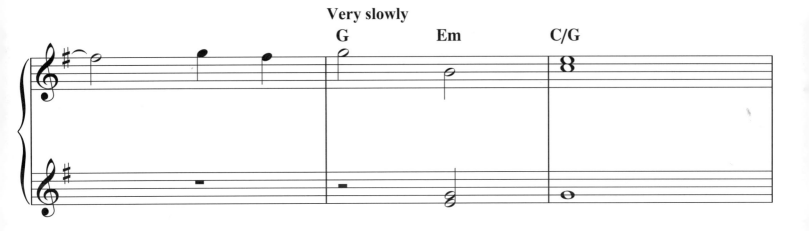

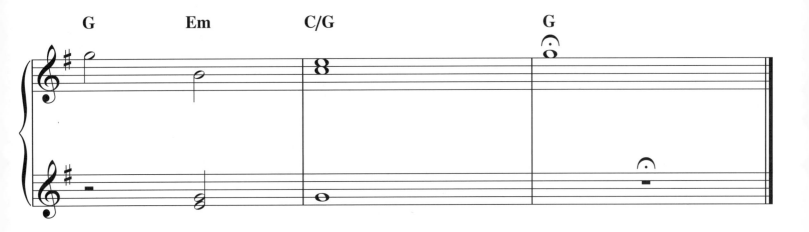

FIXER UPPER

from FROZEN

Music and Lyrics by KRISTEN ANDERSON-LOPEZ
and ROBERT LOPEZ

With comic bounce

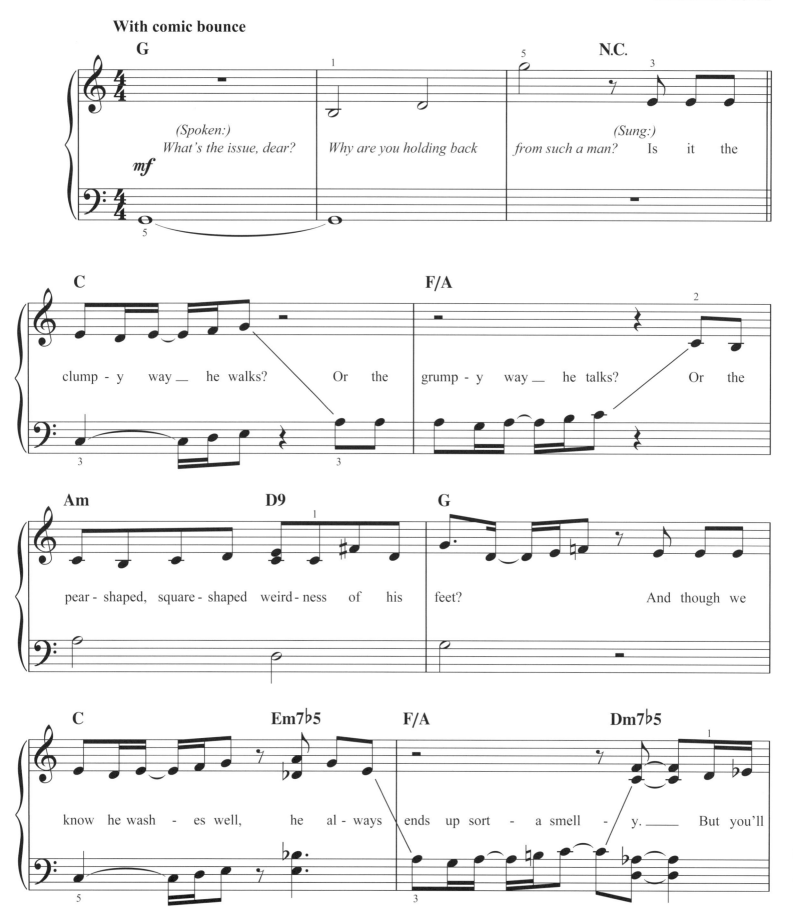

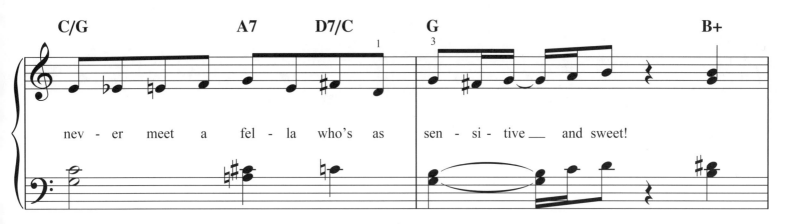

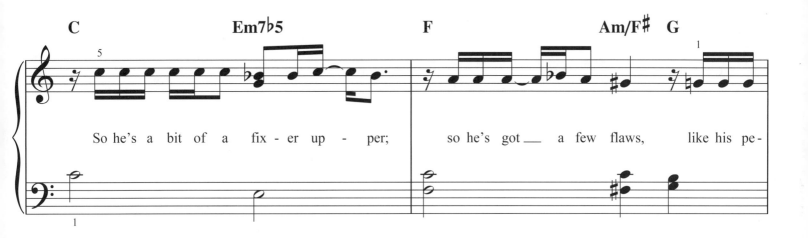

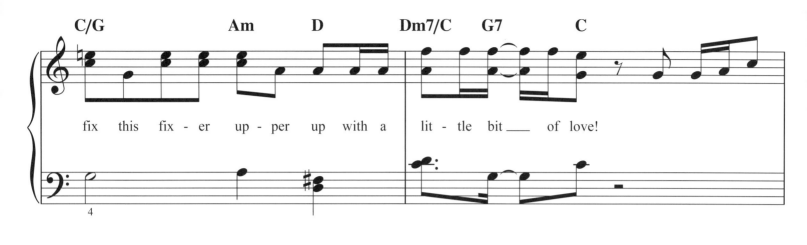

C/G   **Am**   **D**   **Dm7/C**   **G7**   **C**

fix this fix - er up - per up with a   lit - tle bit ___ of love!

A7♯5   **D**   **C**   **F**

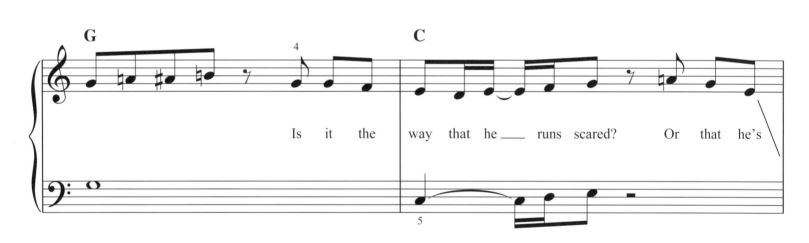

G   **C**

Is it the   way that he ___ runs scared?   Or that he's

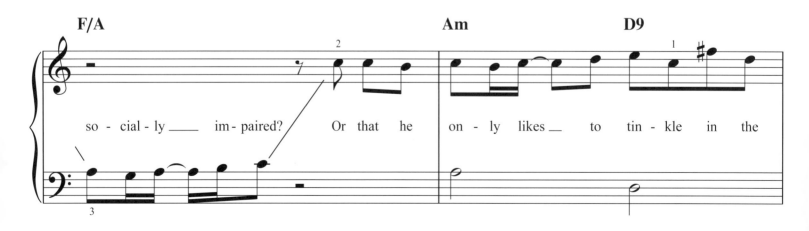

F/A   **Am**   **D9**

so - cial - ly ___ im - paired?   Or that he   on - ly likes ___ to tin - kle in the

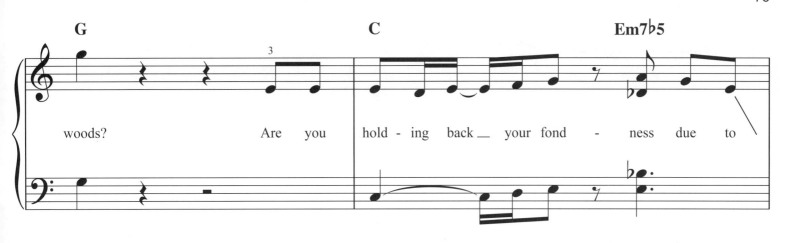

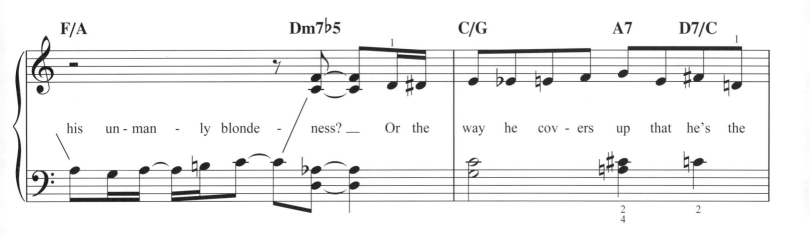

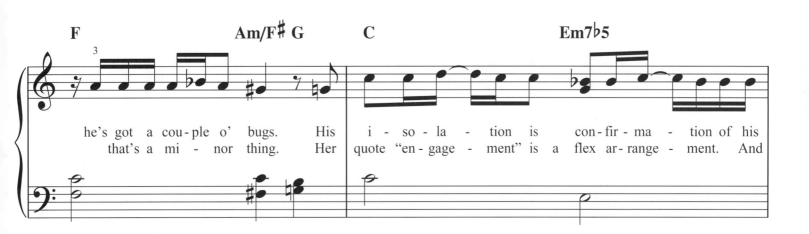

74

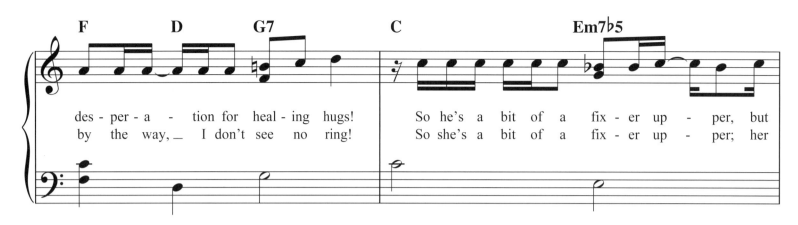
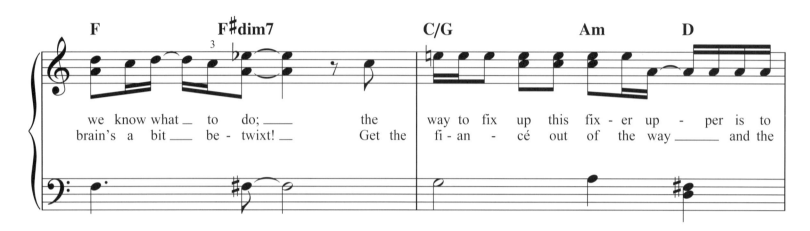

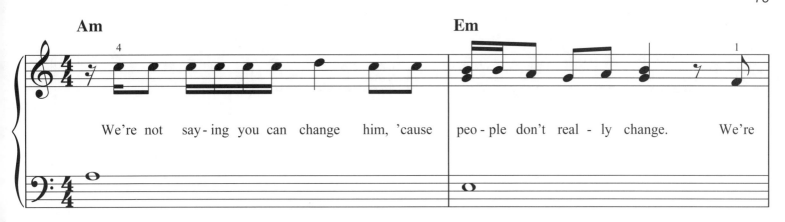

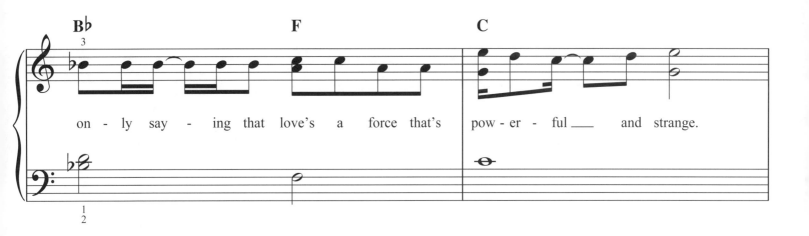

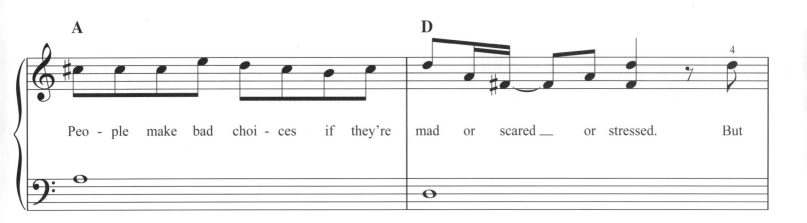

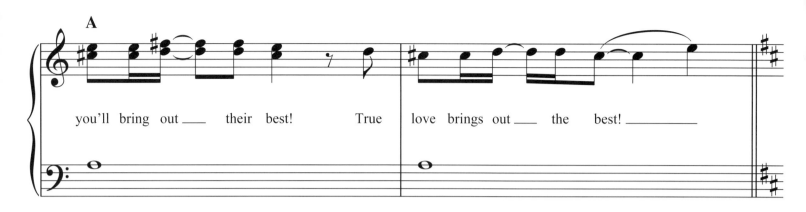

you'll bring out ___ their best! True love brings out ___ the best! ___

Ev-'ry-one's a bit of a fix-er up - per; that's what it's all ___ a-bout! Fa-ther!

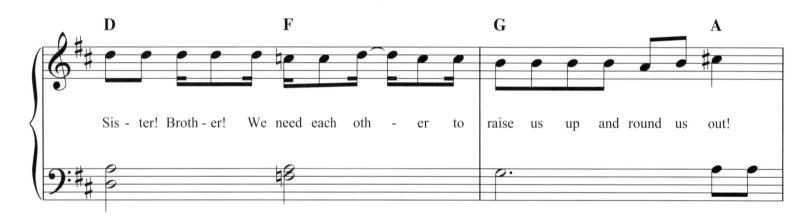

Sis - ter! Broth - er! We need each oth – er to raise us up and round us out!

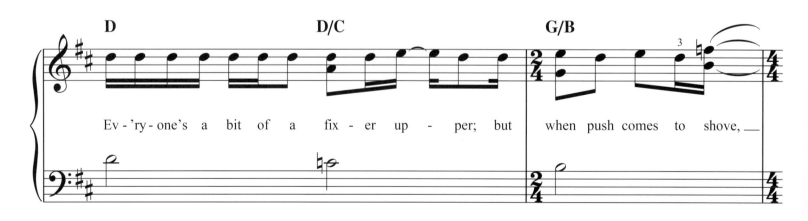

Ev - 'ry-one's a bit of a fix-er up - per; but when push comes to shove, ___

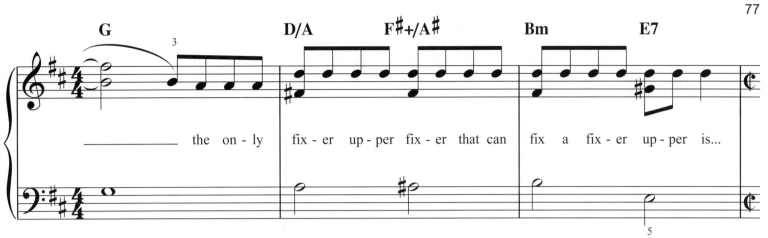

the on - ly fix - er up - per fix - er that can fix a fix - er up - per is...

Double time

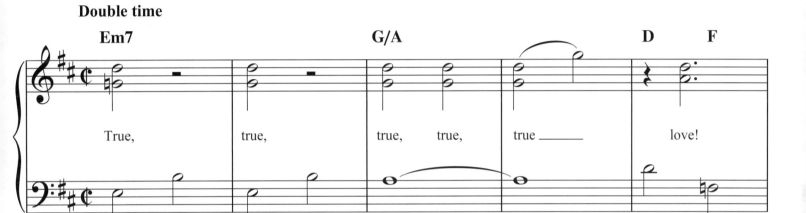

True, true, true, true, true _____ love!

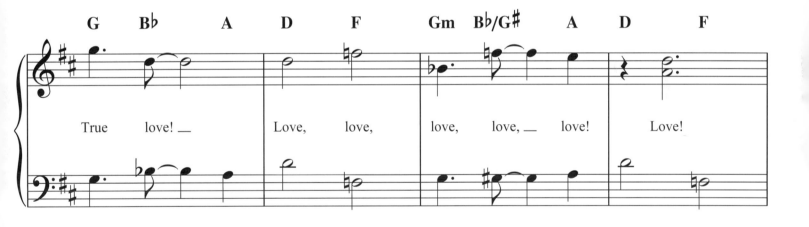

True love! ___ Love, love, love, love, ___ love! Love!

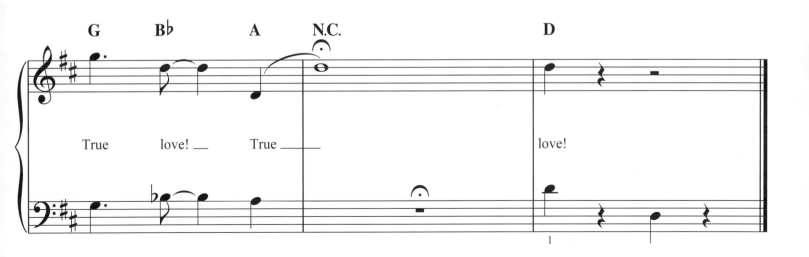

True love! ___ True ___ love!

FOR THE FIRST TIME IN FOREVER

from FROZEN

Music and Lyrics by KRISTEN ANDERSON-LOPEZ
and ROBERT LOPEZ

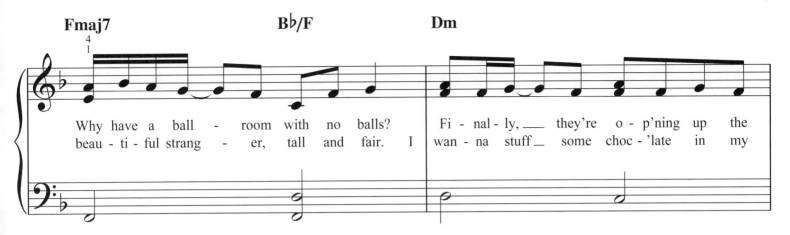

Why have a ball - room with no balls?
beau - ti - ful strang - er, tall and fair. I

Fi - nal - ly, ___ they're o - p'ning up the
wan - na stuff ___ some choc - 'late in my

gates!
face!

There'll be
Then we

ac - tual real ___ live peo - ple;
laugh and talk ___ all eve - ning, which is

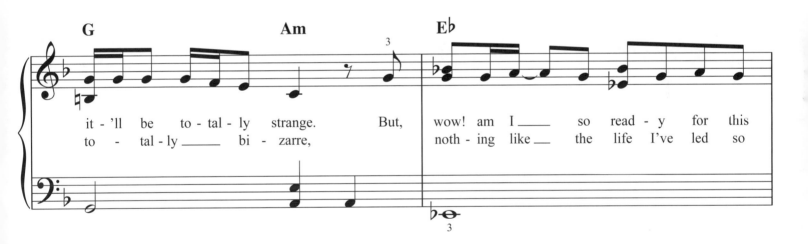

it - 'll be to - tal - ly strange. But,
to - tal - ly ___ bi - zarre,

wow! am I ___ so read - y for this
noth - ing like ___ the life I've led so

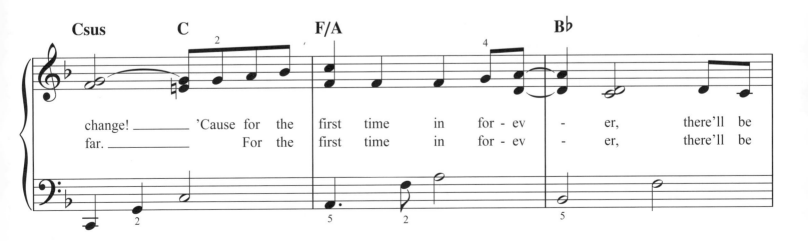

change! ___ 'Cause for the
far. ___ For the

first time in for - ev - er, there'll be
first time in for - ev - er, there'll be

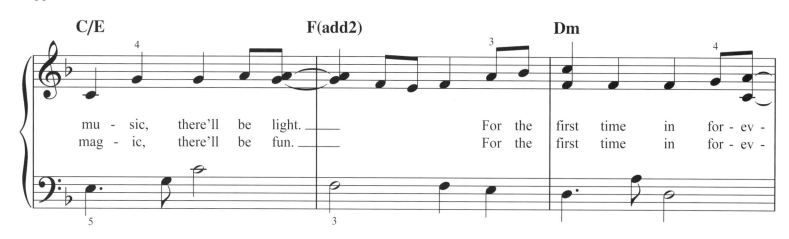

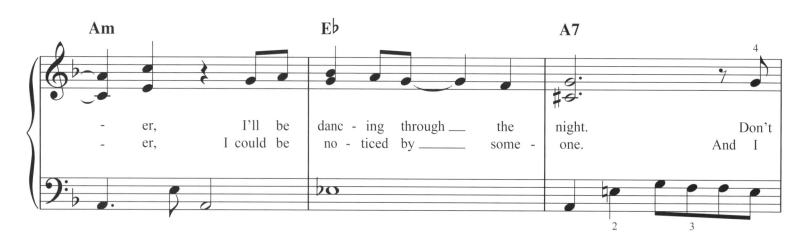

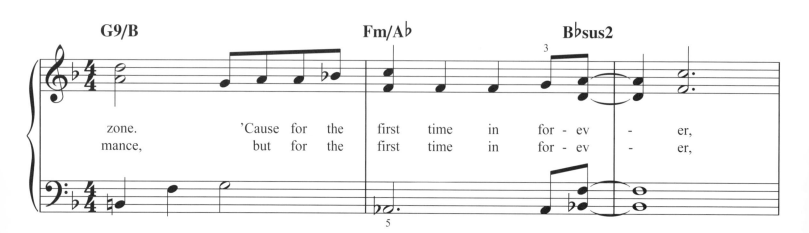

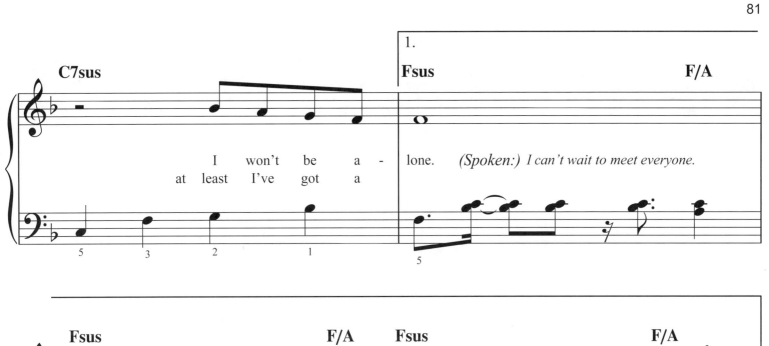

I won't be a - lone.   *(Spoken:) I can't wait to meet everyone.*
at least I've got a

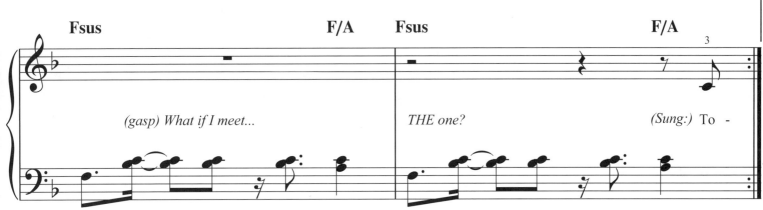

(gasp) What if I meet...   *THE one?*   *(Sung:)* To -

chance.

ELSA: Don't let them in;   don't let them see;   be the good girl ___ you al - ways

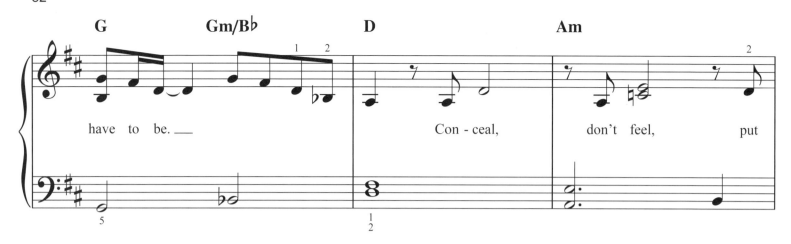

have to be. ___   Con - ceal,   don't feel,   put

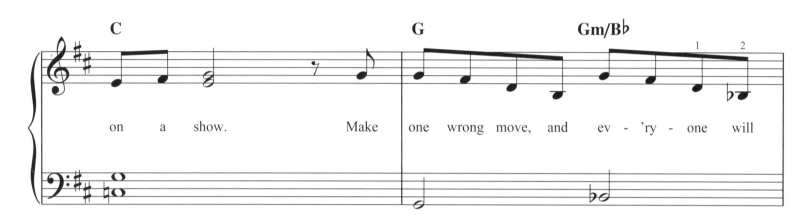

on a show.   Make   one wrong move, and   ev - 'ry - one will

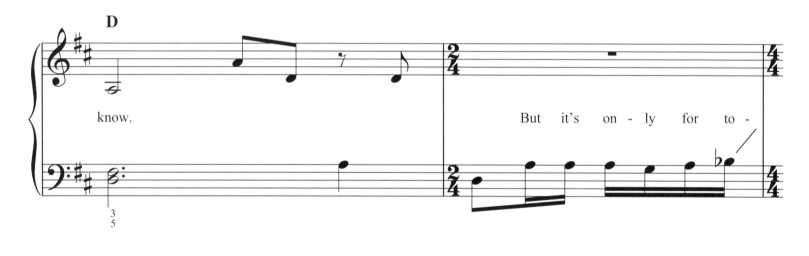

know.   But it's on - ly for to -

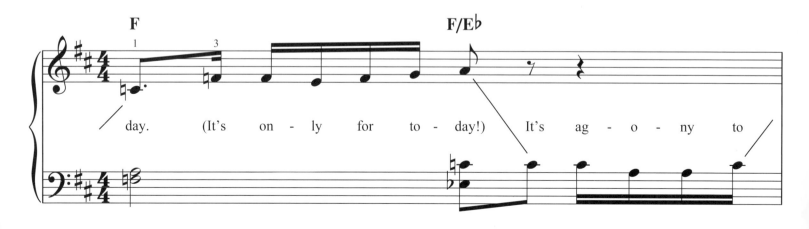

day.   (It's on - ly for to - day!)   It's ag - o - ny to

83

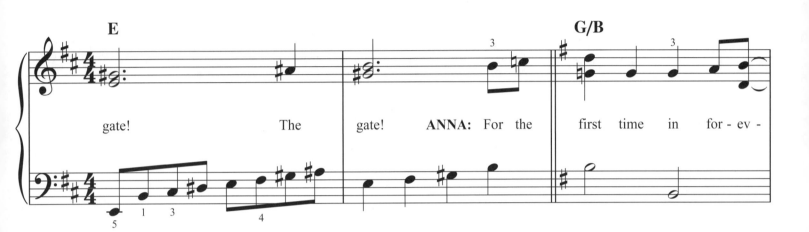

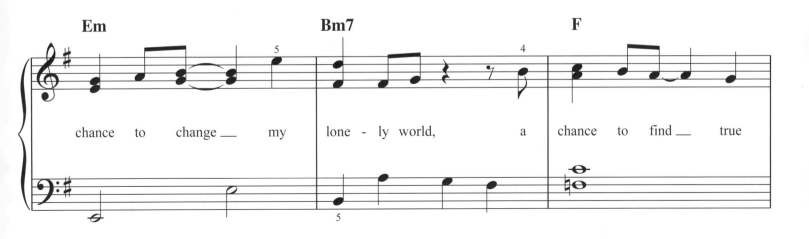

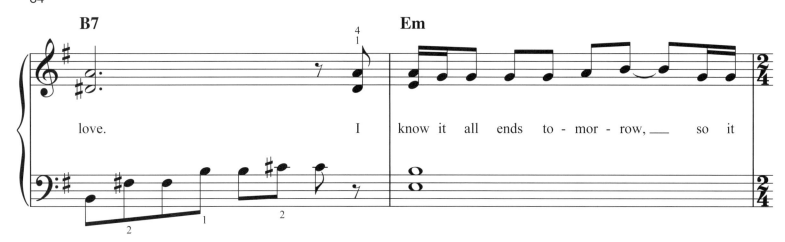

love. I know it all ends to-mor-row, ___ so it

has to be ___ to - day. 'Cause for the first time in for-ev-

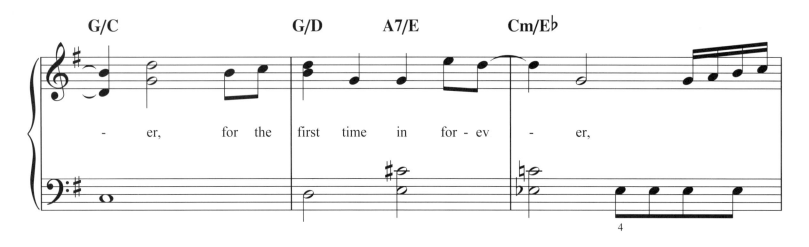

- er, for the first time in for-ev - er,

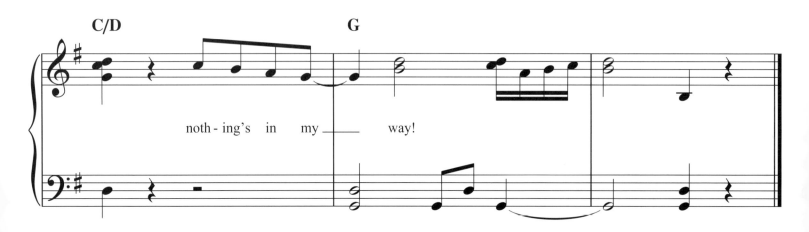

noth-ing's in my ___ way!

A GIRL WORTH FIGHTING FOR

from MULAN

Music by MATTHEW WILDER
Lyrics by DAVID ZIPPEL

For a long time we've been march - ing off to

bat - tle.   In our thun - d'ring herd we

feel a lot like cat - tle. Like the

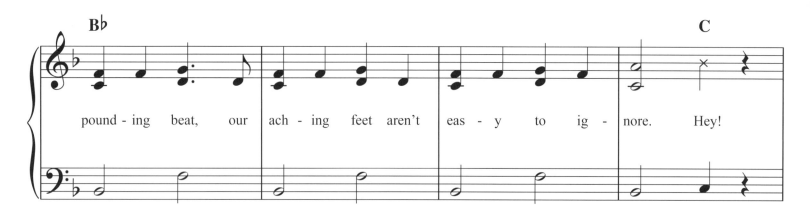

pound - ing beat, our ach - ing feet aren't eas - y to ig - nore. Hey!

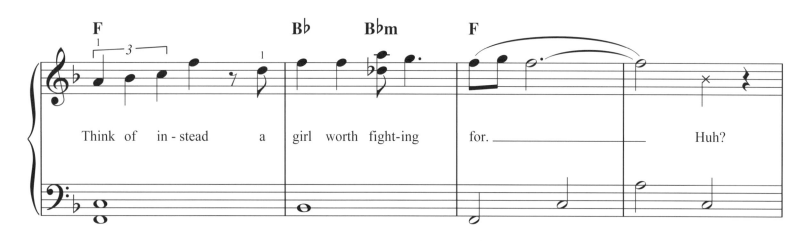

Think of in - stead a girl worth fight-ing for. _____ Huh?

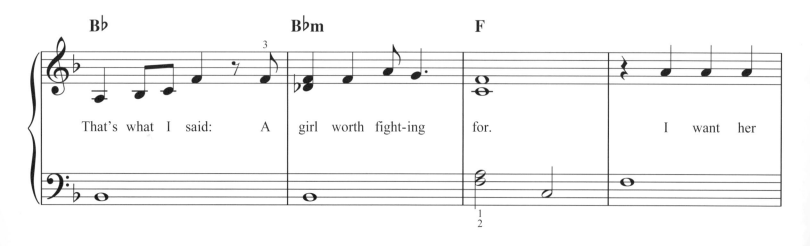

That's what I said: A girl worth fight-ing for. I want her

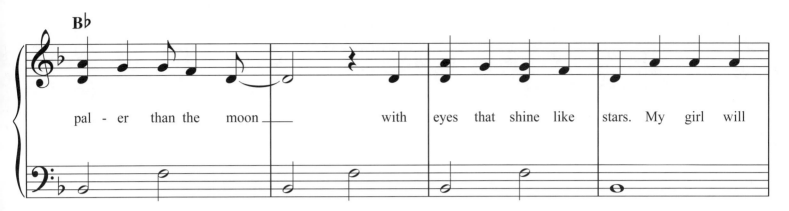

pal - er than the moon ___ with eyes that shine like stars. My girl will

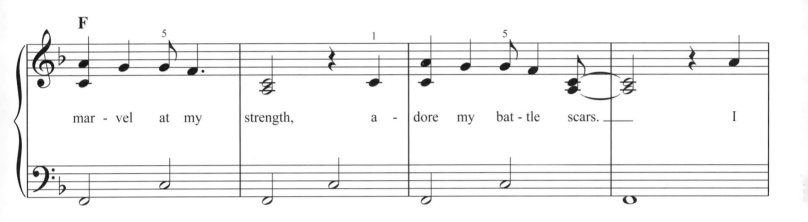

mar - vel at my strength, a - dore my bat - tle scars. ___ I

could - n't care ___ less what she'll wear ___ or what she looks like. ___ It

all de - pends on what she cooks like. Beef, pork, chick - en... Mmmmm...

F(add9)

Bet the

lo - cal girls thought you were quite the charm - er. And I'll

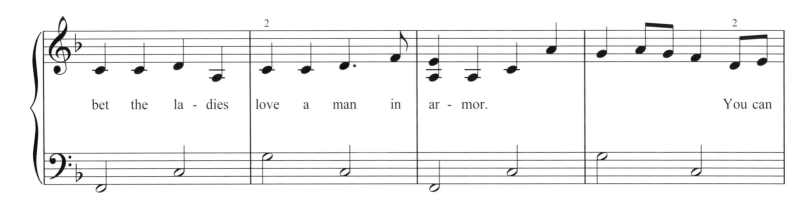

bet the la - dies love a man in ar - mor. You can

B♭   **C**

guess what we have missed the most since we went off to war.

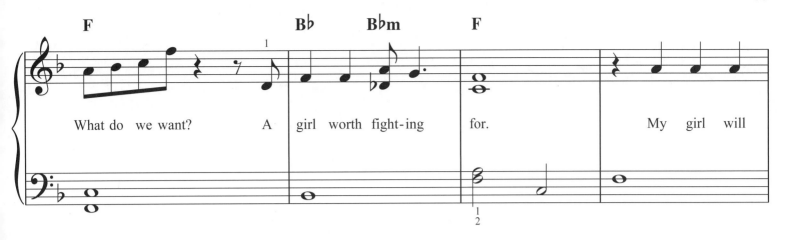

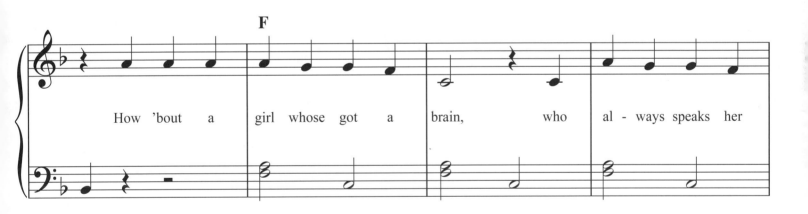

sure to thrill her. _____ He thinks he's such a la - dy kill - er.

I've a girl back home who's un - like an - y

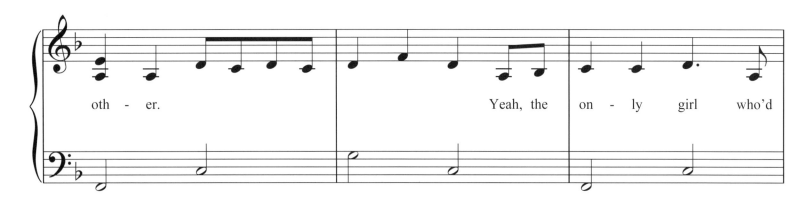

oth - er. Yeah, the on - ly girl who'd

love him is his moth - er. But when we come home in

91

vic - to - ry they'll line up at the door.

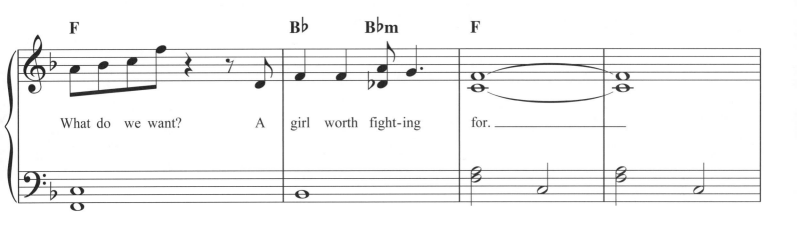

What do we want? A girl worth fight-ing for. _____

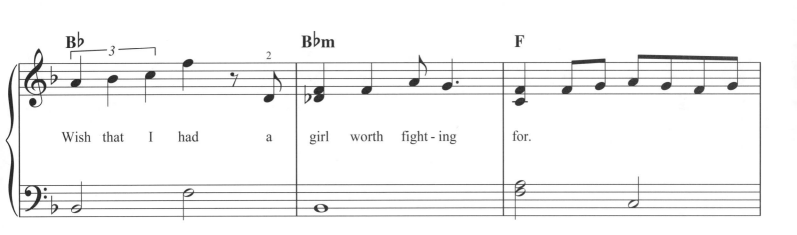

Wish that I had a girl worth fight - ing for.

(Whistle) _____ A girl worth fight - ing...

GO THE DISTANCE
from HERCULES

Music by ALAN MENKEN
Lyrics by DAVID ZIPPEL

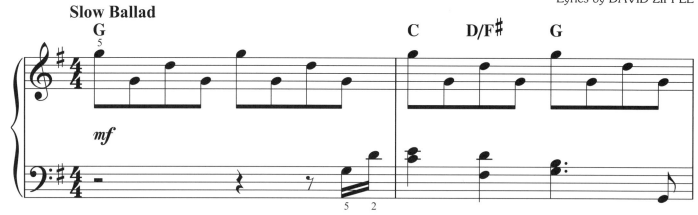

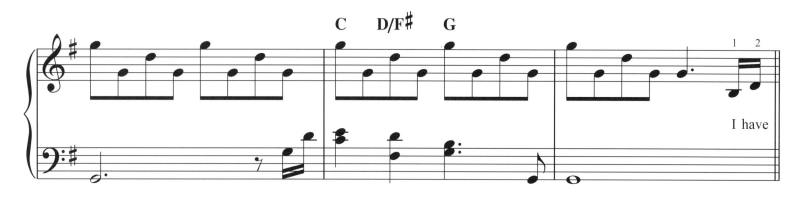

I have

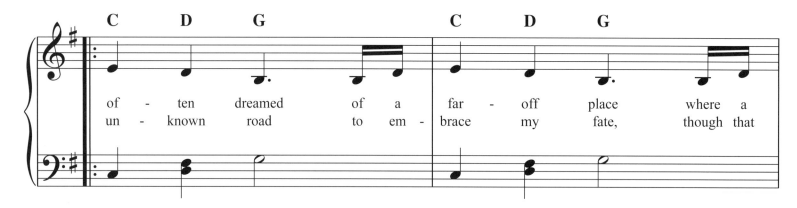

of - ten dreamed of a far - off place where a
un - known road to em - brace my fate, though that

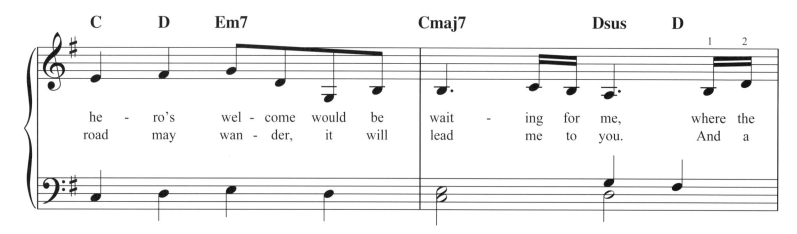

he - ro's wel - come would be wait - ing for me, where the
road may wan - der, it will lead me to you. And a

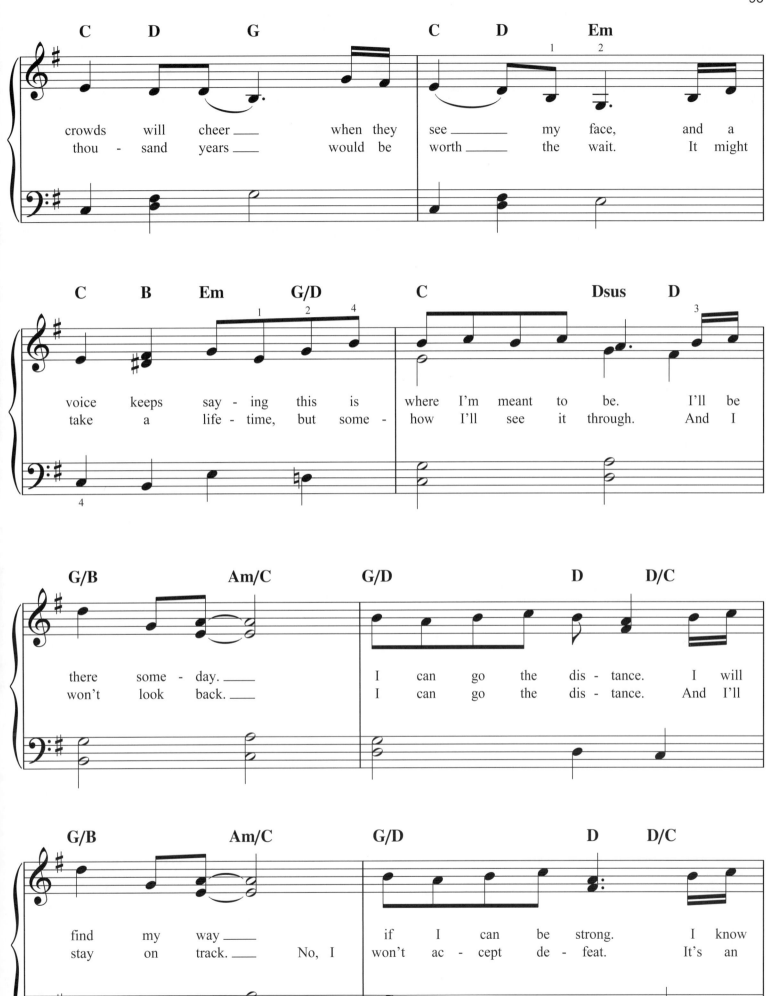

94

ev - 'ry mile ___ will be | worth my | while. ___ When I
up - hill slope, ___ but I

go the dis - tance, I'll be | right where I be -

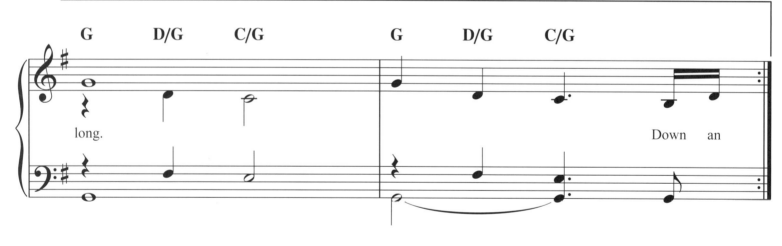

long. Down an

2.

won't lose hope ___ till I | go the dis - tance and my

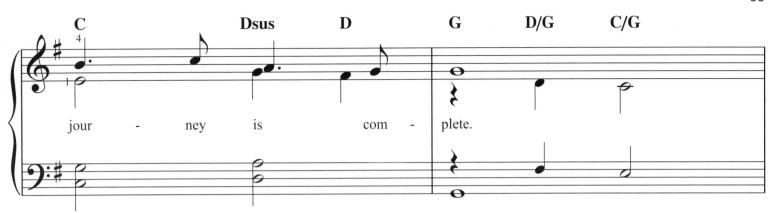

jour - ney is com - plete.

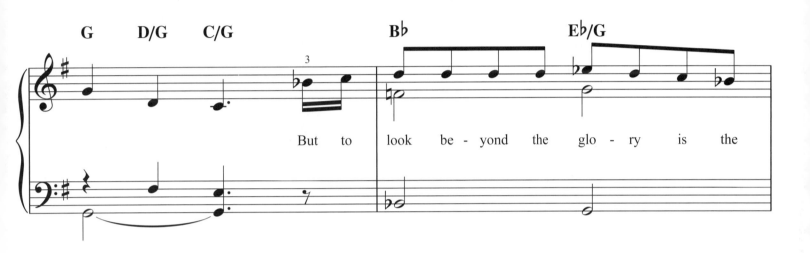

But to look be - yond the glo - ry is the

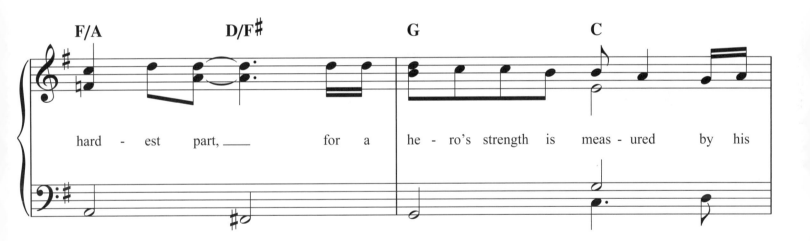

hard - est part, _____ for a he - ro's strength is meas - ured by his

heart. _____ Like a shoot - ing star, _____

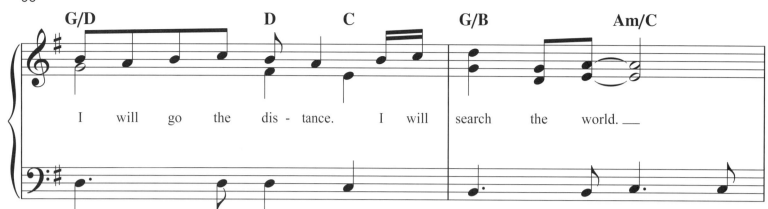

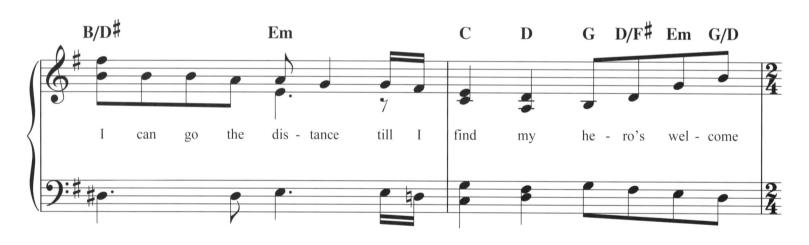

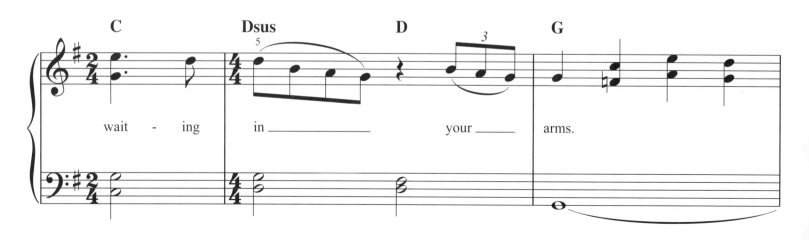

I will search the world. ___ I will face it's harms ___

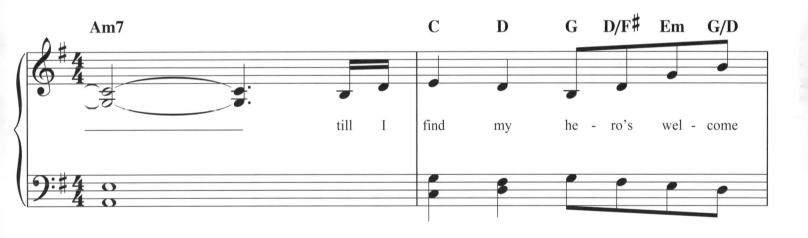

___ till I find my he - ro's wel - come

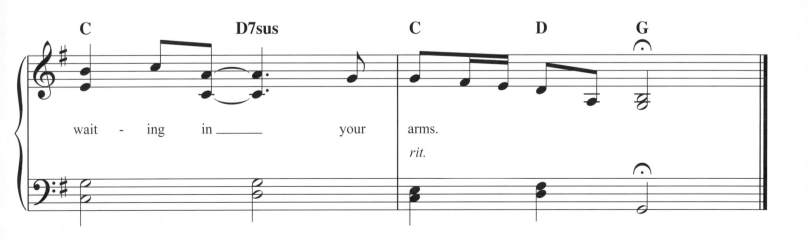

wait - ing in ___ your arms.

rit.

HAKUNA MATATA

from THE LION KING (2019)

Music by ELTON JOHN
Lyrics by TIM RICE

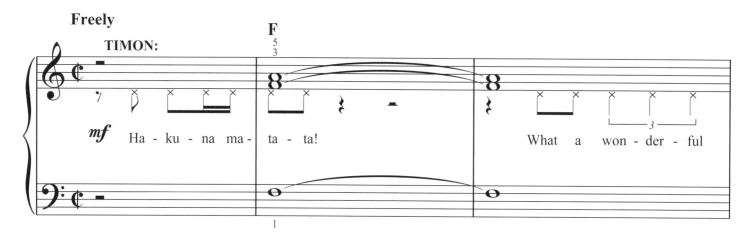

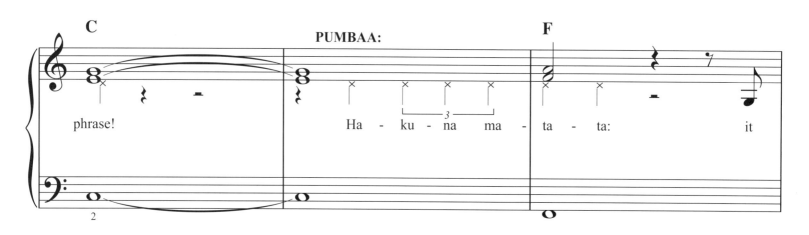

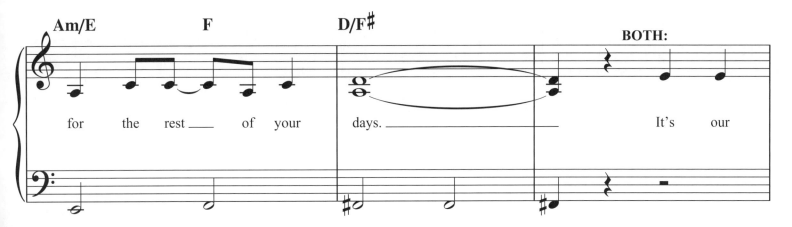

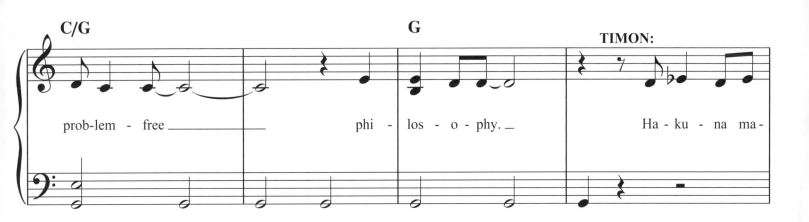

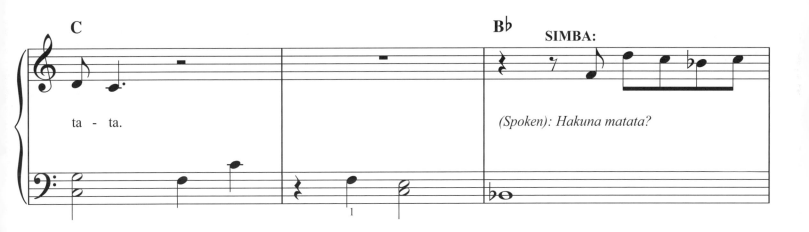

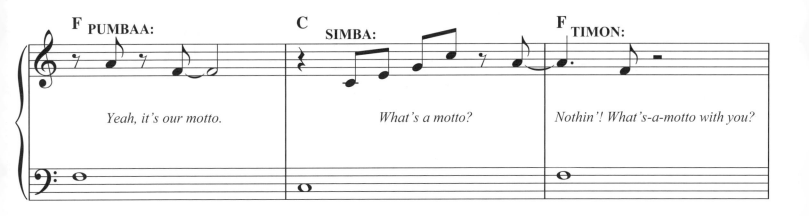

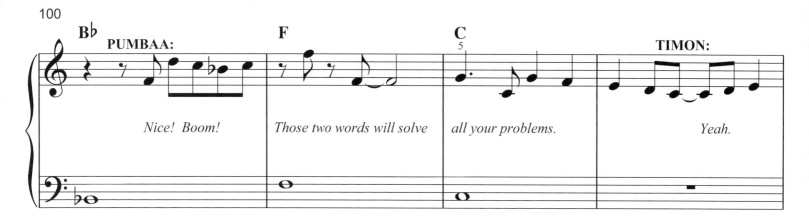

PUMBAA:

Nice! Boom! *Those two words will solve* *all your problems.* **TIMON:** *Yeah.*

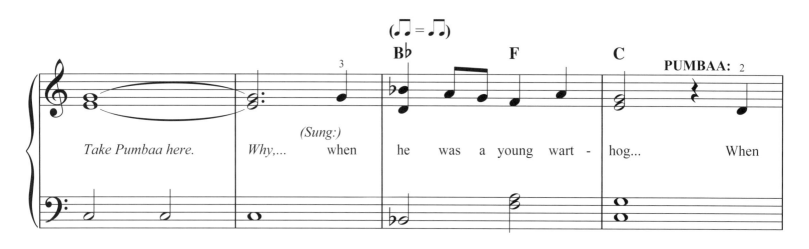

Take Pumbaa here. *Why,...* *(Sung:)* *when* *he was a young wart - hog...* **PUMBAA:** *When*

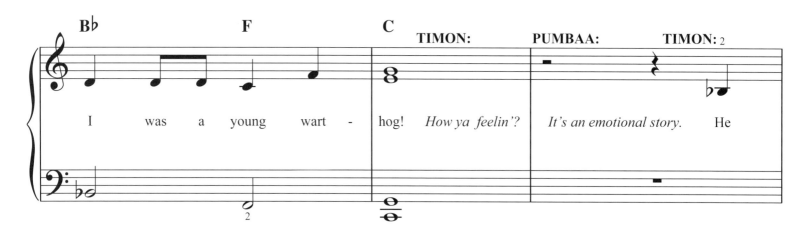

I was a young wart - hog! **TIMON:** *How ya feelin'?* **PUMBAA:** *It's an emotional story.* **TIMON:** *He*

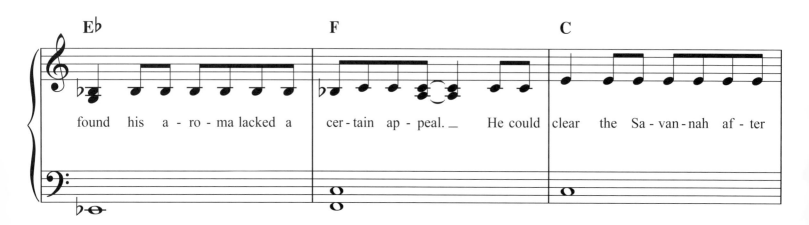

found his a - ro - ma lacked a *cer - tain ap - peal. __ He could* *clear the Sa - van - nah af - ter*

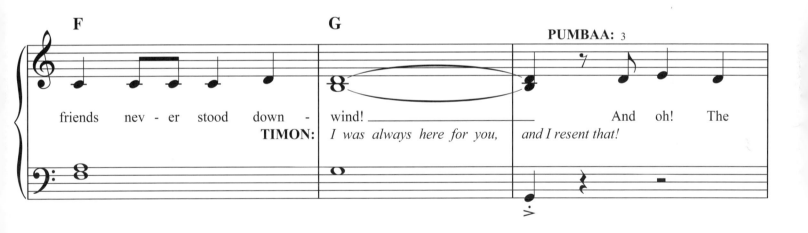

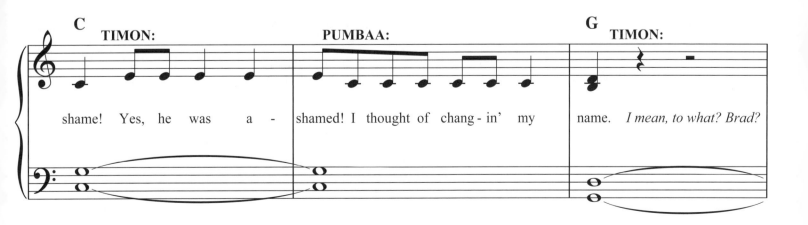

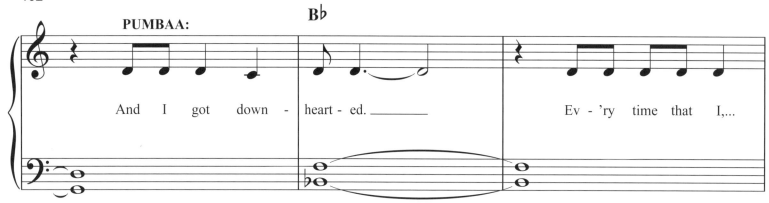

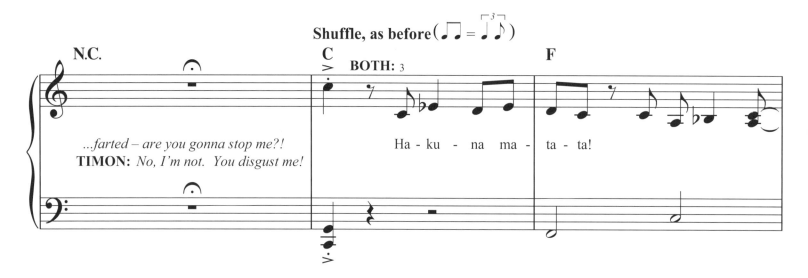

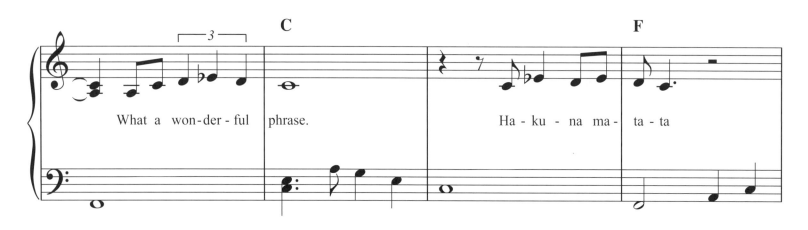

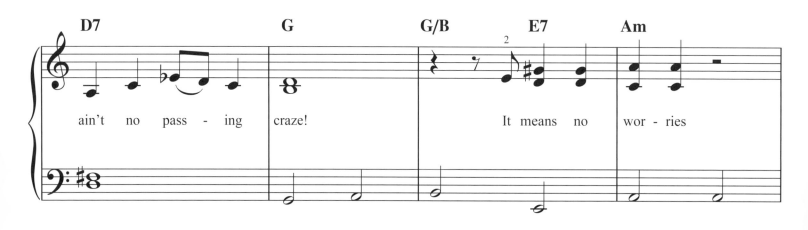

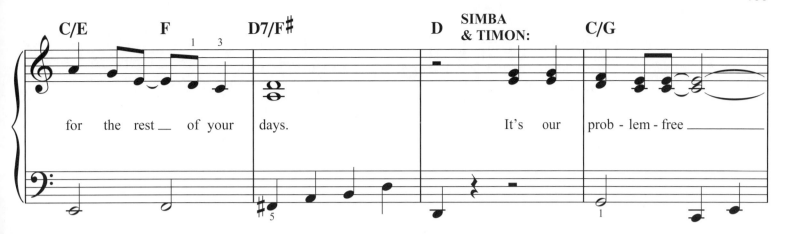

for the rest __ of your days.   It's our prob-lem-free ____

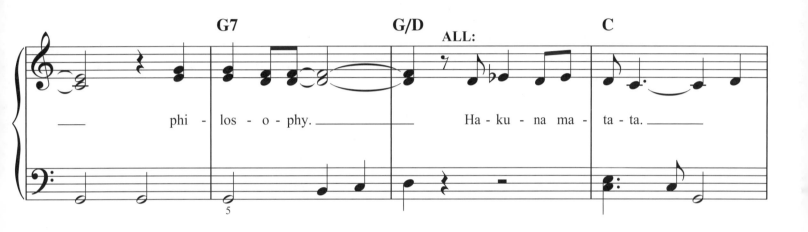

____ phi - los - o - phy. ____   Ha - ku - na ma - ta - ta. ____

Ha - ku - na ma - ta - ta.   Ha-

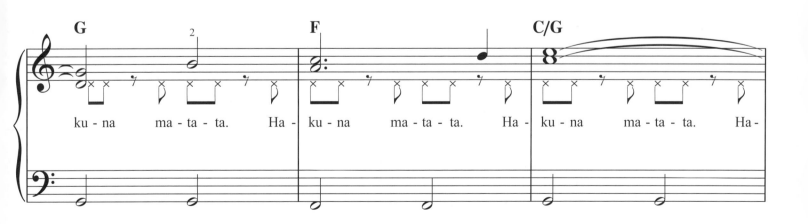

ku - na ma - ta - ta.   Ha - ku - na ma - ta - ta.   Ha - ku - na ma - ta - ta.   Ha-

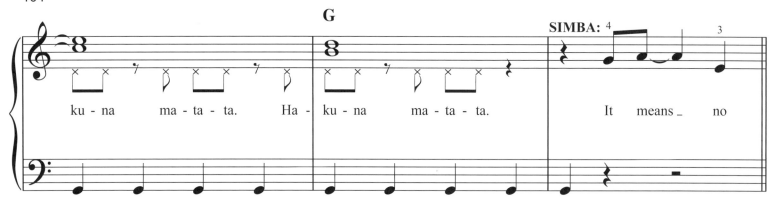

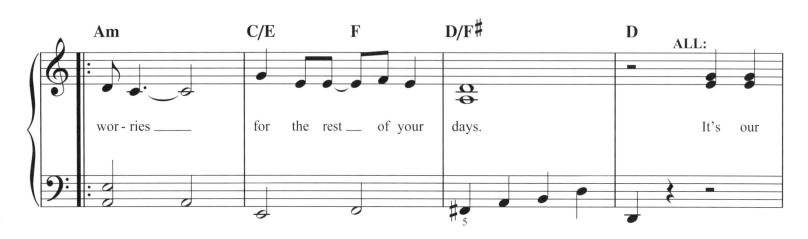

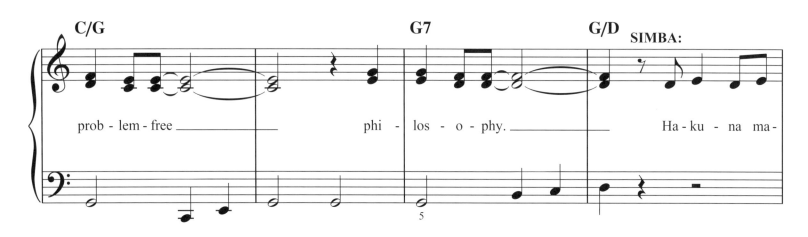

HOW FAR I'LL GO

from MOANA

Music and Lyrics by
LIN-MANUEL MIRANDA

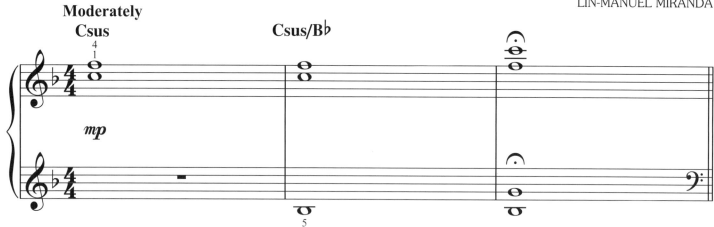

I've been _ star - ing at the edge of the wa - ter _ long _ as I can re -

mem - ber, _ nev - er real - ly know - ing why. I wish _ I could be the per - fect

daugh - ter, _ but I come back to the wa - ter _ no mat - ter how hard I try. Ev - 'ry

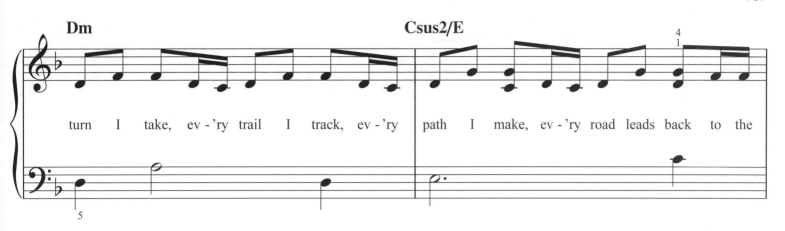

turn I take, ev-'ry trail I track, ev-'ry path I make, ev-'ry road leads back to the

place I know where I can-not go, where I long ___ to be. See the

knows ___ how far it

line where the sky meets the sea, it calls ___ me, and no one knows ___ how far it

goes. ___ If the wind in my sail on the sea stays be-hind ___ me, one day I'll

Dm7   **B♭m6**   **F**

know. _____   If I go, there's just no tell-ing how far I'll go. I ____ know _ ev-'ry-bod-y on this

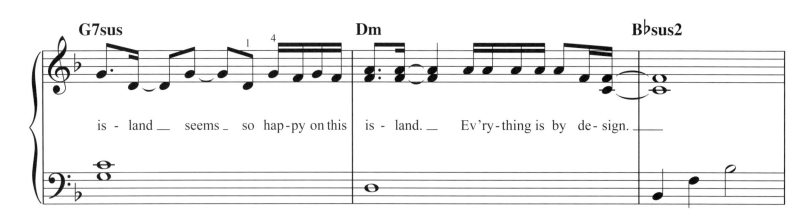

G7sus   **Dm**   **B♭sus2**

is - land __ seems _ so hap-py on this is - land. __ Ev'ry-thing is by de-sign. ____

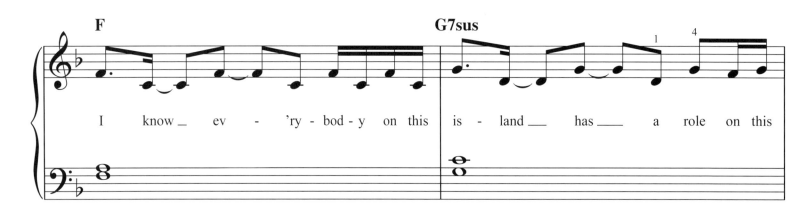

F   **G7sus**

I know __ ev - 'ry-bod-y on this is - land __ has ___ a role on this

Dm   **B♭**

is - land, __ so may-be I can roll with mine. ___   I can

Dm ... **Csus2/E**

lead with pride, I can make us strong. I'll be sat - is - fied if I play a - long, but the

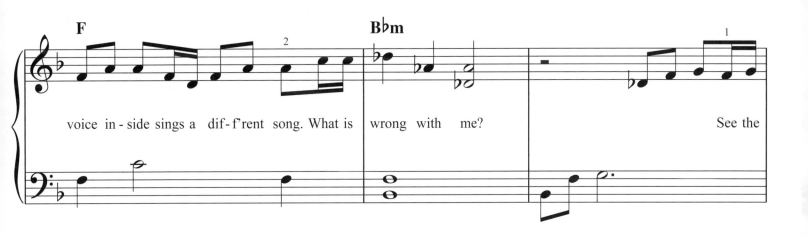

F ... **B♭m**

voice in - side sings a dif - f'rent song. What is wrong with me? See the

F ... **Csus** ... **C** ... **Dm7**

light as it shines on the sea: it's blind - ing, but no one knows _____ how deep it

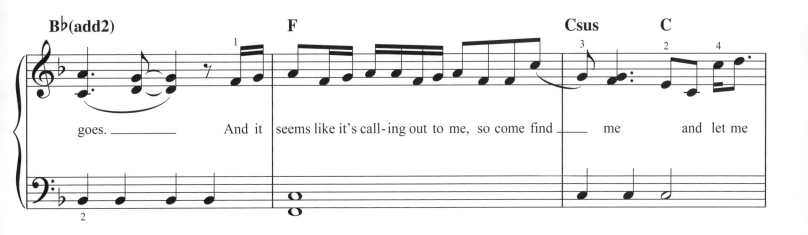

B♭(add2) ... **F** ... **Csus** ... **C**

goes. _____ And it seems like it's call-ing out to me, so come find ____ me and let me

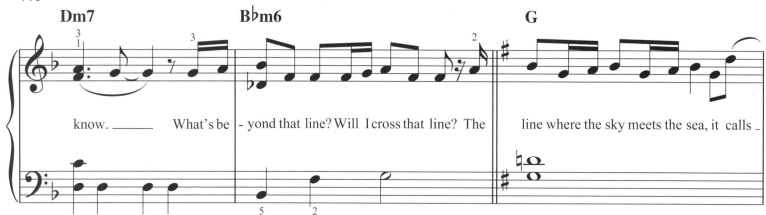

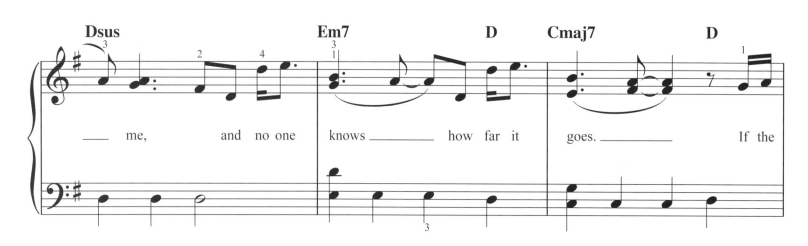

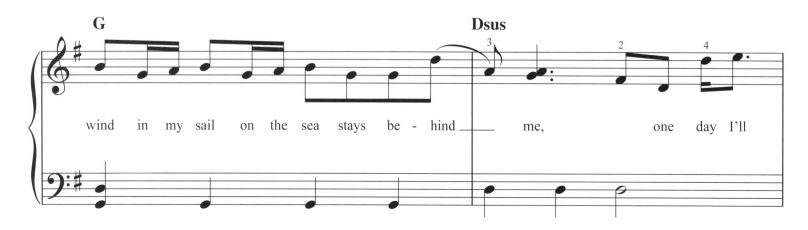

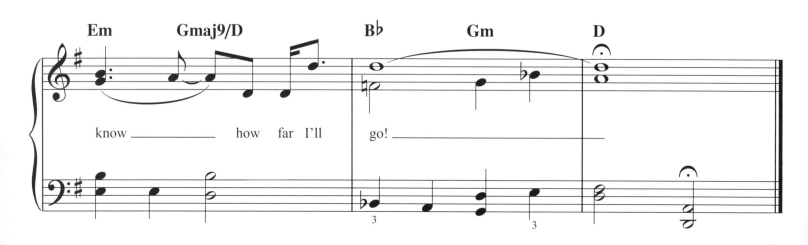

HAWAIIAN ROLLER COASTER RIDE

from LILO & STITCH

Words and Music by ALAN SILVESTRI
and MARK KEALI'I HO'OMALU

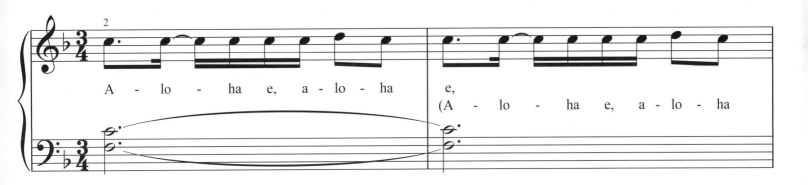

112

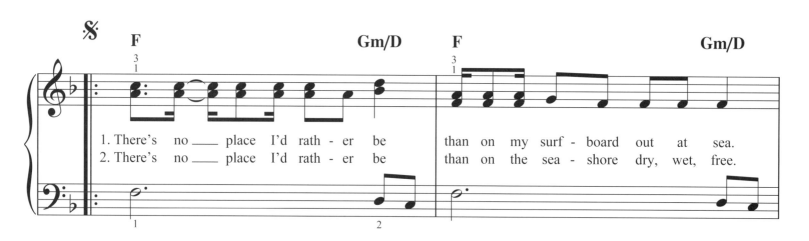

1. There's no place I'd rath-er be than on my surf-board out at sea.
2. There's no place I'd rath-er be than on the sea-shore dry, wet, free.

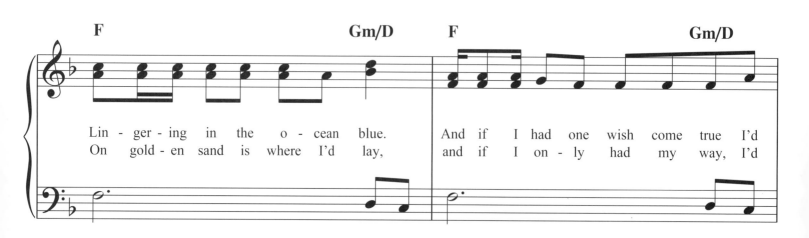

Lin - ger - ing in the o - cean blue. And if I had one wish come true I'd
On gold - en sand is where I'd lay, and if I on - ly had my way, I'd

113

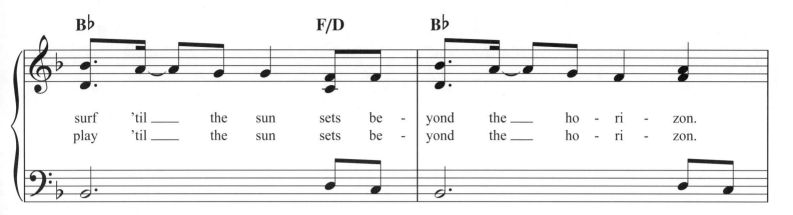

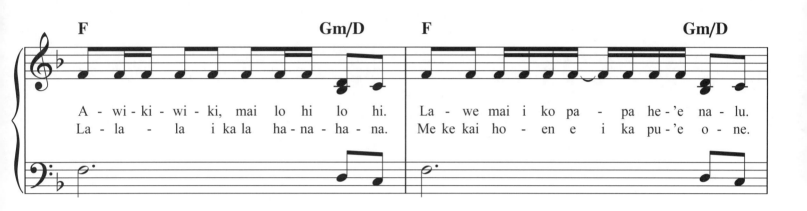

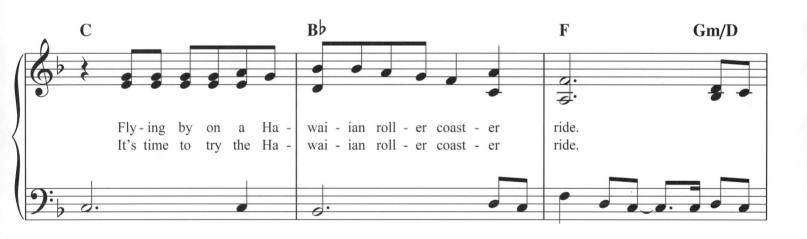

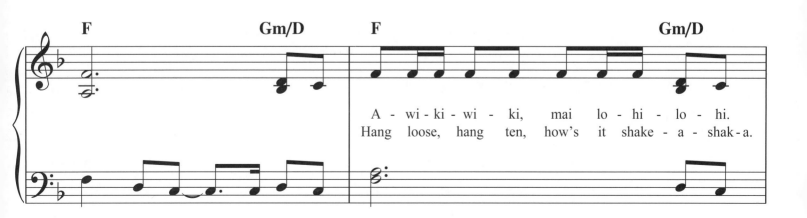

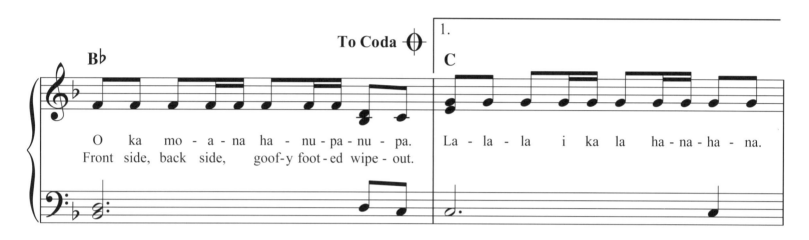

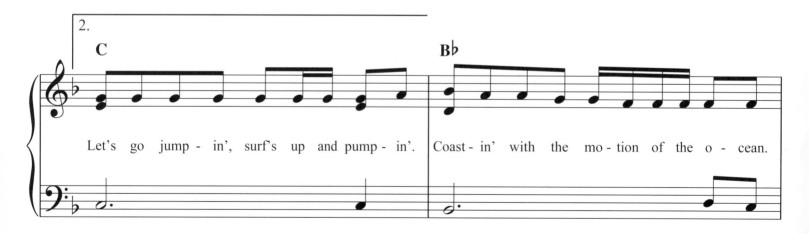

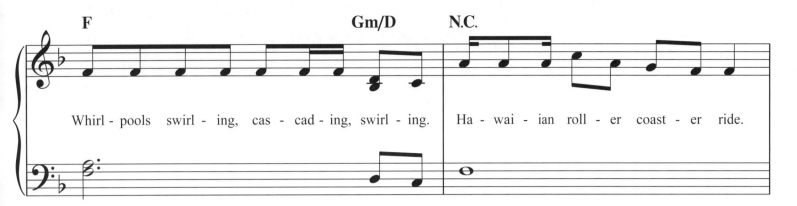

I JUST CAN'T WAIT TO BE KING

from THE LION KING (2019)

Music by ELTON JOHN
Lyrics by TIM RICE

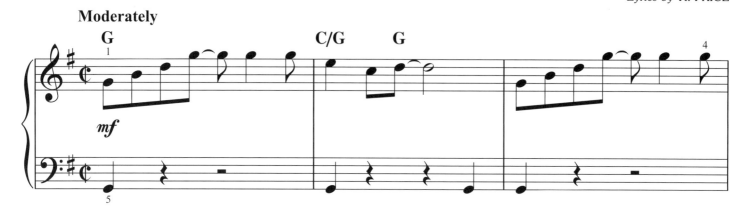

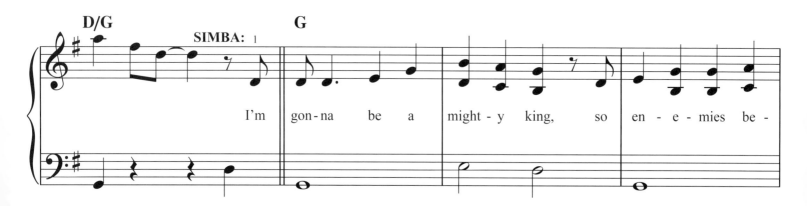

I'm gon-na be a might-y king, so en-e-mies be-

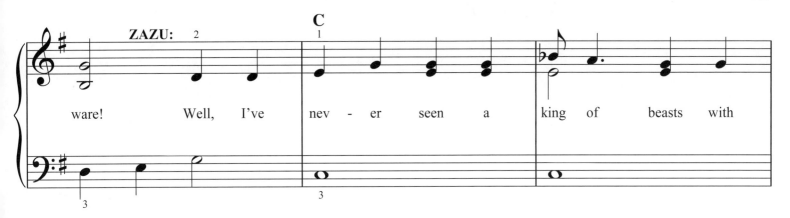

ware! Well, I've nev - er seen a king of beasts with

quite so lit - tle hair. I'm gon - na be the mane e - vent, like

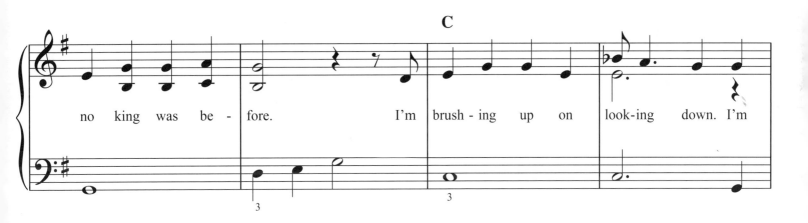

no king was be - fore. I'm brush - ing up on look - ing down. I'm

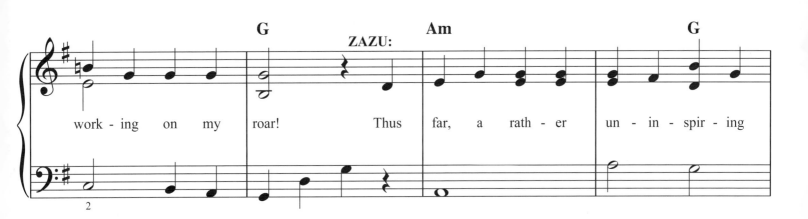

work - ing on my roar! Thus far, a rath - er un - in - spir - ing

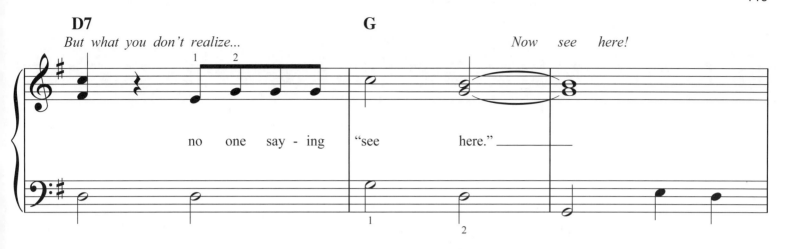

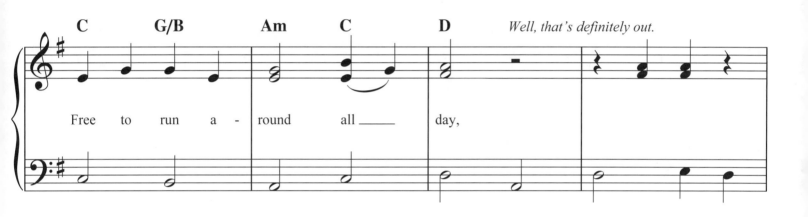

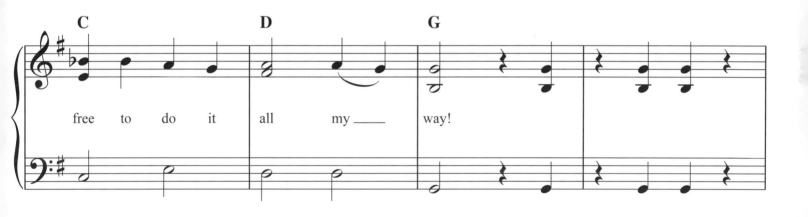

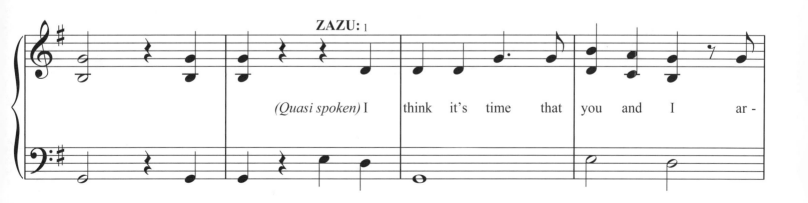

120

ranged a heart - to - heart. *(Sung)* Kings don't need ad - vice from lit - tle

horn - bills, for a start. *(Quasi spoken)* If this is where the

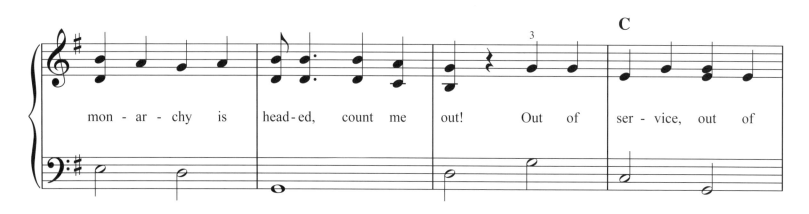

mon - ar - chy is head - ed, count me out! Out of ser - vice, out of

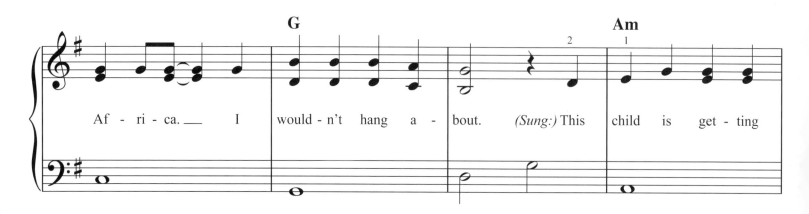

Af - ri - ca. ___ I would - n't hang a - bout. *(Sung:)* This child is get - ting

wild - ly   out   of   wing!   Oh, I   just   can't ____

wait   to   be   king!

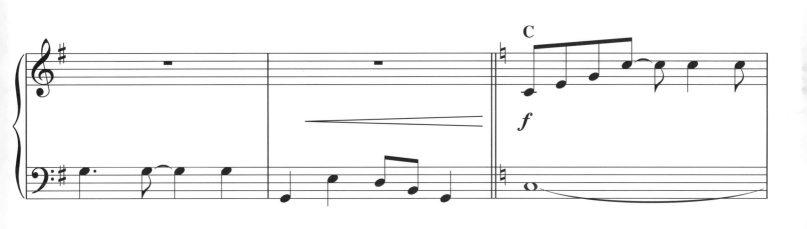

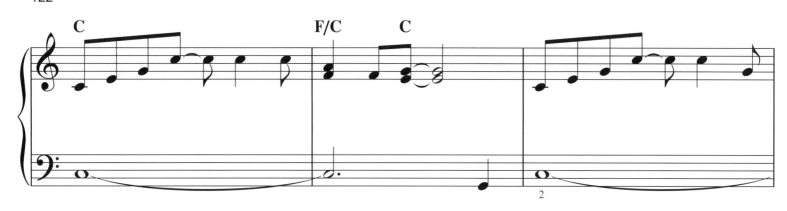

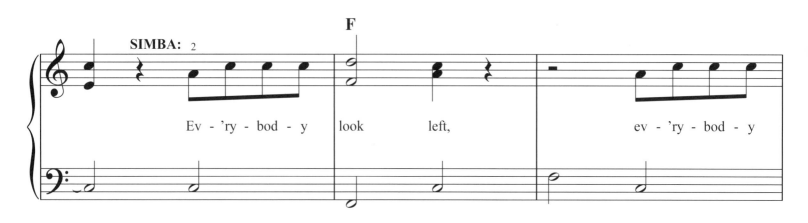

Ev - 'ry - bod - y look left, ev - 'ry - bod - y

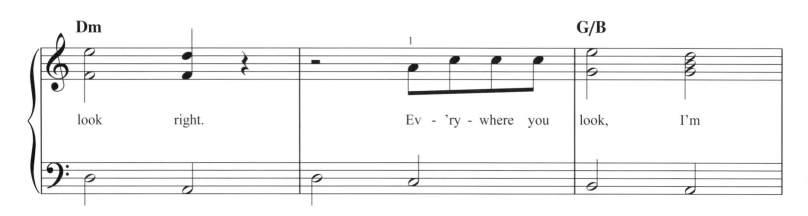

look right. Ev - 'ry - where you look, I'm

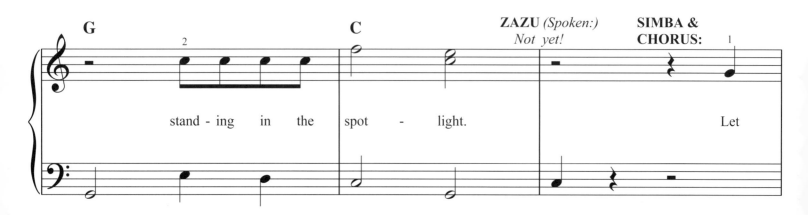

stand - ing in the spot - light. Let

ZAZU *(Spoken:)*
Not yet!

SIMBA & CHORUS:

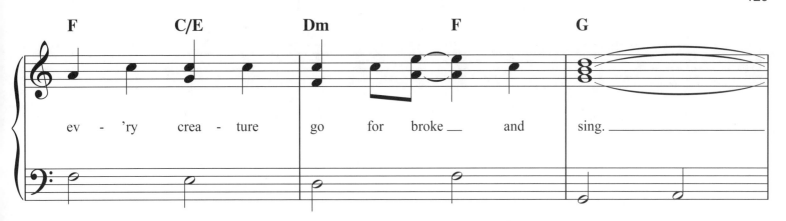

ev - 'ry crea - ture go for broke __ and sing. ___

___ Let's hear it in the herd and on __ the wing. ___

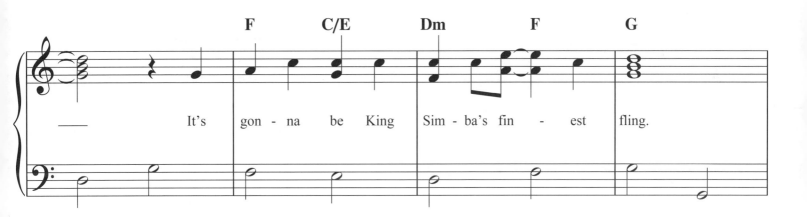

___ It's gon - na be King Sim - ba's fin - est fling.

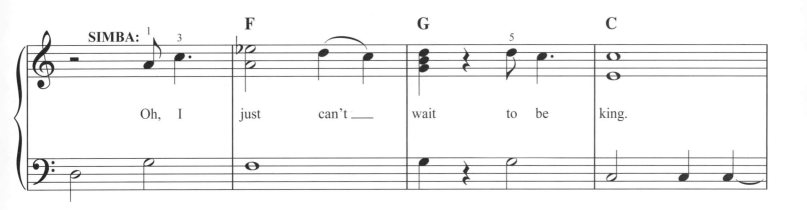

SIMBA: Oh, I just can't __ wait to be king.

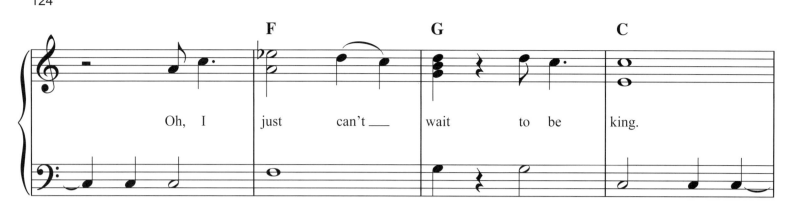

Oh, I just can't ___ wait to be king.

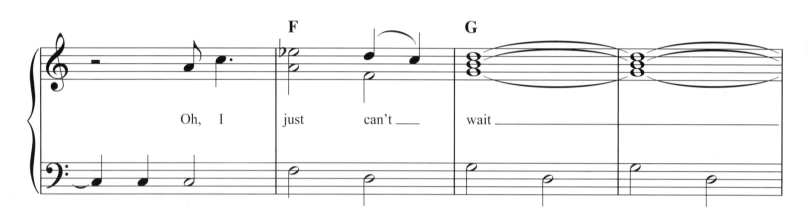

Oh, I just can't ___ wait ___

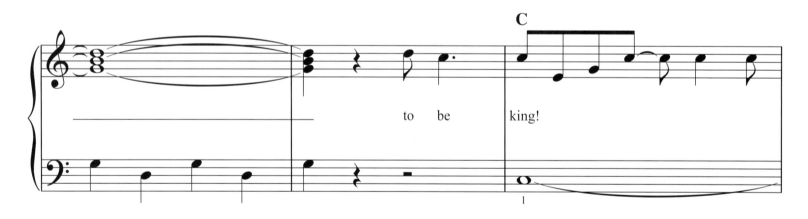

___ to be king!

I WON'T SAY

(I'm in Love)
from HERCULES

Music by ALAN MENKEN
Lyrics by DAVID ZIPPEL

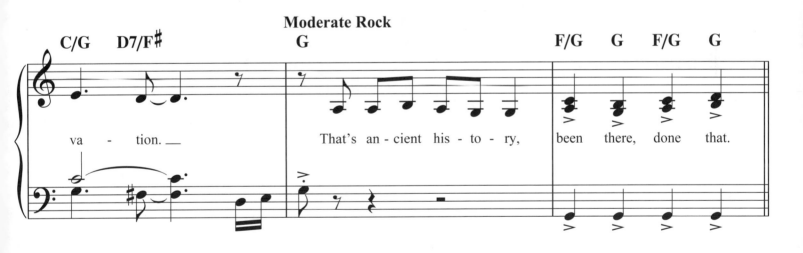

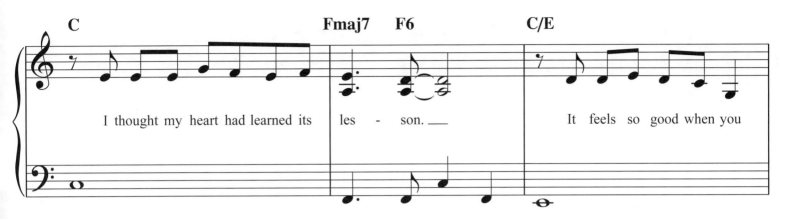

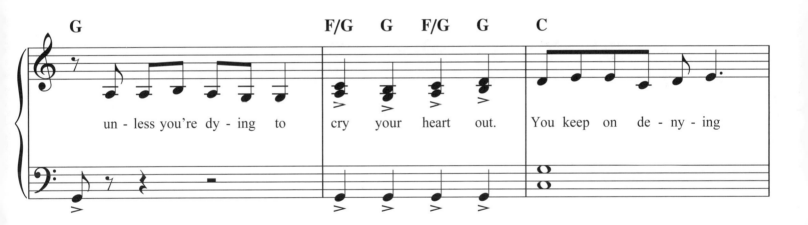

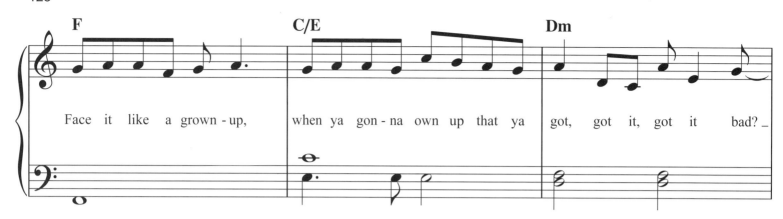

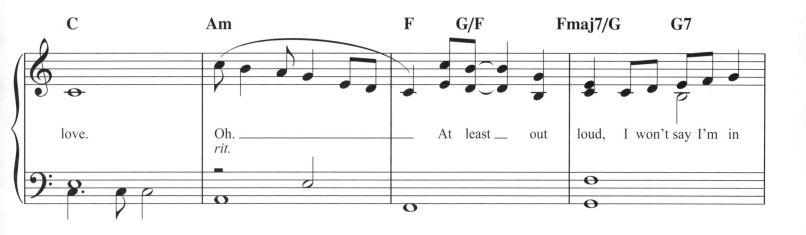

I SEE THE LIGHT
from TANGLED

Music by ALAN MENKEN
Lyrics by GLENN SLATER

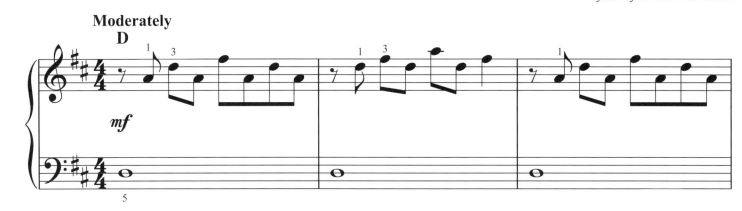

All those days,
Now I'm here,
watch - ing from the win - dows.
blink - ing in the star - light.

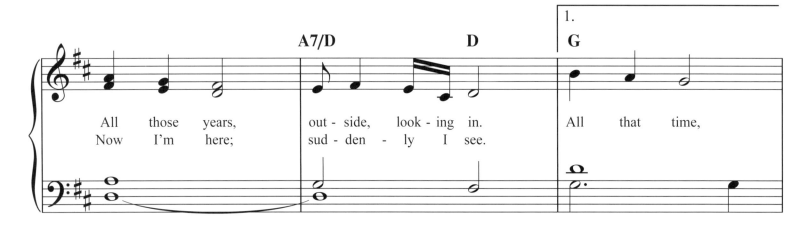

All those years,
Now I'm here;
out - side, look - ing in.
sud - den - ly I see.

1.
All that time,

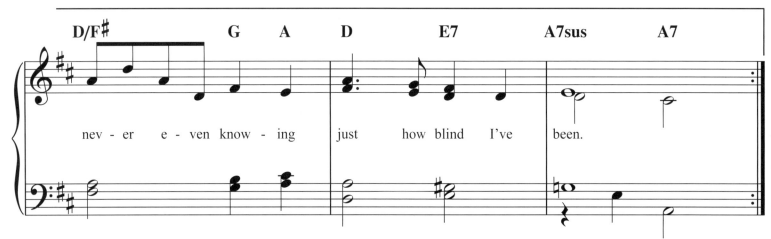

nev - er e - ven know - ing just how blind I've been.

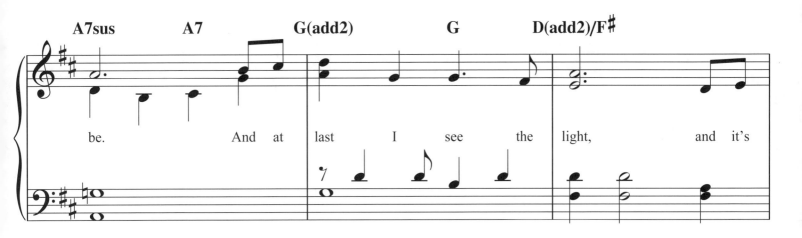

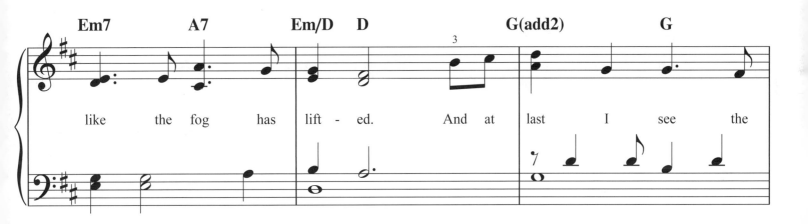

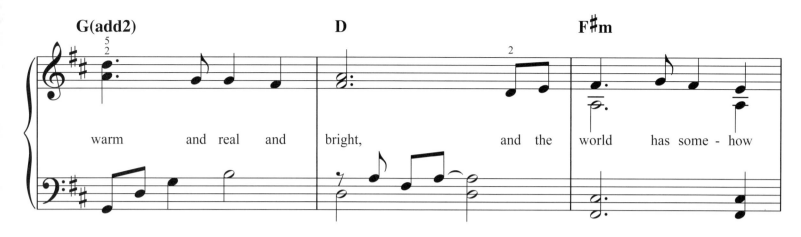

warm and real and bright, and the world has some - how

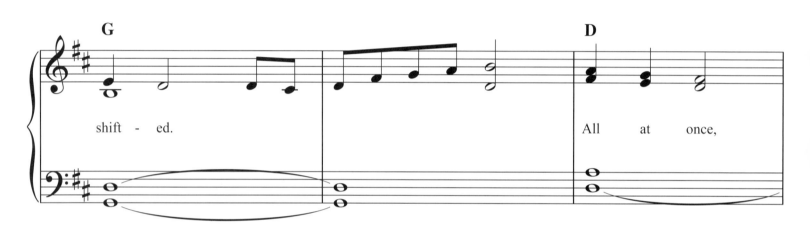

shift - ed. All at once,

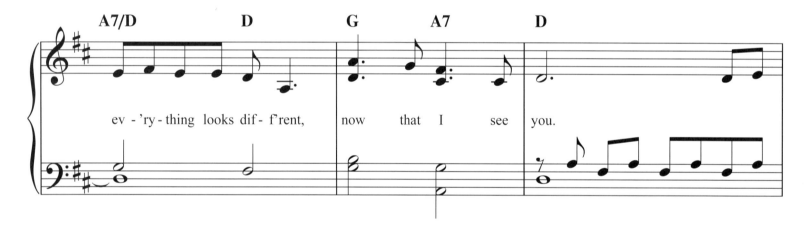

ev - 'ry - thing looks dif - f'rent, now that I see you.

All those days, chas - ing down a day - dream.

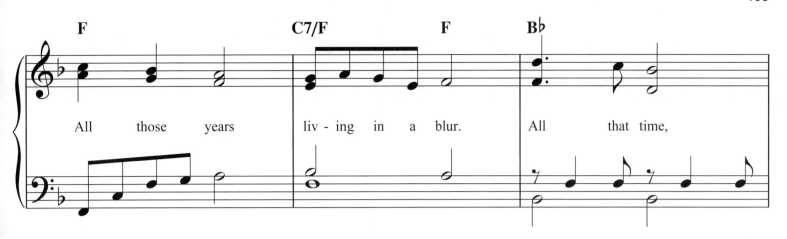

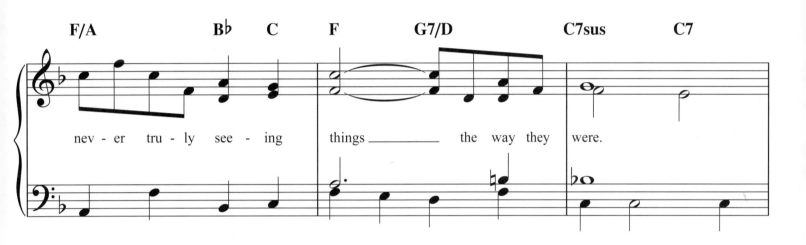

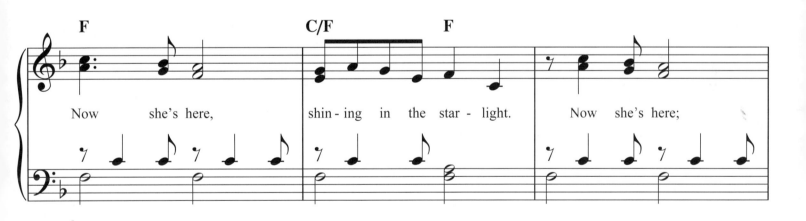

134

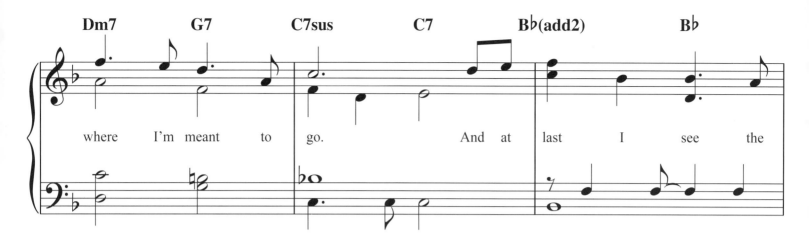

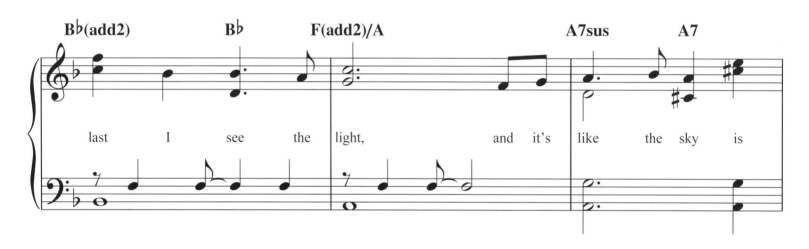

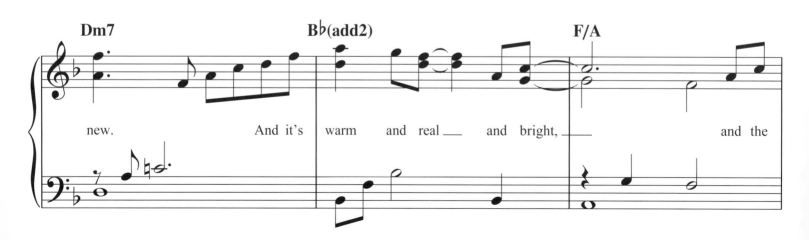

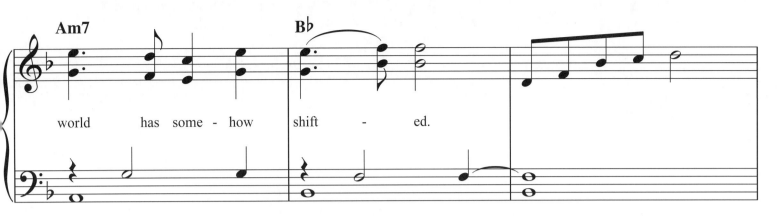

world has some-how shift - ed.

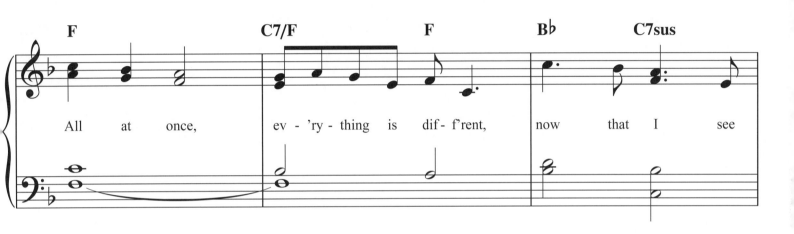

All at once, ev-'ry-thing is dif-f'rent, now that I see

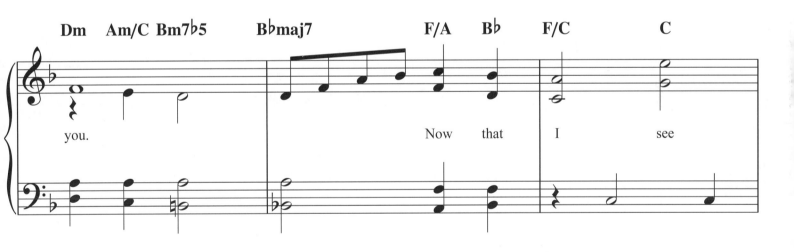

you. Now that I see

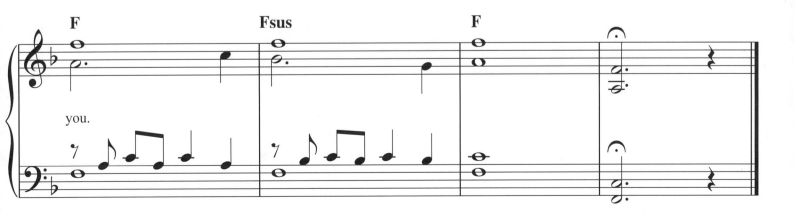

you.

I'LL MAKE A MAN OUT OF YOU

from MULAN

Music by MATTHEW WILDER
Lyrics by DAVID ZIPPEL

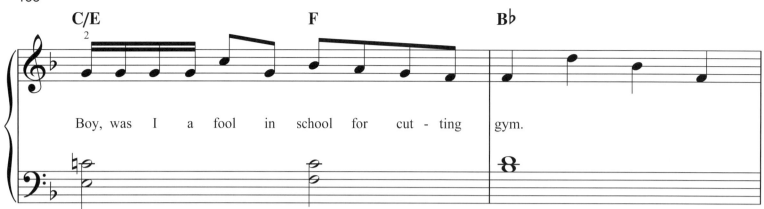

Boy, was I a fool in school for cut-ting gym.

This guy's got 'em scared to death. Hope he does-n't see right through me.

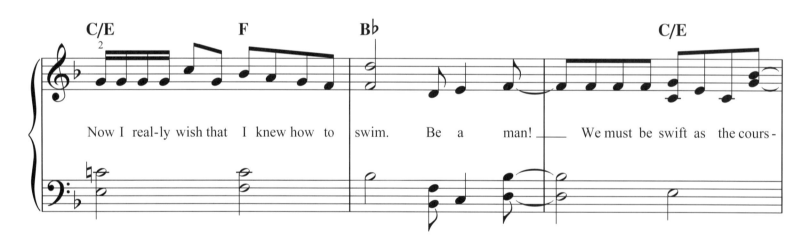

Now I real-ly wish that I knew how to swim. Be a man! We must be swift as the cours-

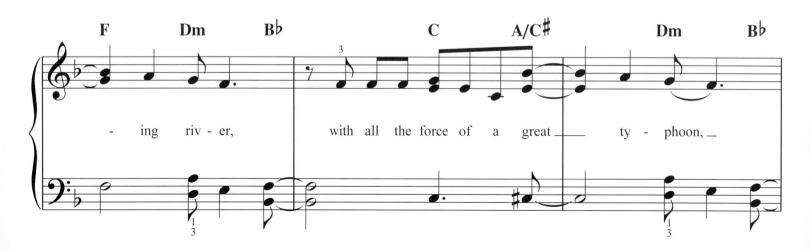

-ing riv-er, with all the force of a great ty-phoon,

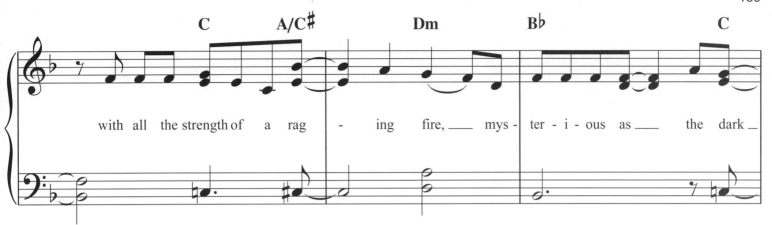

with all the strength of a rag - ing fire, __ mys - ter - i - ous as __ the dark __

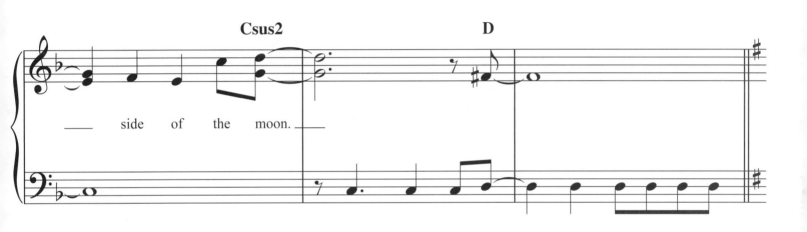

__ side of the moon. __

Time is rac - ing toward __ us 'til the Huns ar - rive.

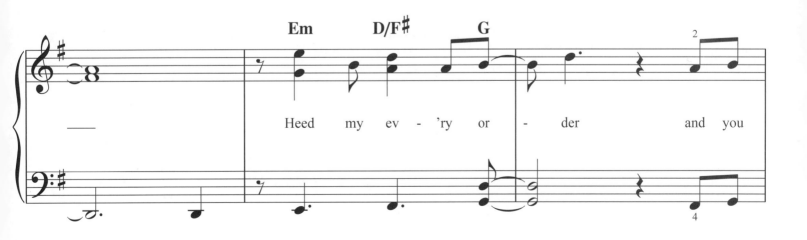

__ Heed my ev - 'ry or - der and you

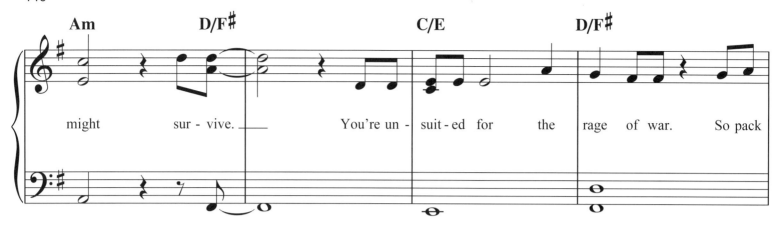

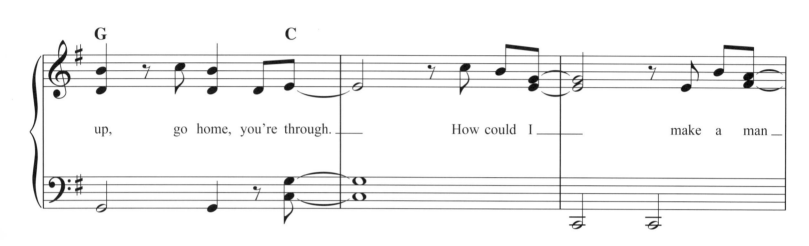

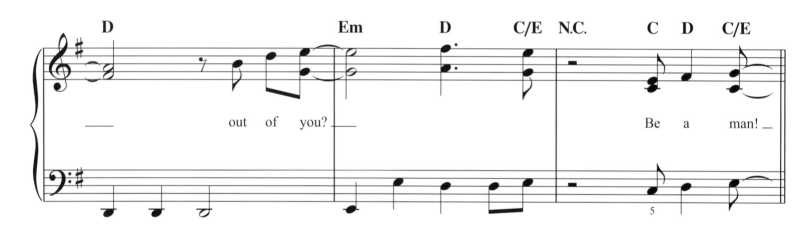

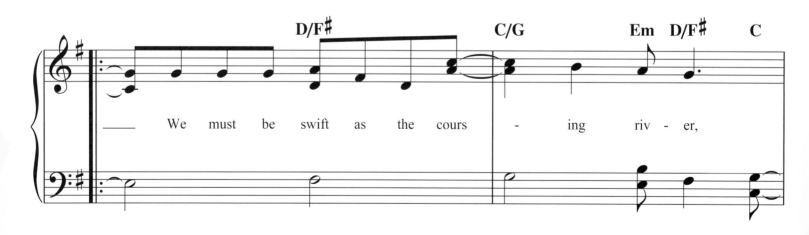

I'VE GOT A DREAM

from TANGLED

Music by ALAN MENKEN
Lyrics by GLENN SLATER

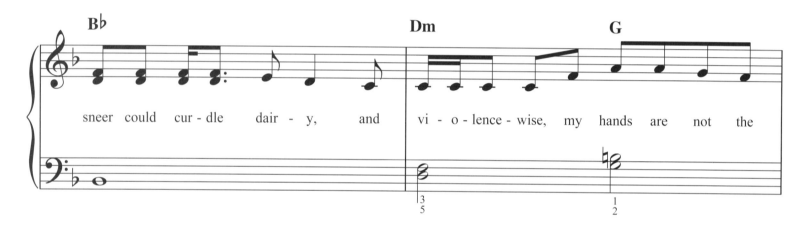

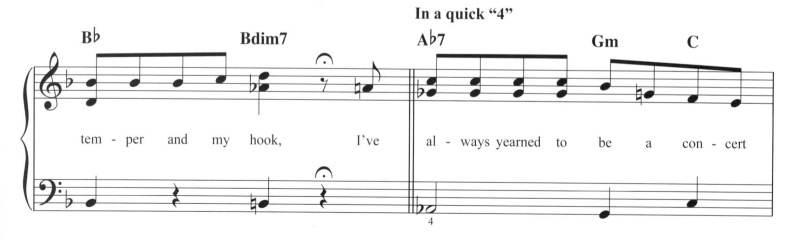

143

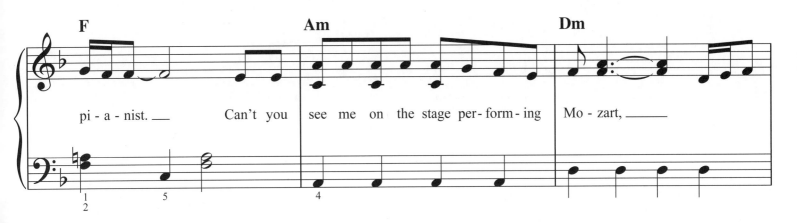

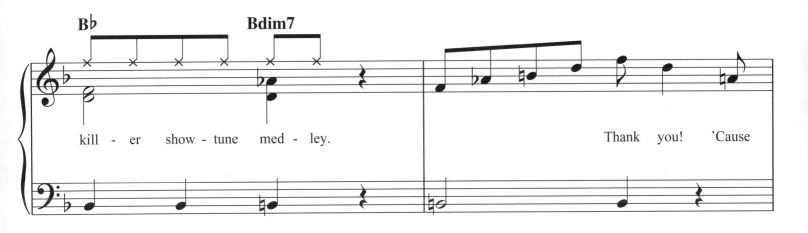

144

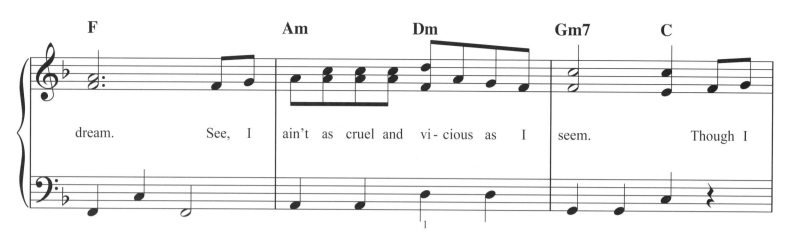

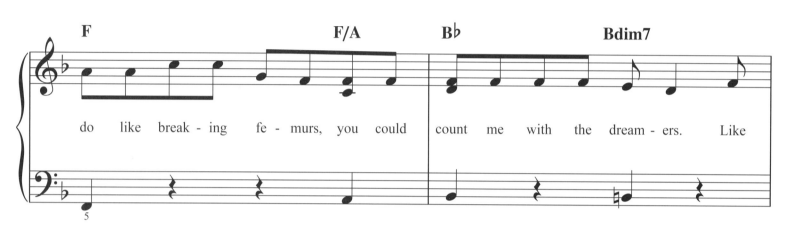

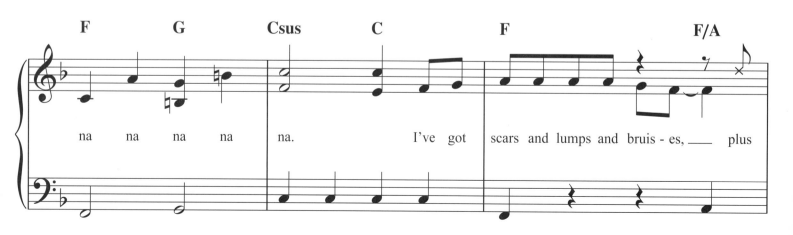

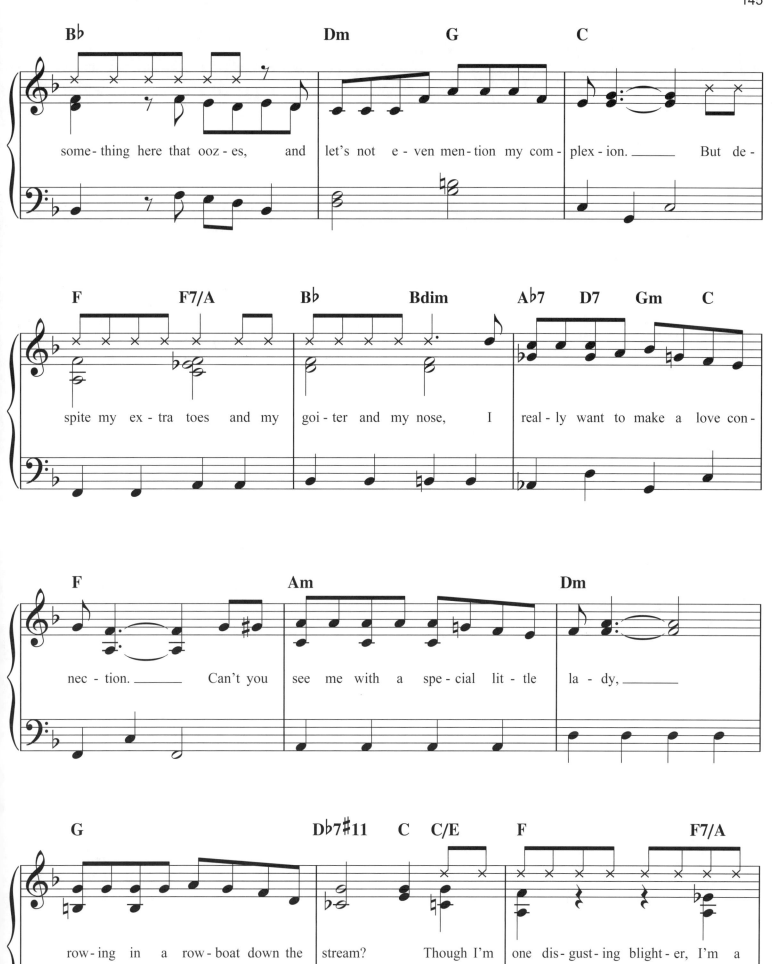

lov - er, not a fight - er, 'cause way down deep in - side, I've got a dream. I've got a

dream, _____ I've got a dream, and I know one day ro - mance will reign su -

preme! Though my face leaves peo - ple scream - ing, there's a child be - hind it dream - ing. Like

ev - 'ry - bod - y else, I've got a dream. Tor would like to quit and be a

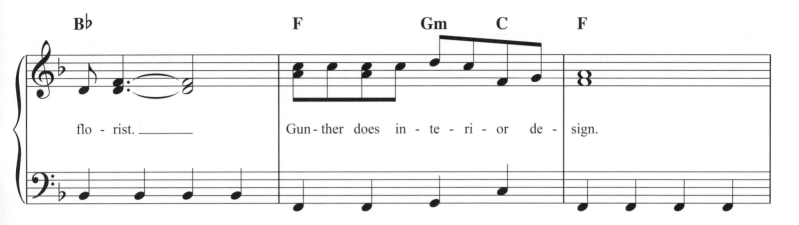

florist. _____ Gun - ther does in - te - ri - or de - sign.

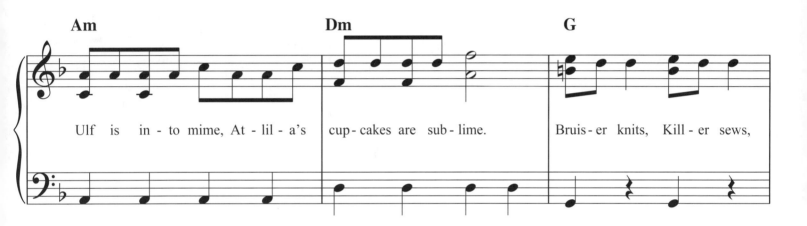

Ulf is in - to mime, At - lil - a's cup - cakes are sub - lime. Bruis - er knits, Kill - er sews,

Fang does lit - tle pup - pet shows, and Vla - di - mir col - lects cer - am - ic u - ni - corns.

rit.

I have dreams like you, no, real - ly! Just much less touch - y feel - y. They

a tempo

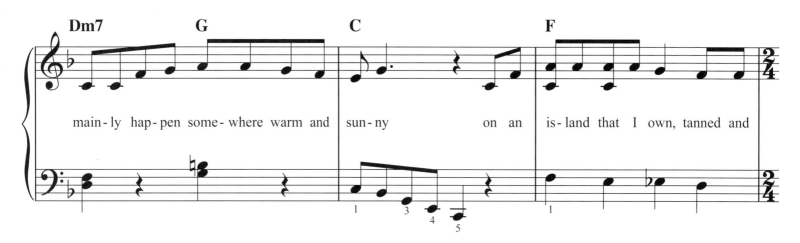

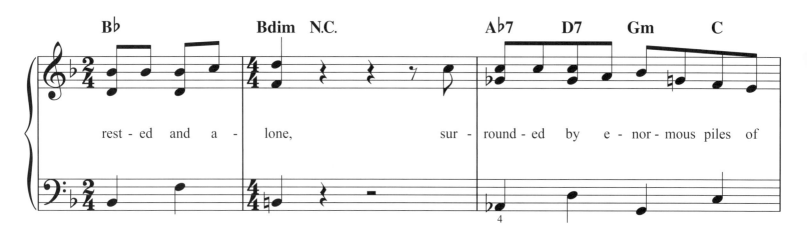

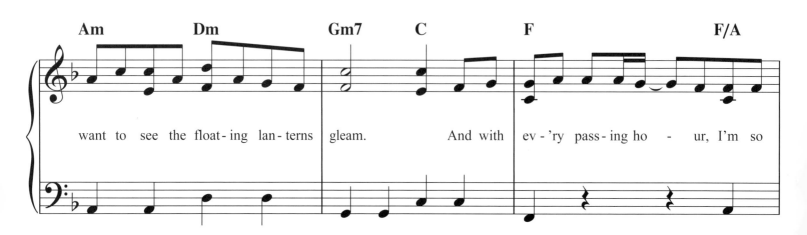

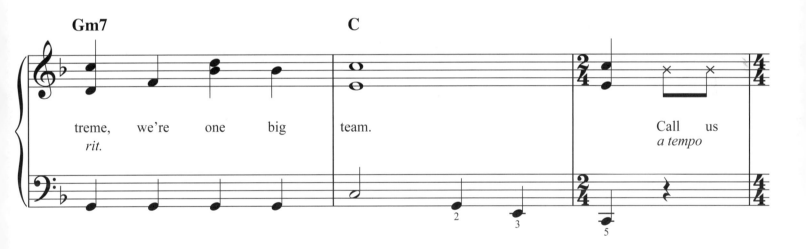

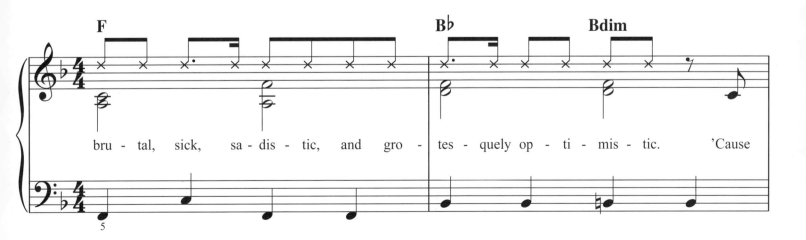

way down deep in - side, we've got a dream, I've got a dream, I've got a

dream, I've got a dream, I've got a dream, I've got a dream, I've got a

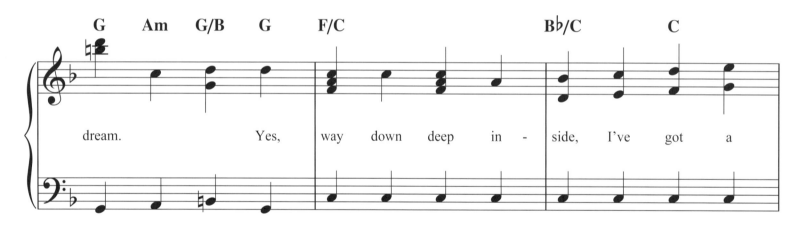

dream. Yes, way down deep in - side, I've got a

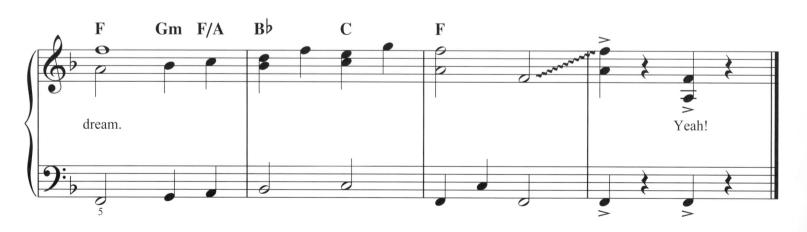

dream. Yeah!

IN SUMMER
from FROZEN

Music and Lyrics by KRISTEN ANDERSON-LOPEZ
and ROBERT LOPEZ

152

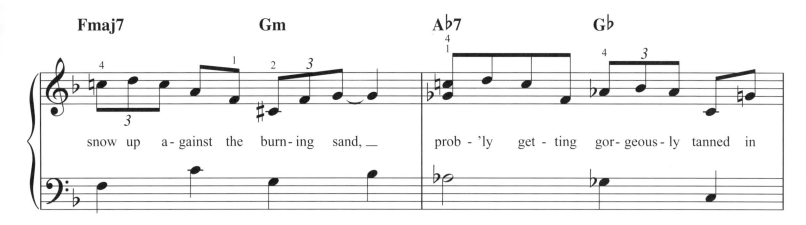

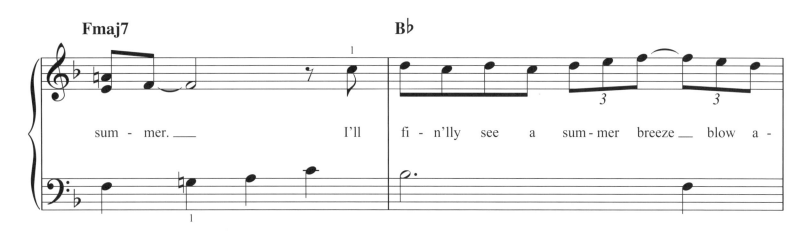

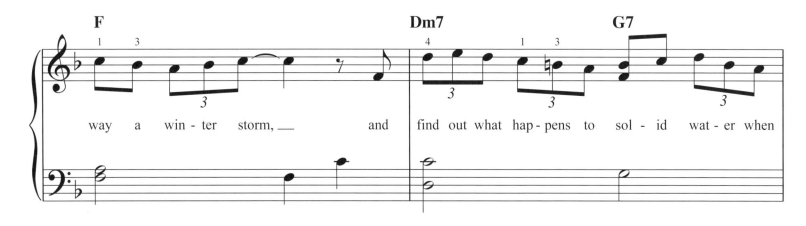

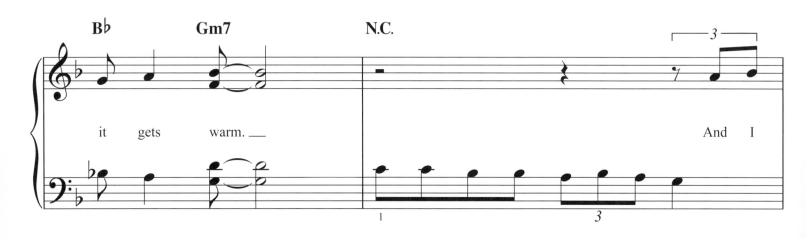

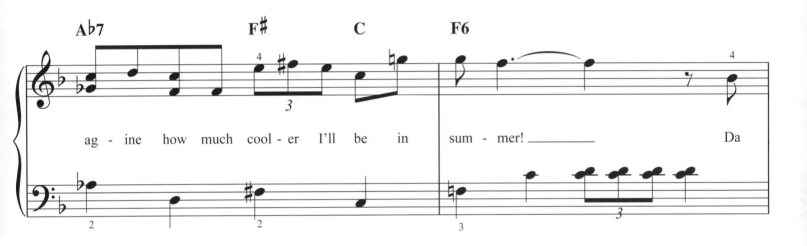

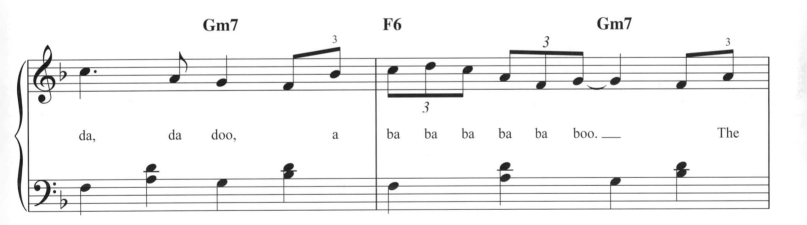

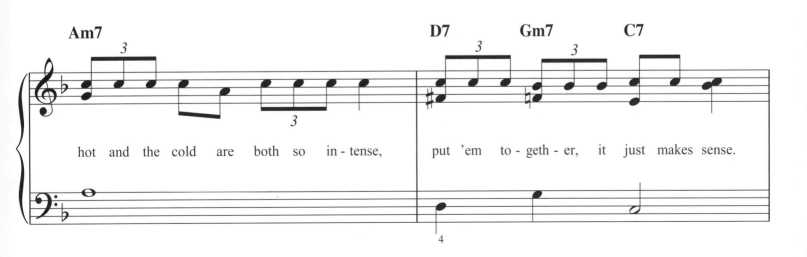

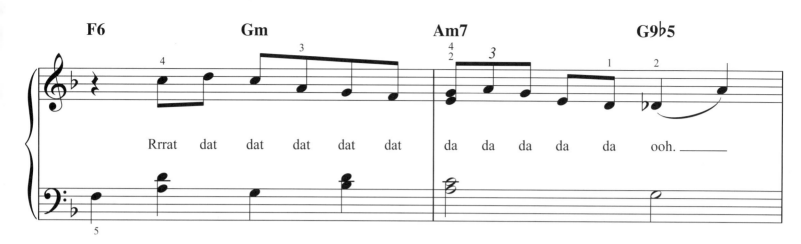

Rrrat dat dat dat dat dat da da da da da ooh. _____

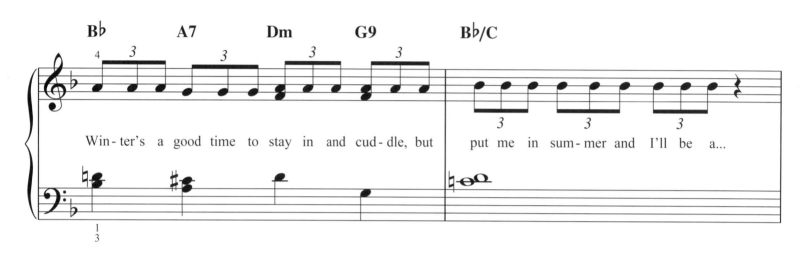

Win - ter's a good time to stay in and cud - dle, but put me in sum - mer and I'll be a...

(Spoken:) happy snowman! *(Sung:) When life gets rough, I like to*

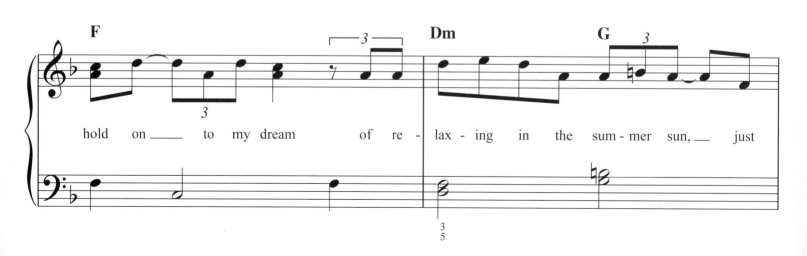

hold on _____ to my dream of re - lax - ing in the sum - mer sun, _____ just

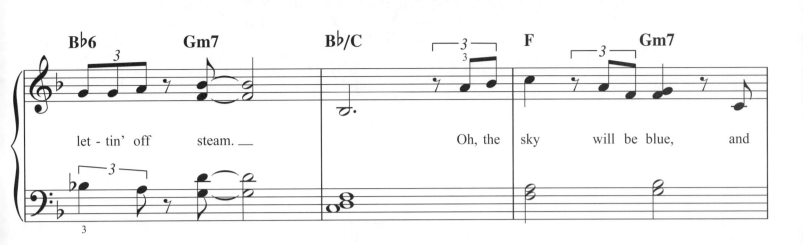

let - tin' off   steam. __   Oh, the   sky   will be blue,   and

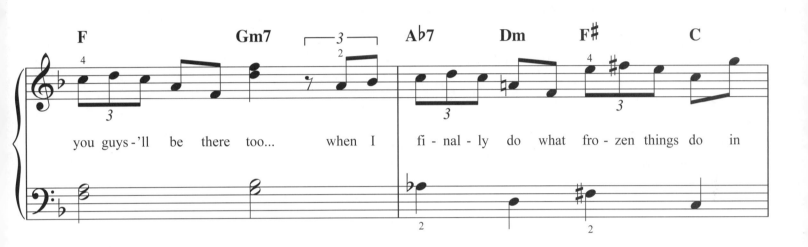

you guys -'ll   be   there too...   when I   fi - nal - ly   do   what   fro - zen things do   in

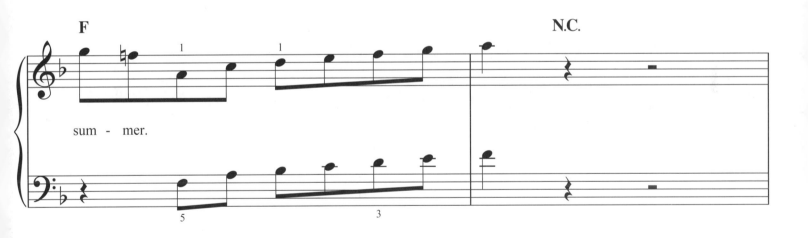

sum - mer.

In   sum - mer! _____

AN INNOCENT WARRIOR
from MOANA

By OPETAIA FOA'I

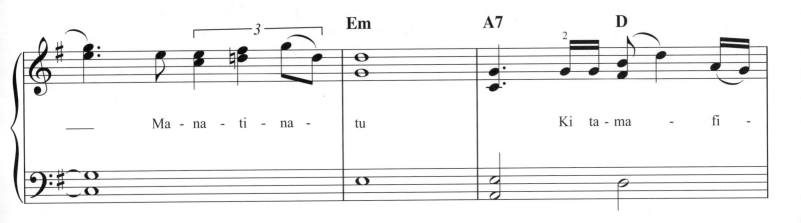

Ma - na - ti - na - tu   Ki ta - ma - fi -

ne   Ma - un ai   te lu - ma - nai

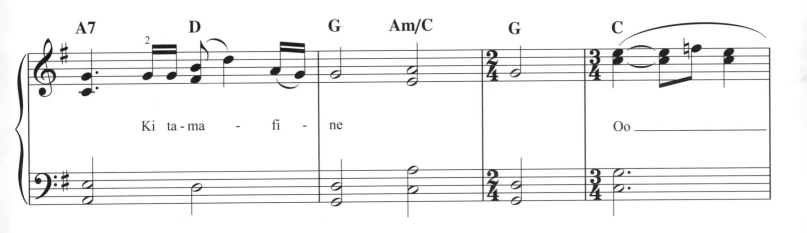

Ki ta - ma - fi - ne   Oo

Oo   O ma - ta e ma - ta - ge

JUST AROUND THE RIVERBEND

from POCAHONTAS

Music by ALAN MENKEN
Lyrics by STEPHEN SCHWARTZ

What I love most a-bout riv-ers is: you

can't step in the same riv-er twice. The wa-ter's al-ways chang-ing, al-ways

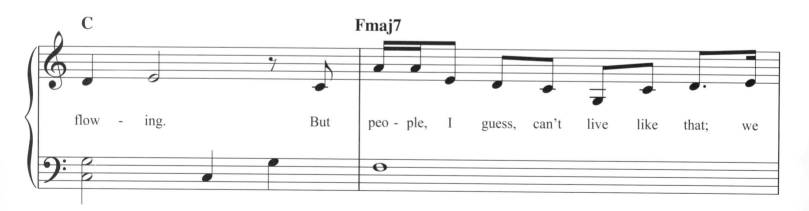

flow - ing. But peo - ple, I guess, can't live like that; we

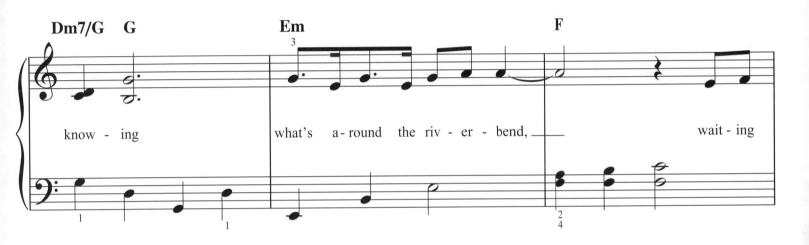

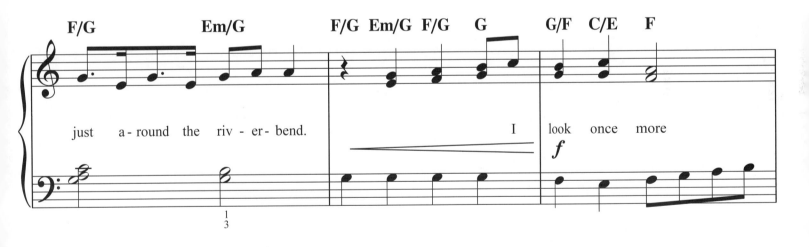

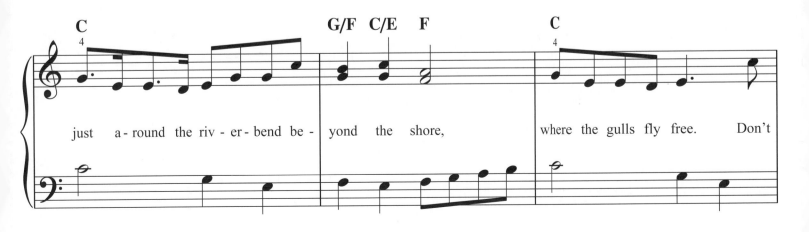

know what for, what I dream the day might send just a-round the riv-er-bend __

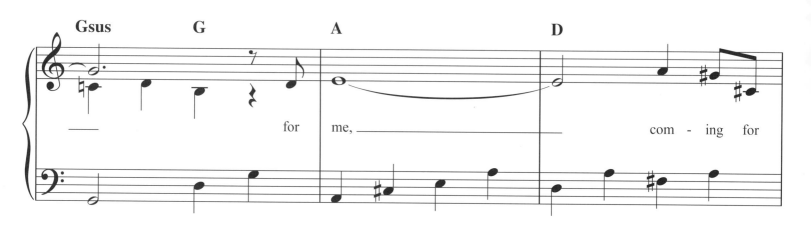

__ for me, __ com-ing for

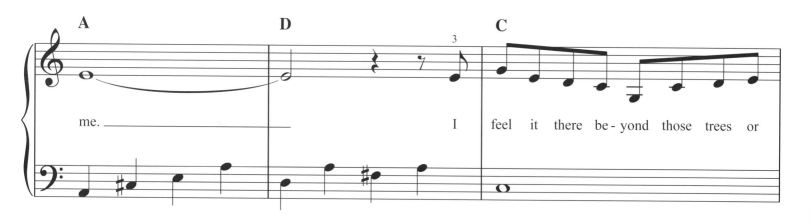

me. __ I feel it there be-yond those trees or

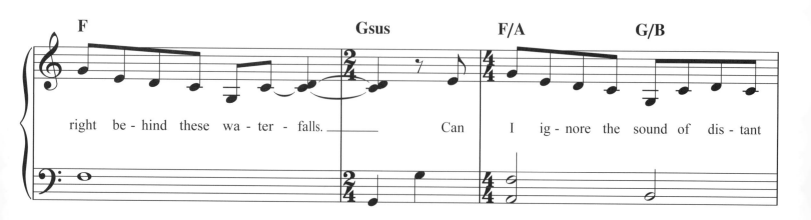

right be-hind these wa-ter-falls. __ Can I ig-nore the sound of dis-tant

drum - ming   for a   hand - some stur - dy hus - band who builds   hand - some stur - dy walls   and

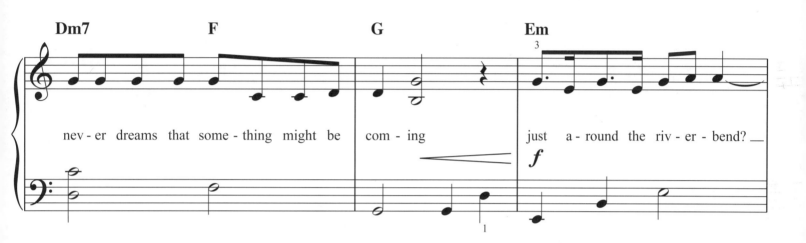

nev - er dreams that some - thing might be   com - ing   just a - round the riv - er - bend? __

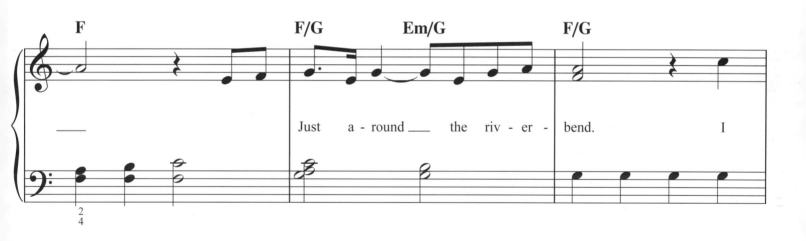

__   Just a - round __ the riv - er - bend.   I

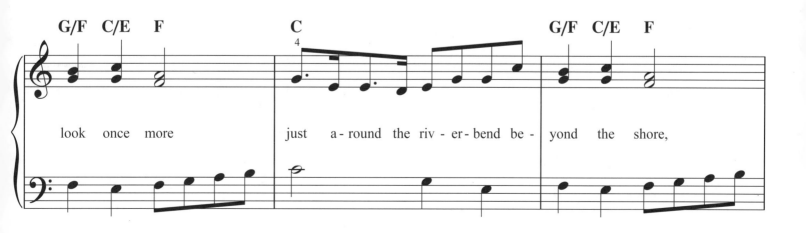

look once more   just a - round the riv - er - bend be - yond the shore,

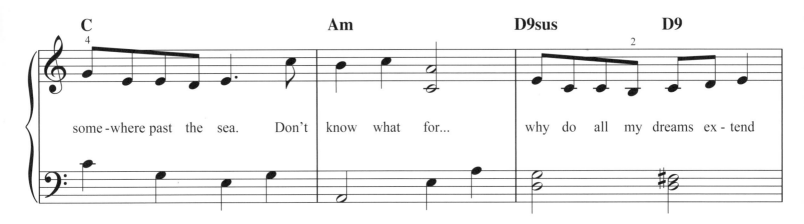

Slowly

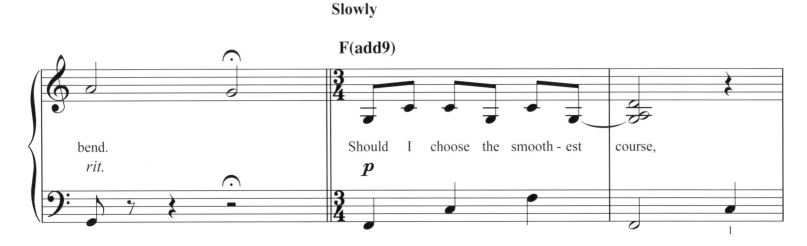

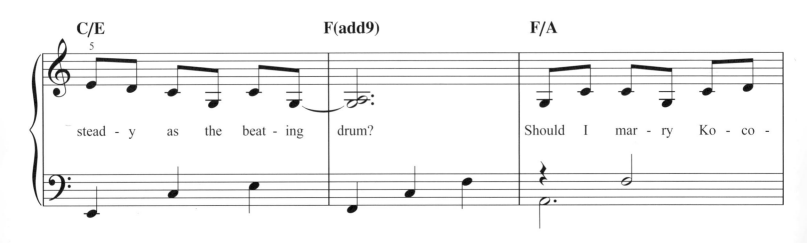

um? _____ Is all my dream - ing at an end? Or

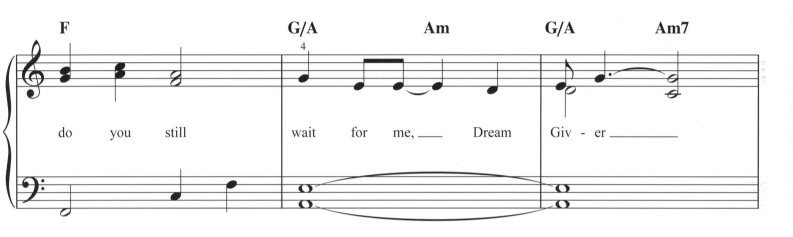

do you still wait for me, ___ Dream Giv - er _____

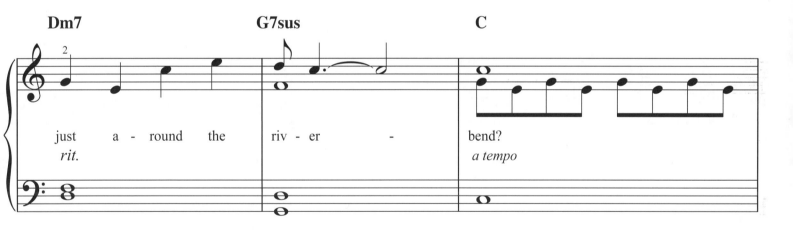

just a - round the riv - er - bend?

rit.   *a tempo*

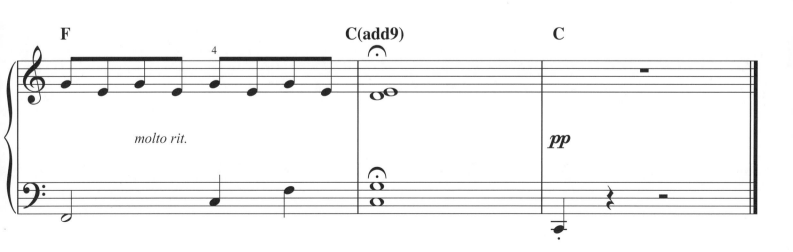

molto rit.   *pp*

LET IT GO
from FROZEN

Music and Lyrics by KRISTEN ANDERSON-LOPEZ
and ROBERT LOPEZ

Half-time feel, mysterious

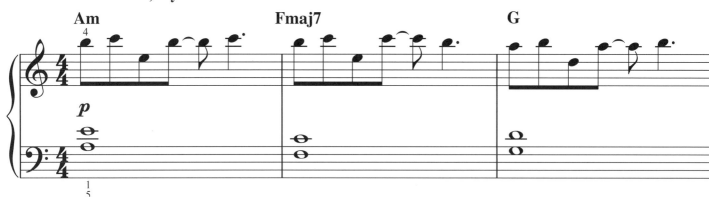

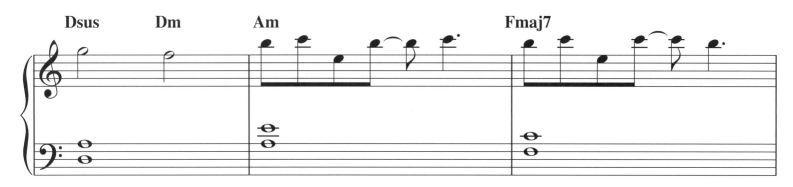

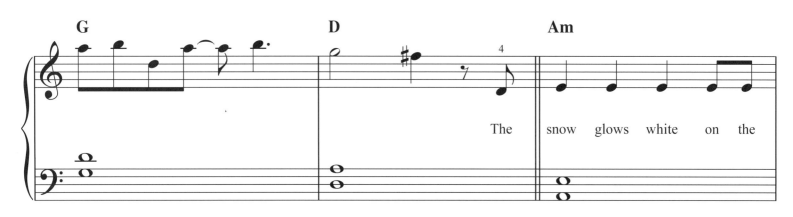

The snow glows white on the

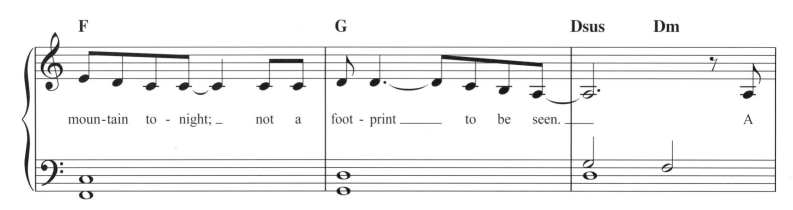

moun-tain to-night;_ not a foot-print _____ to be seen. ___ A

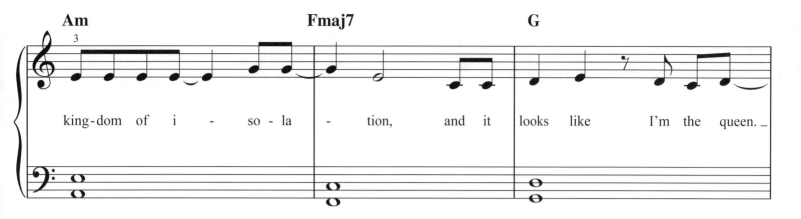

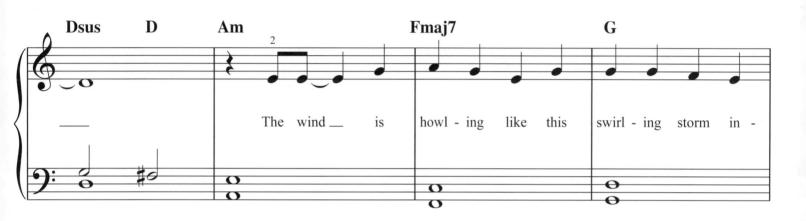

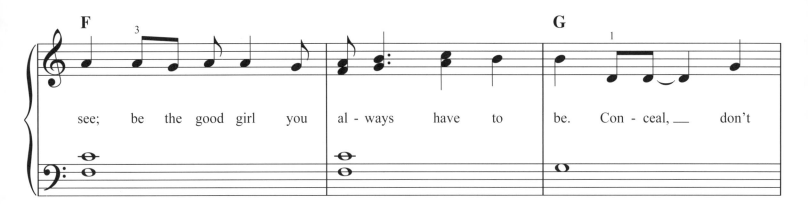

see; be the good girl you al - ways have to be. Con - ceal, __ don't

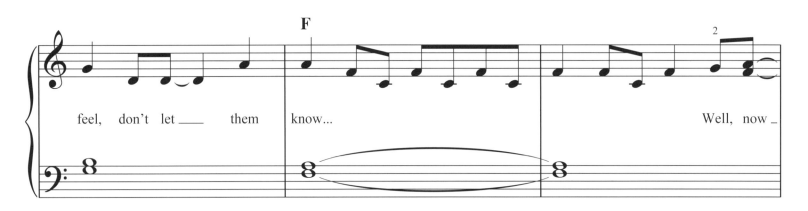

feel, don't let __ them know... Well, now __

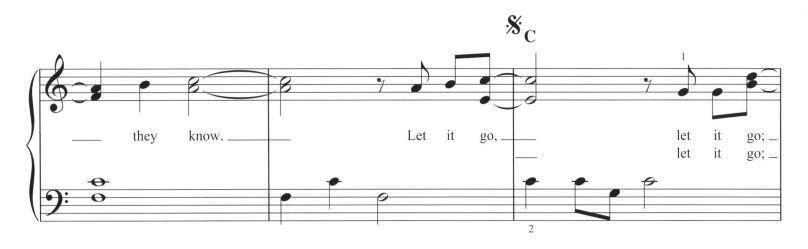

__ they know. __ Let it go, __ let it go;

let it go; __

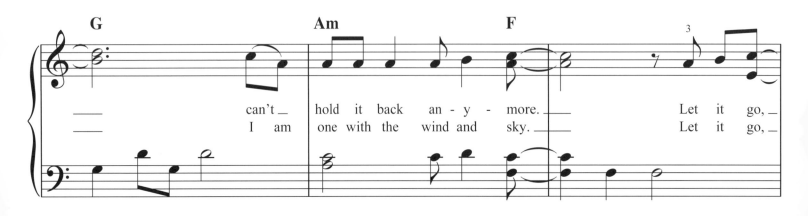

can't __ hold it back an - y - more. Let it go, __

I am one with the wind and sky. Let it go, __

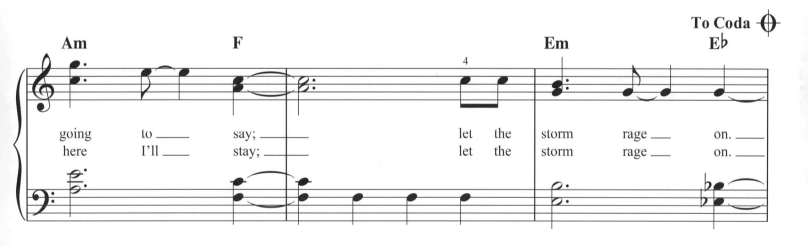

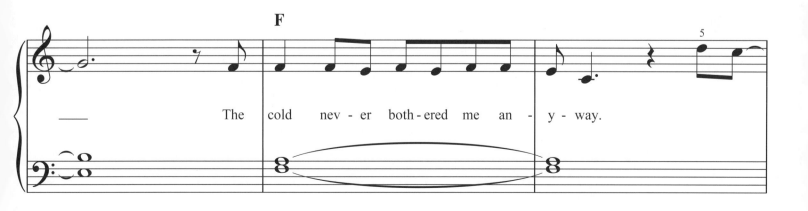

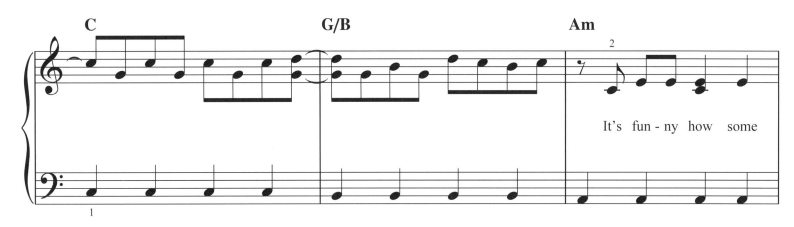

C   G/B   Am

It's fun - ny how some

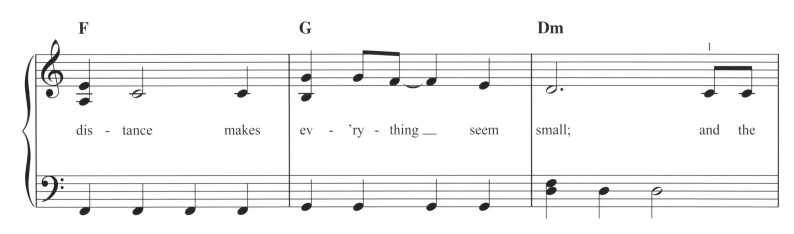

F   G   Dm

dis - tance   makes   ev - 'ry - thing __ seem   small;   and the

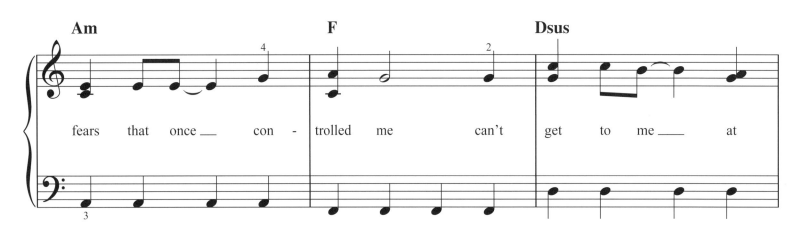

Am   F   Dsus

fears that once __ con - trolled me   can't   get to me ___ at

D   G

all.   It's time __ to   see what I can

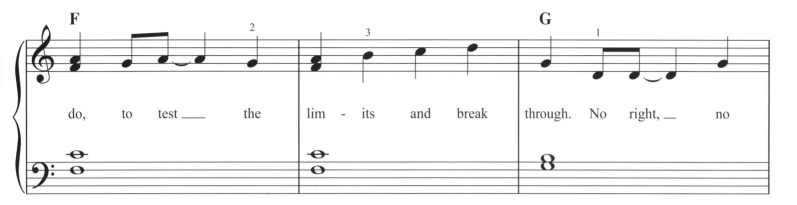

do, to test ___ the lim - its and break through. No right, ___ no

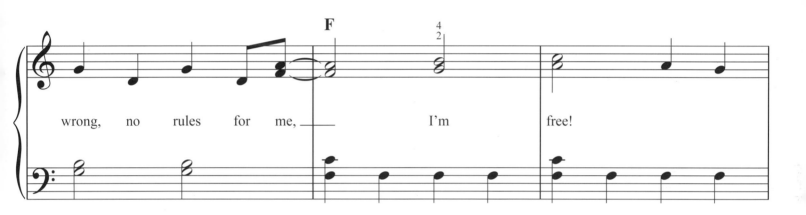

wrong, no rules for me, ___ I'm free!

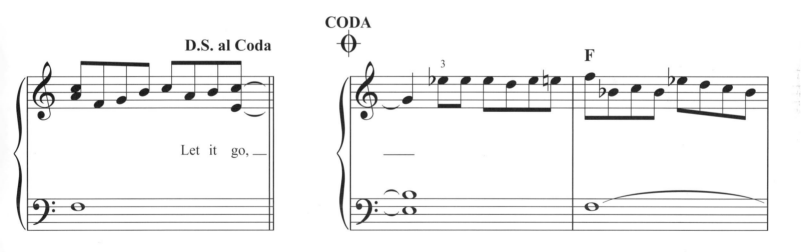

Let it go, ___

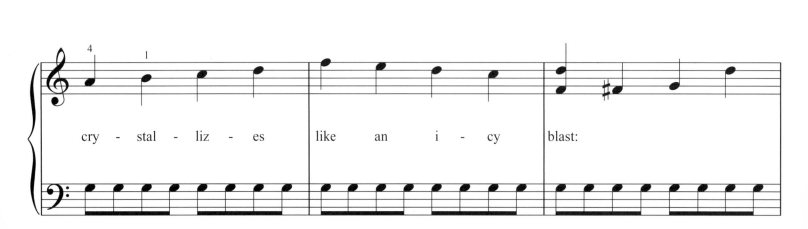

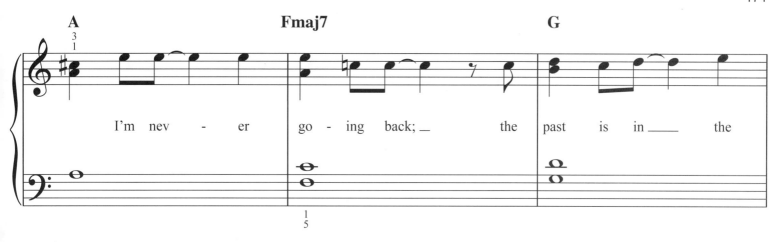

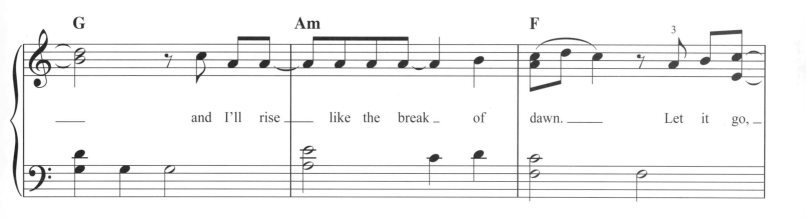

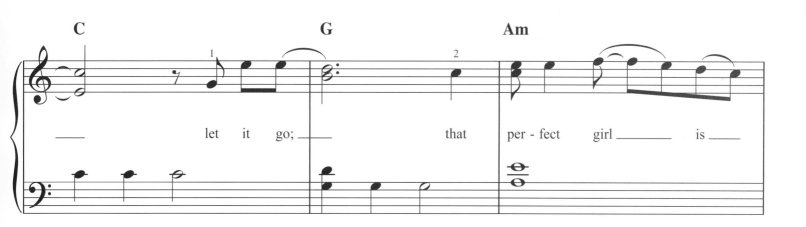

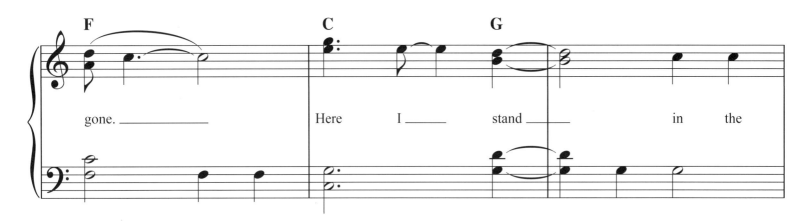

gone. _____ Here I ___ stand _____ in the

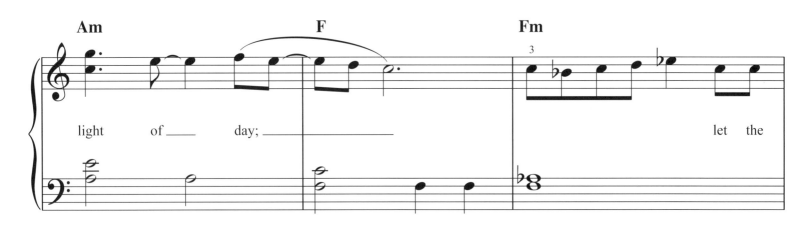

light of ___ day; _____ let the

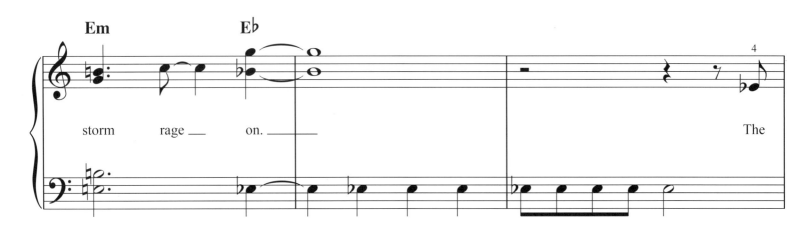

storm rage ___ on. _____ The

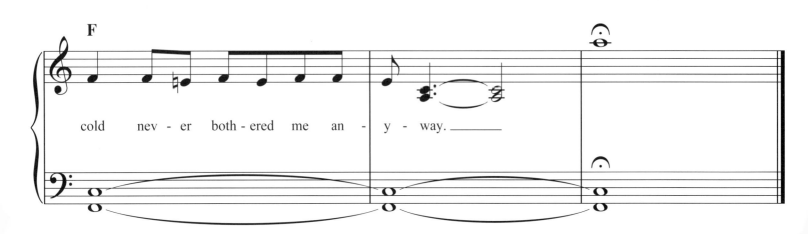

cold nev - er both - ered me an - y - way. _____

KISS THE GIRL

from THE LITTLE MERMAID

Music by ALAN MENKEN
Lyrics by HOWARD ASHMAN

Moderately

There you see her

sit-ting there a-cross the way. She don't got a lot to say,

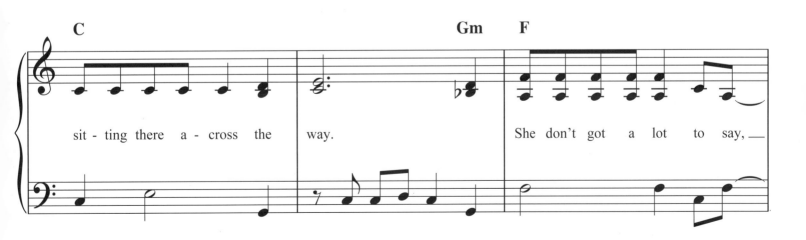

but there's some - thing a - bout her.

And you

don't know why, ___ but you're dy - ing to try. You wan - na kiss the girl.

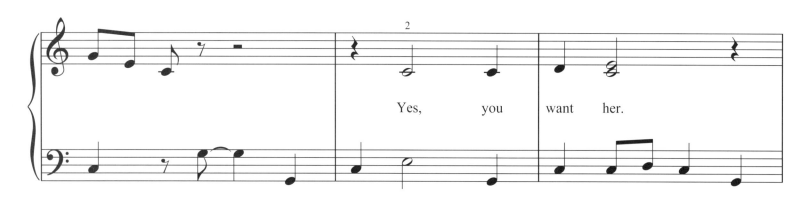

Yes, you want her.

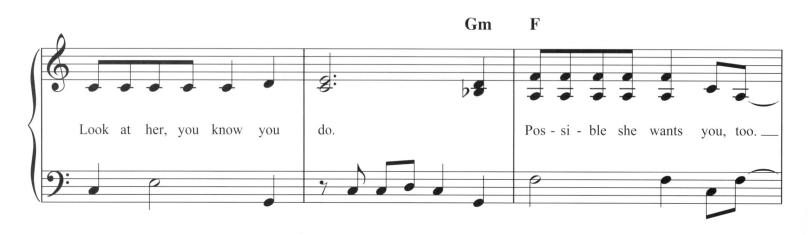

Look at her, you know you do. Pos - si - ble she wants you, too. ___

ain't that sad.___ Ain't it a shame, too bad.___ He gon-na miss the girl.___

Now's your mo - ment, float - ing in a blue la -

goon. Boy, you bet - ter do it soon, ___ no time will be

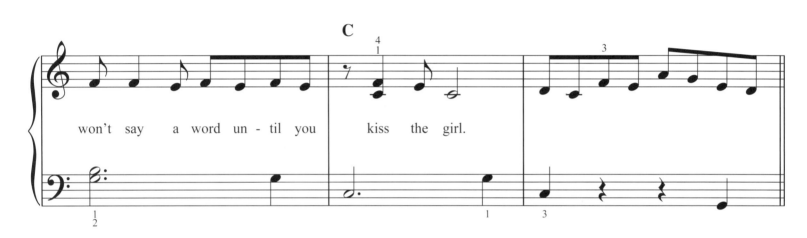

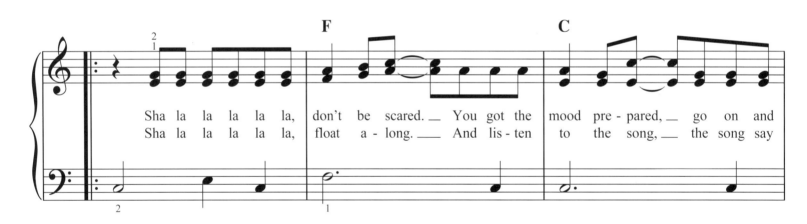

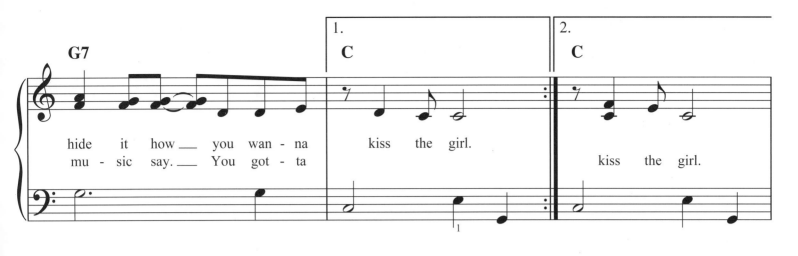

KNOW WHO YOU ARE

from MOANA

Music by OPETAIA FOA'I,
LIN-MANUEL MIRANDA and MARK MANCINA
Lyrics by OPETAIA FOA'I
and LIN-MANUEL MIRANDA

I have crossed the ho - ri - zon to   find you.

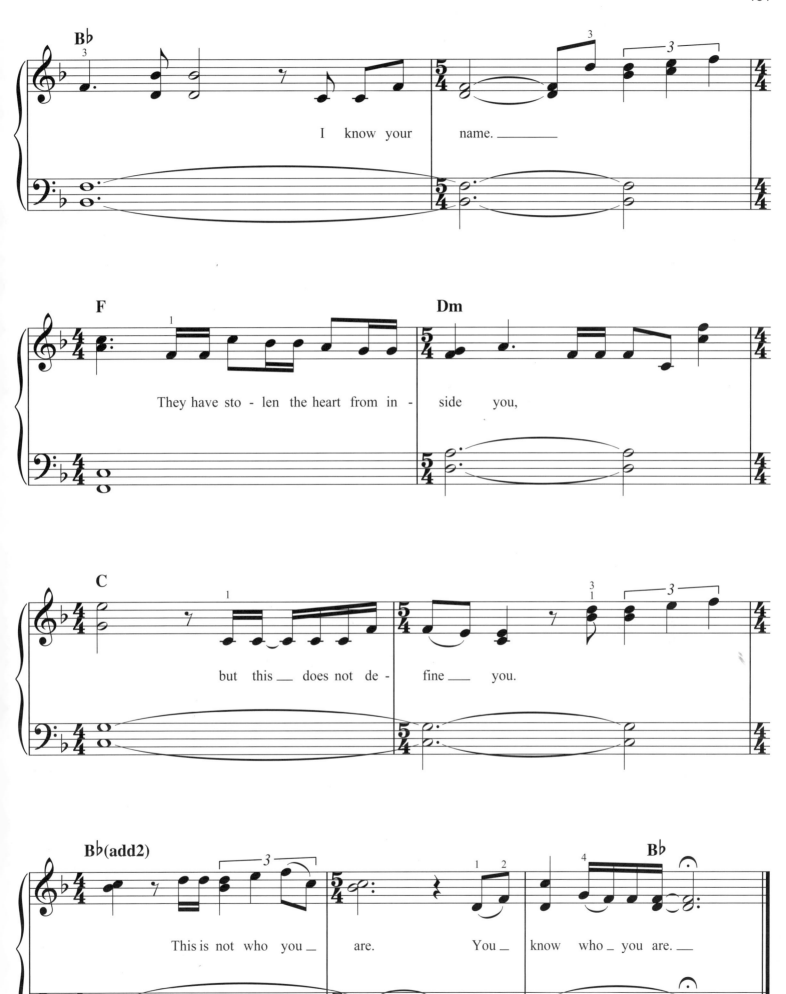

LOGO TE PATE
from MOANA

By OPETAIA FOA'I

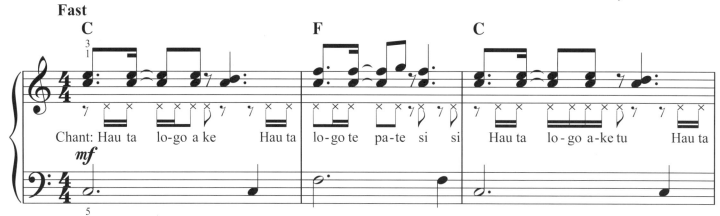

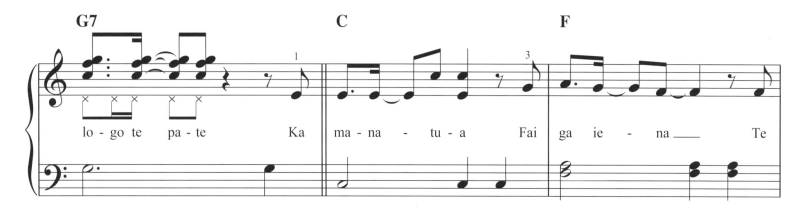

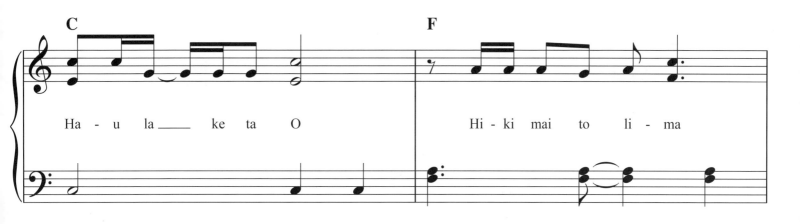

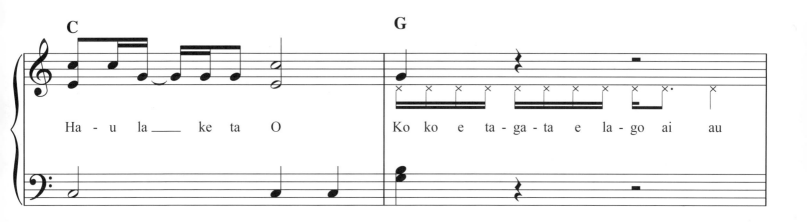

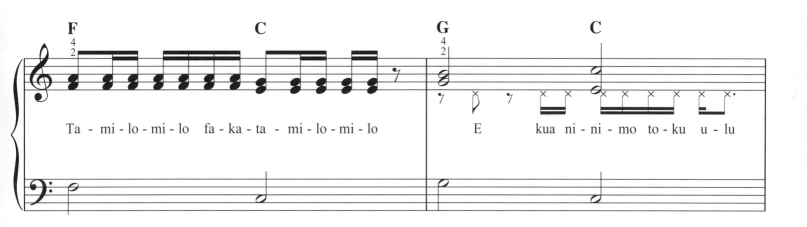

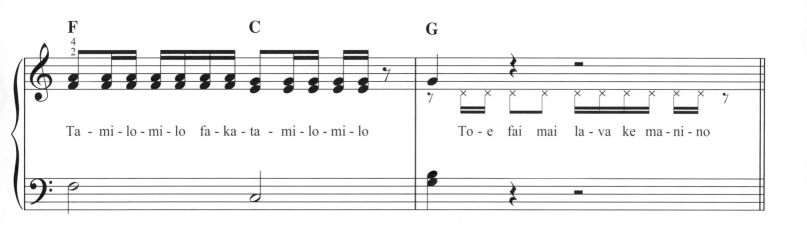

Ka - ta - ka - ta mai   Hi - hi - va mai   Fa - ka - lo - go kite pa - te   Ma te

lu - e - lu - e

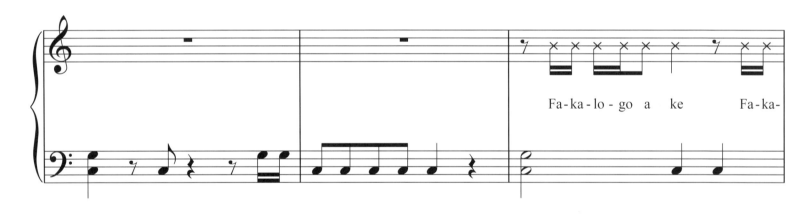

Fa - ka - lo - go a ke   Fa - ka -

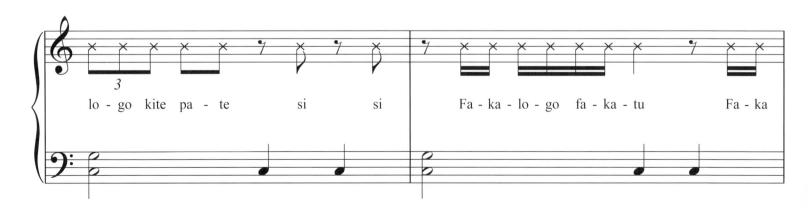

lo - go kite pa - te si si   Fa - ka - lo - go fa - ka - tu   Fa - ka

lo - go kite pa - te

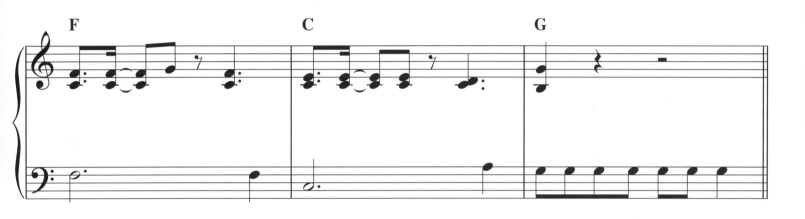

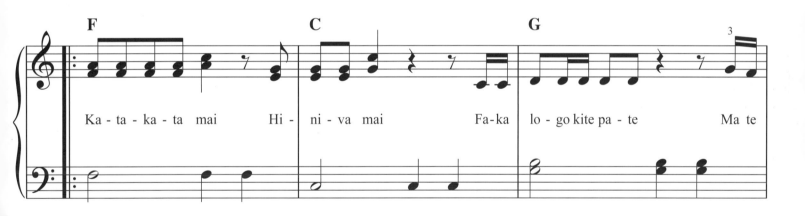

Ka - ta - ka - ta mai   Hi - ni - va mai   Fa - ka lo - go kite pa - te   Ma te

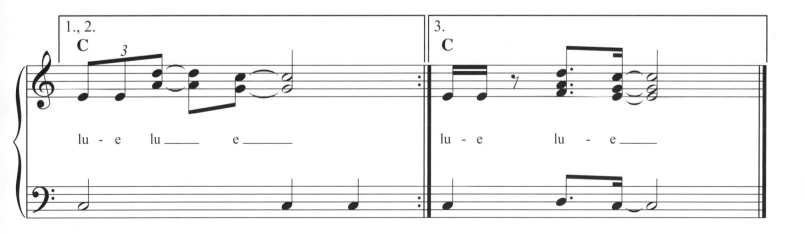

lu - e lu____ e_____   lu - e lu - e_____

LOVE IS AN OPEN DOOR
from FROZEN

Music and Lyrics by KRISTEN ANDERSON-LOPEZ
and ROBERT LOPEZ

187

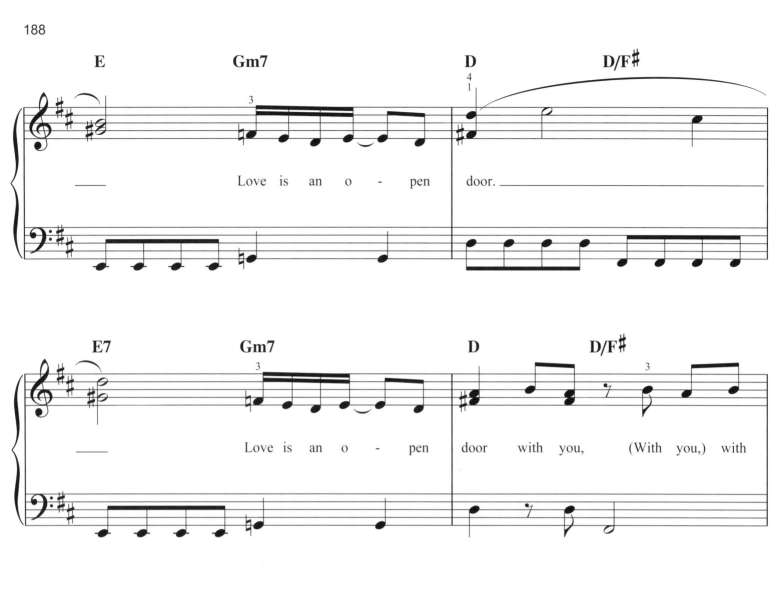

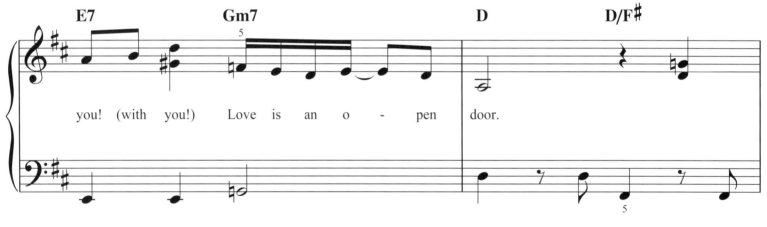

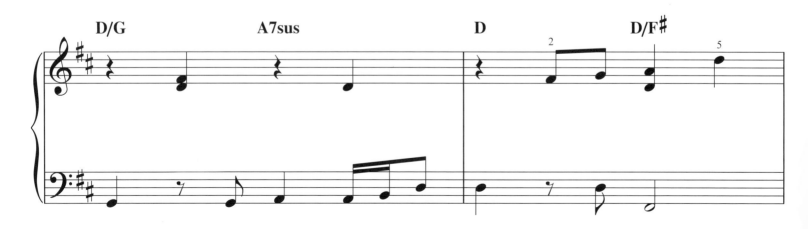

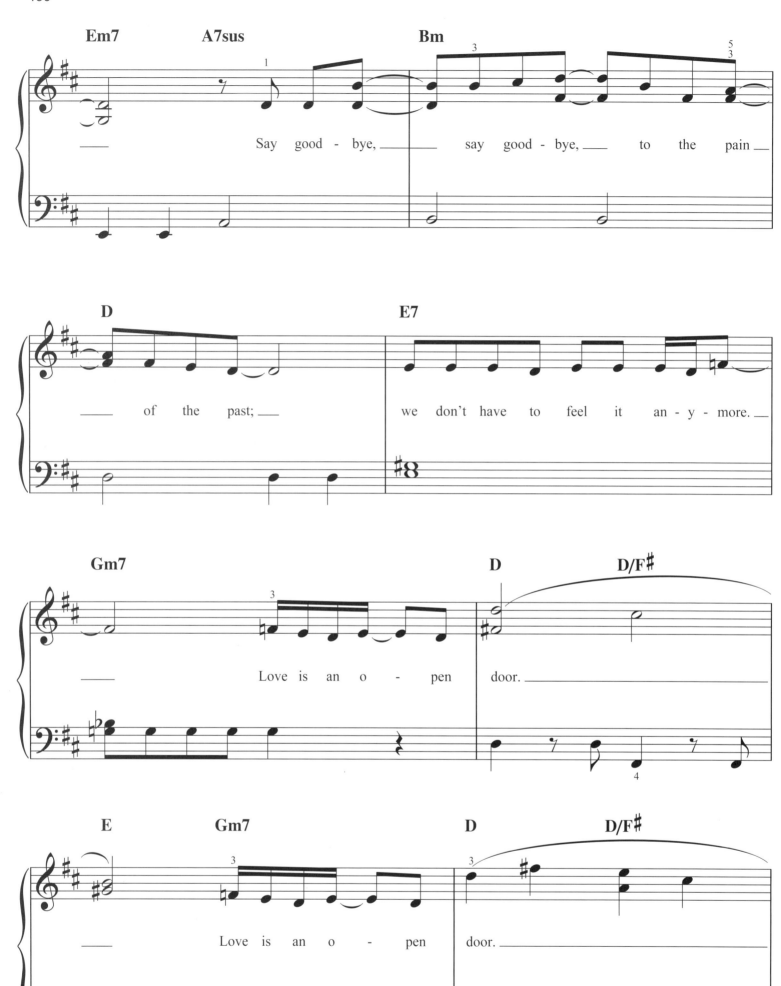

ONE JUMP AHEAD
from ALADDIN

Music by ALAN MENKEN
Lyrics by TIM RICE

Very bright two

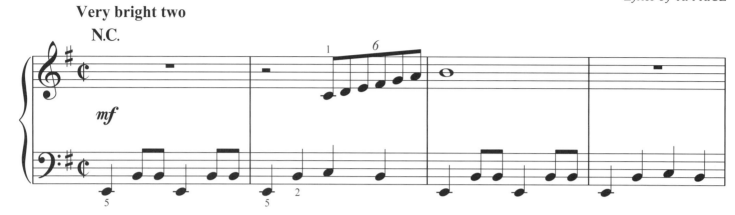

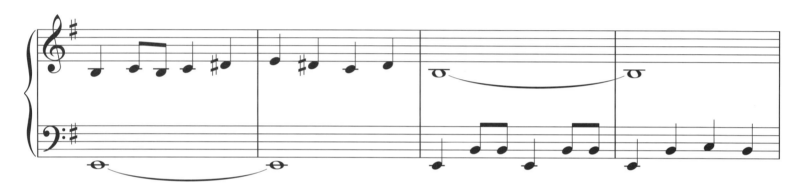

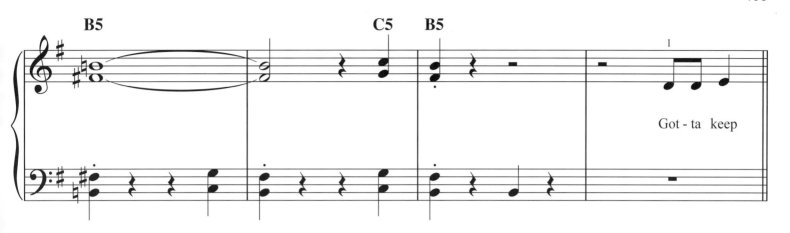

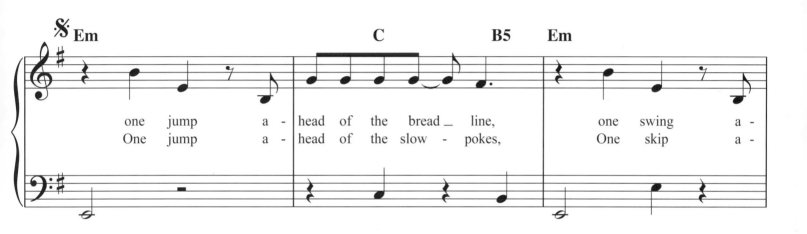

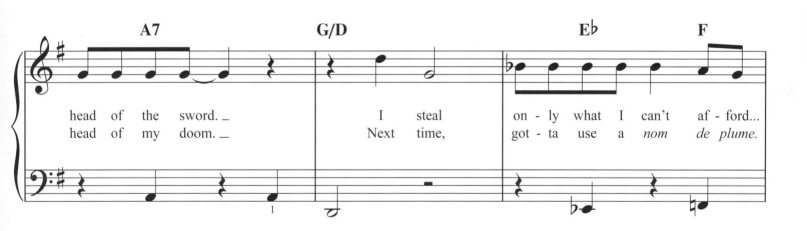

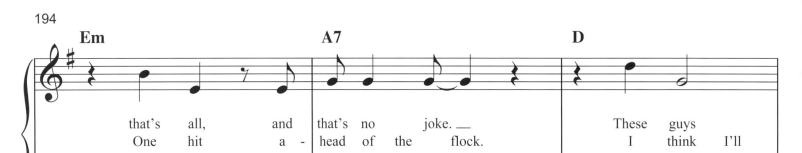

that's all, and that's no joke. ___ These guys
One hit a - head of the flock. I think I'll

don't ap - pre - ci - ate I'm broke.
take a stroll a - round the block.

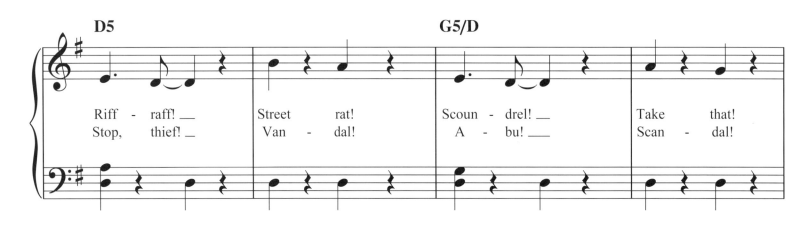

Riff - raff! ___ Street rat! Scoun - drel! ___ Take that!
Stop, thief! ___ Van - dal! A - bu! ___ Scan - dal!

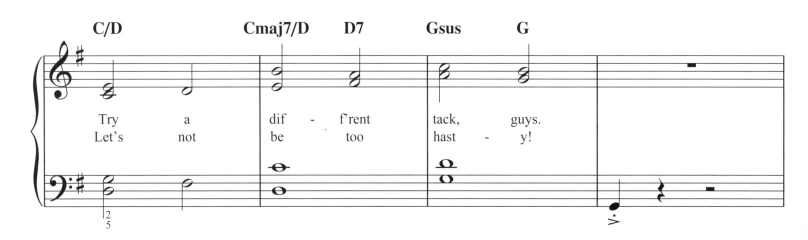

Try a dif - f'rent tack, guys.
Let's not be too hast - y!

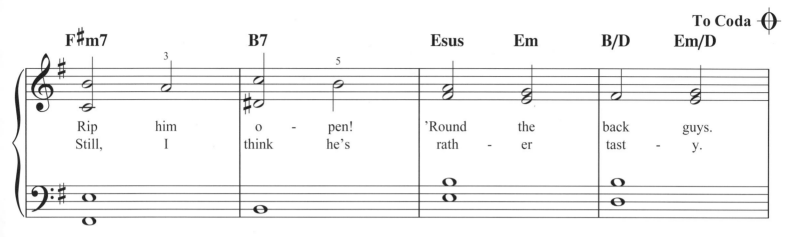

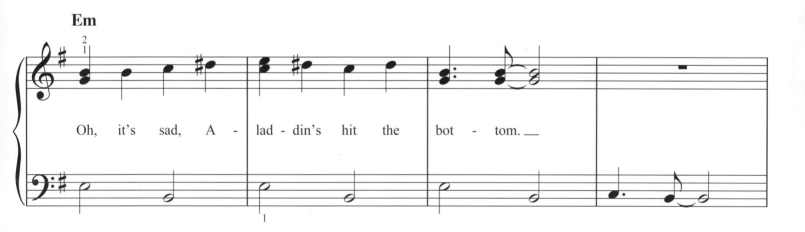

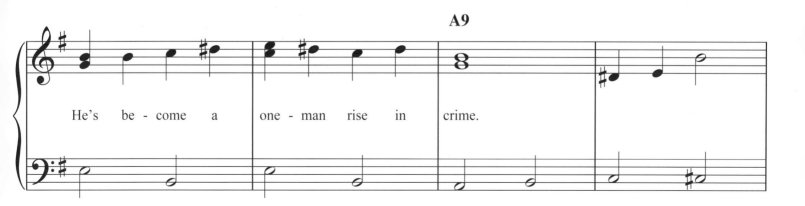

196

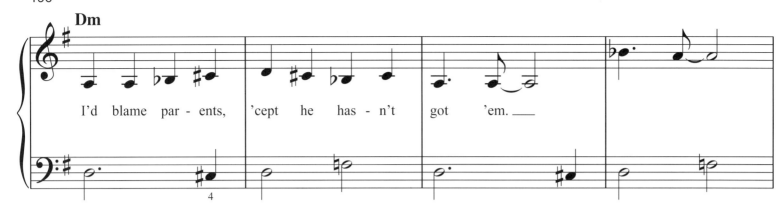

I'd blame par - ents, 'cept he has - n't got 'em. __

Got - ta eat to live, got - ta steal to eat. Tell you all a - bout it when I got the

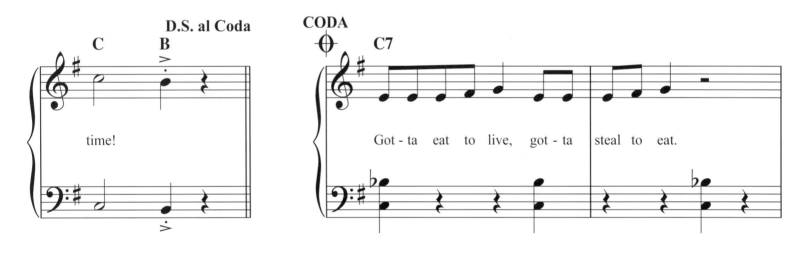

D.S. al Coda

time!

CODA

C7

Got - ta eat to live, got - ta steal to eat.

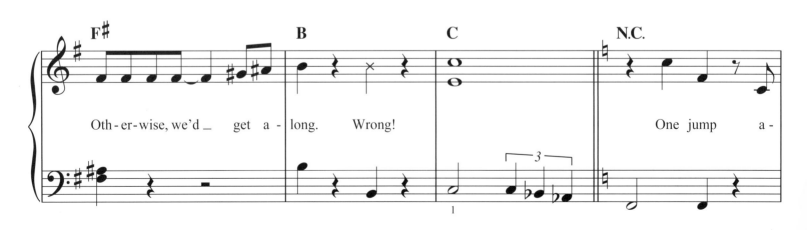

Oth - er - wise, we'd __ get a - long. Wrong! One jump a -

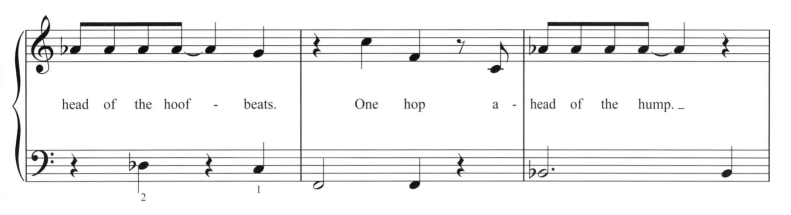

head of the hoof - beats. One hop a - head of the hump. _

Cm

One trick a - head of dis - as - ter. They're quick, but

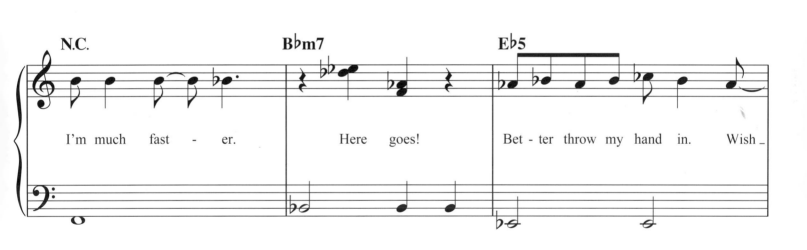

N.C. **B♭m7** **E♭5**

I'm much fast - er. Here goes! Bet - ter throw my hand in. Wish _

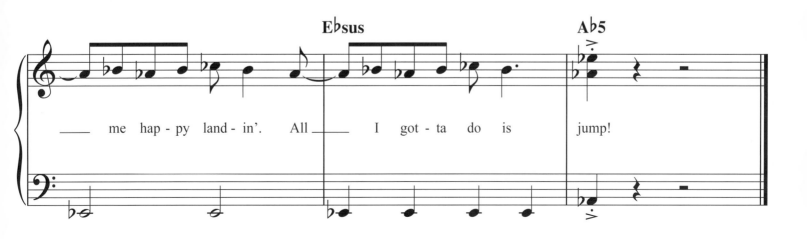

E♭sus **A♭5**

___ me hap - py land - in'. All ___ I got - ta do is jump!

PART OF YOUR WORLD
from THE LITTLE MERMAID

Music by ALAN MENKEN
Lyrics by HOWARD ASHMAN

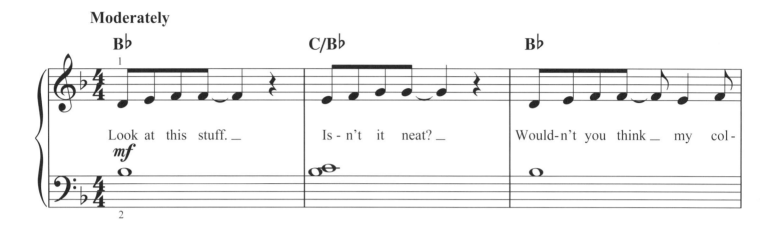

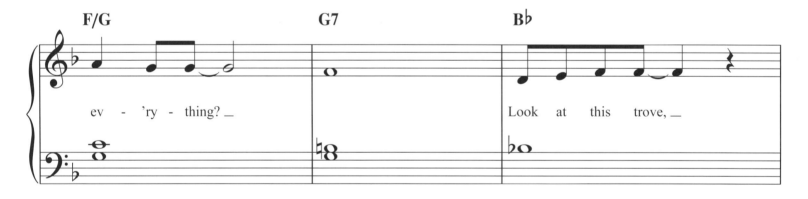

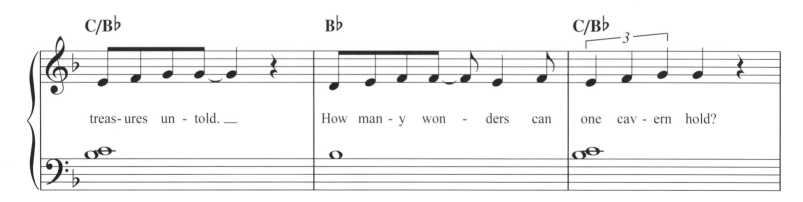

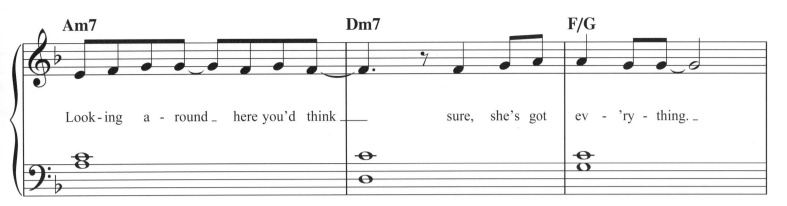

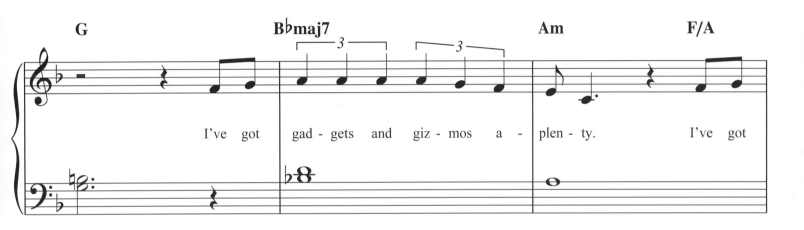

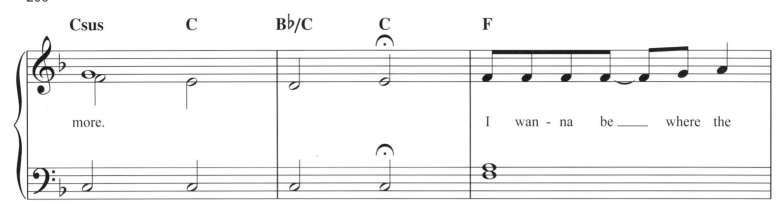

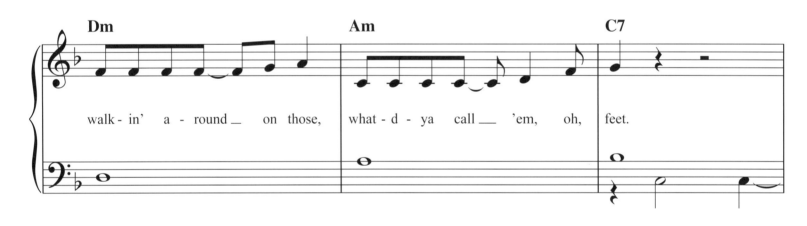

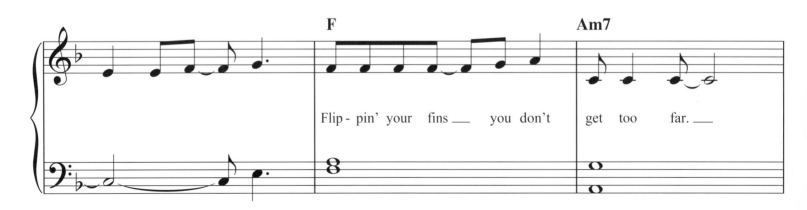

Legs are re - quired _____ for jump - in', danc - in'. Stroll - in' a - long _ down the,

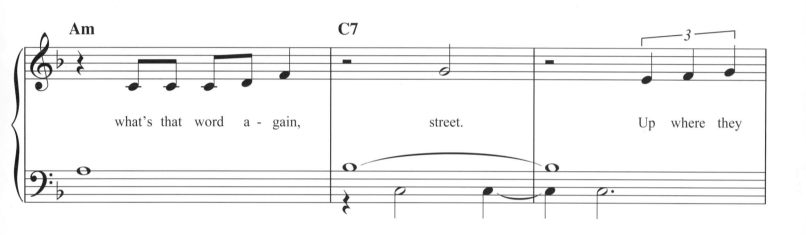

what's that word a - gain, street. Up where they

walk, up where they run, up where they stay all day _ in the sun. _

_ Wan - der - in' free, wish I could be part of that

world. _____ What would I give if I could

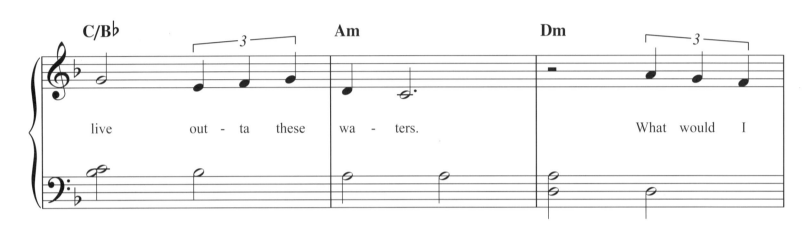

live out - ta these wa - ters. What would I

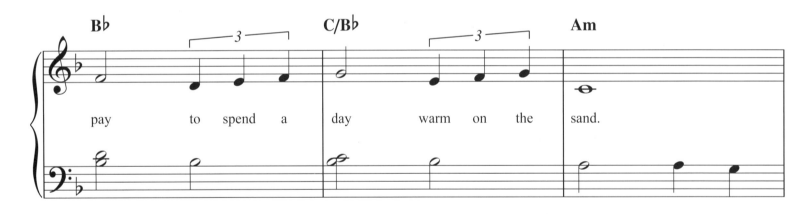

pay to spend a day warm on the sand.

Bet - cha on land they un - der - stand. Bet they don't

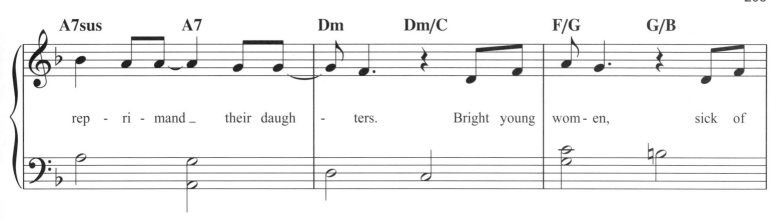

rep - ri - mand _ their daugh - ters. Bright young wom - en, sick of

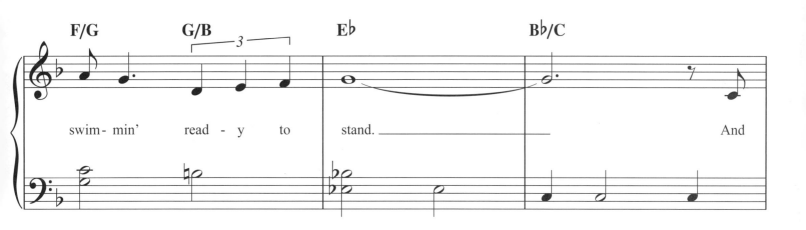

swim - min' read - y to stand. _____ And

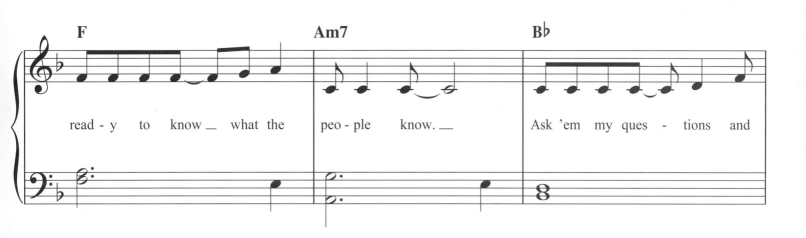

read - y to know _ what the peo - ple know. _ Ask 'em my ques - tions and

get some an - swers. What's a fire, ___ and why does it, what's the word,

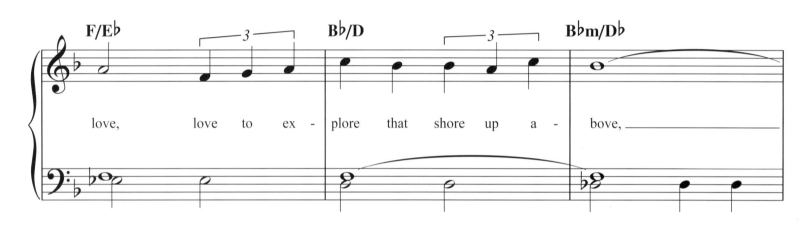

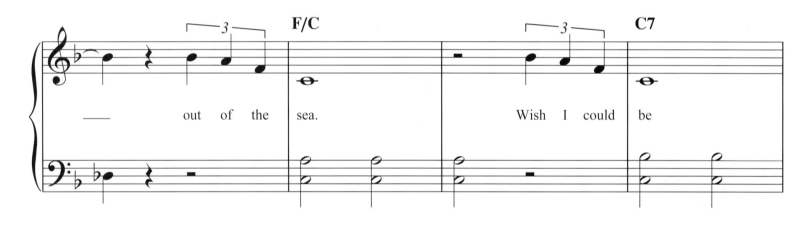

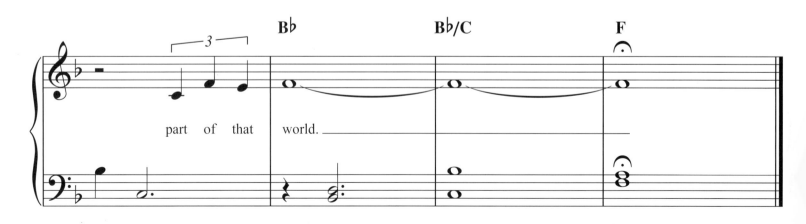

REFLECTION

from MULAN

Music by MATTHEW WILDER
Lyrics by DAVID ZIPPEL

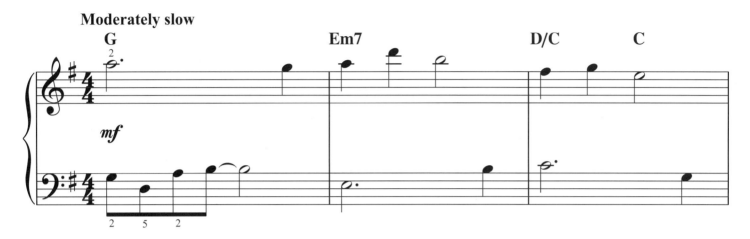

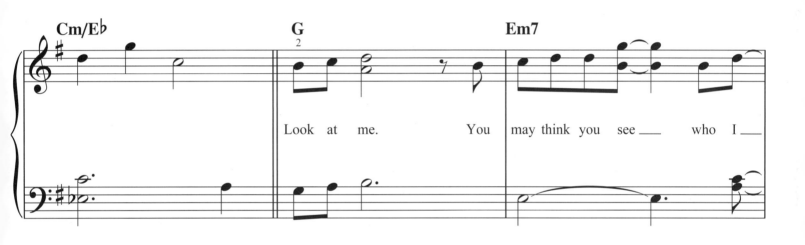

Look at me. You may think you see ___ who I ___

___ real - ly am, ___ but you'll nev - er know me. Ev - 'ry day it's

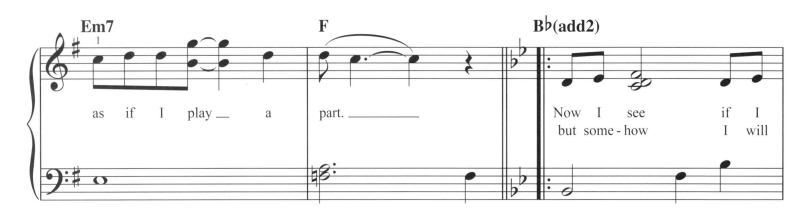

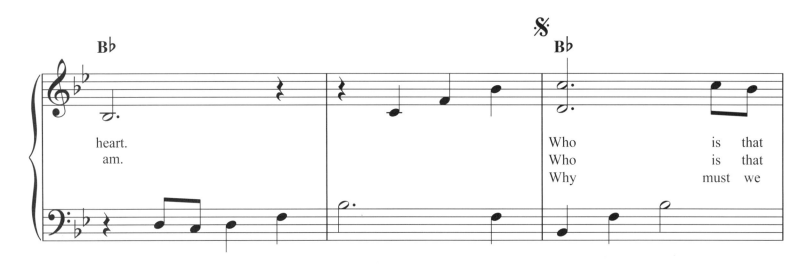

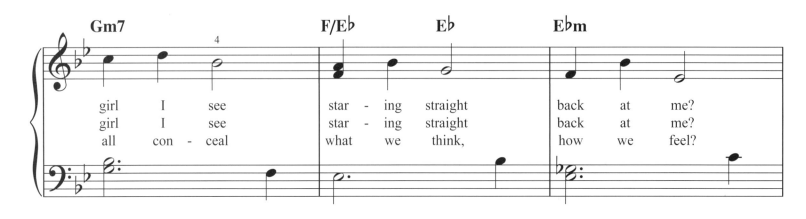

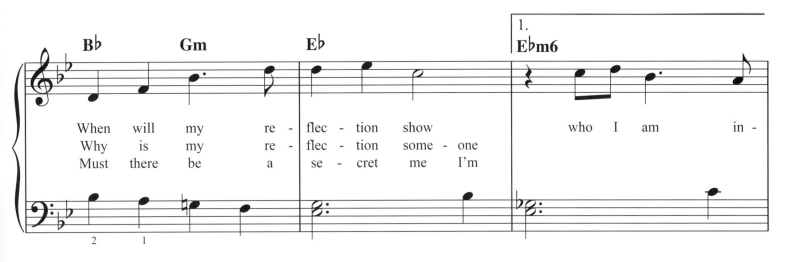

Bb   Gm   Eb   1. Ebm6

When will my re- | flec - tion show | who I am in -
Why is my re- | flec - tion some - one |
Must there be a | se - cret me I'm |

Bb/D   Gm   G

side? | | I am now in a

Em7   Am   D7

world where I ____ have to | hide my heart ___ | and what I be - lieve in,

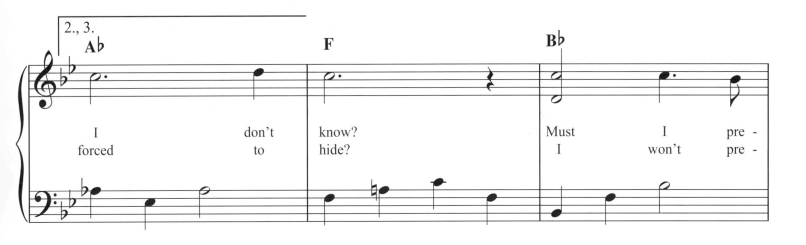

2., 3.
Ab   F   Bb

I don't | know? | Must I pre -
forced to | hide? | I won't pre -

208

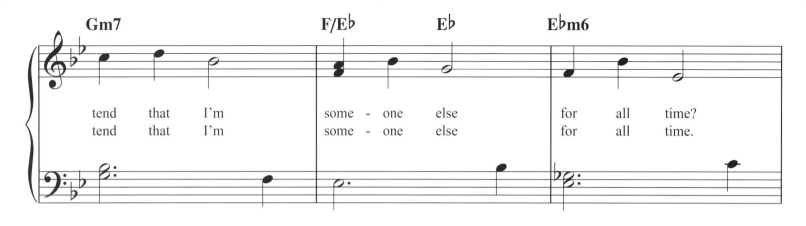

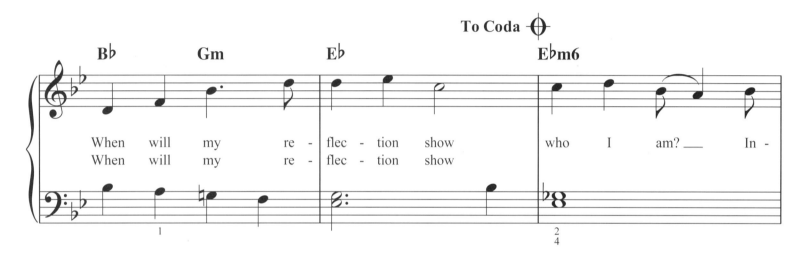

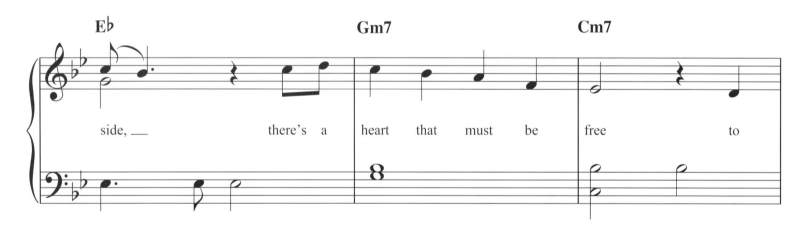

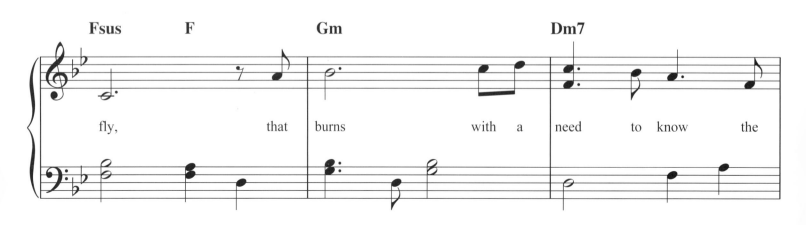

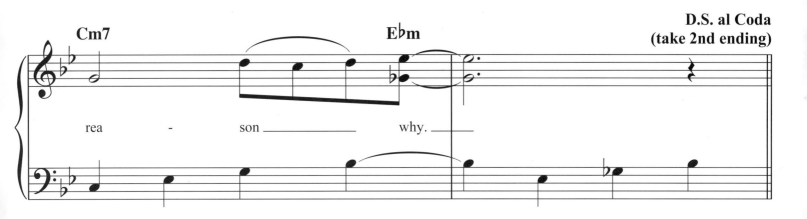

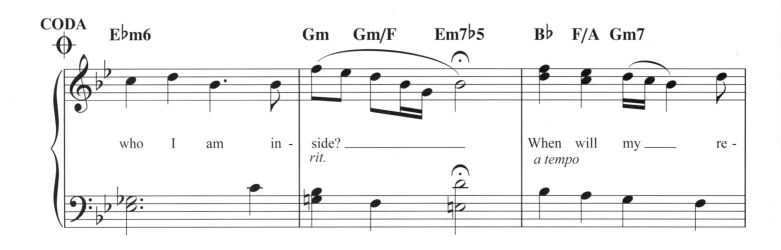

SHINY
from MOANA

Music by LIN-MANUEL MIRANDA
and MARK MANCINA
Lyrics by LIN-MANUEL MIRANDA

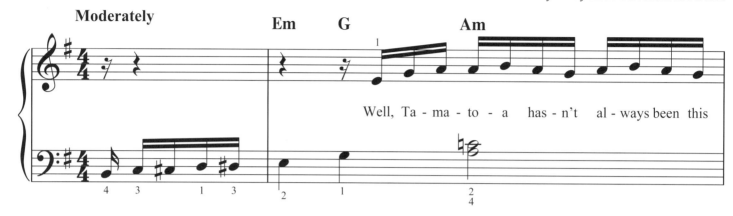

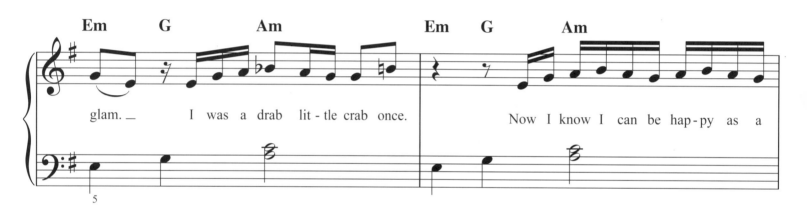

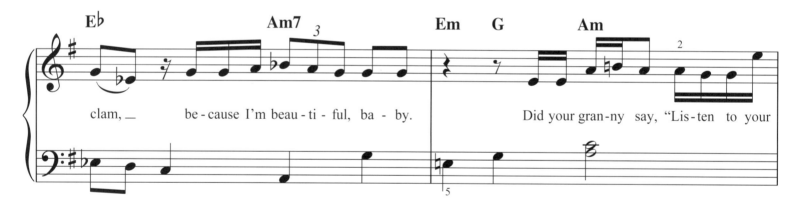

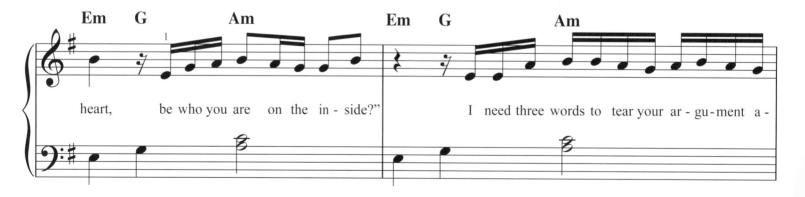

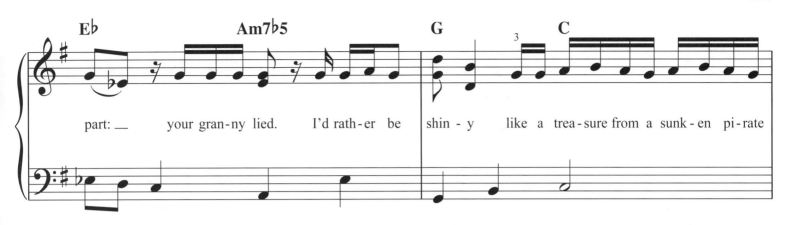

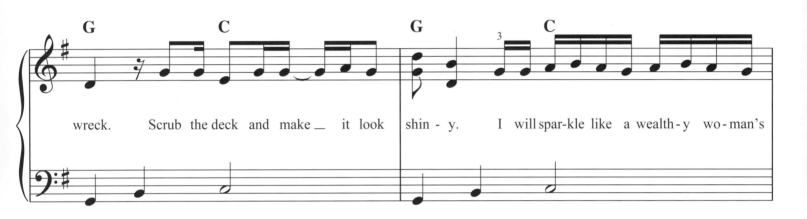

Am · · · D · · · Eb5

____ glit- ters. Mm, fish din-ners! I just love | free food,... _ and you look like | sea - food...

Em G Am

Well, well, well. Lit-tle Mau-i's hav-ing trou-ble with his

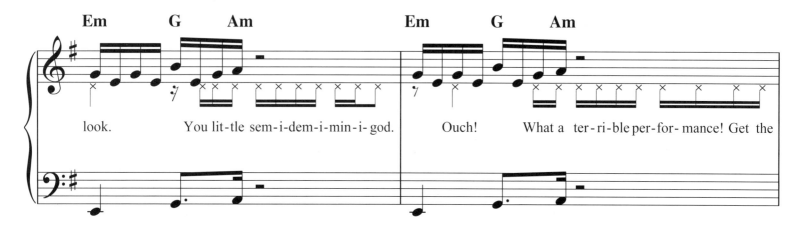

Em G Am · · · Em G Am

look. You lit-tle sem-i-dem-i-min-i-god. | Ouch! What a ter-ri-ble per-for-mance! Get the

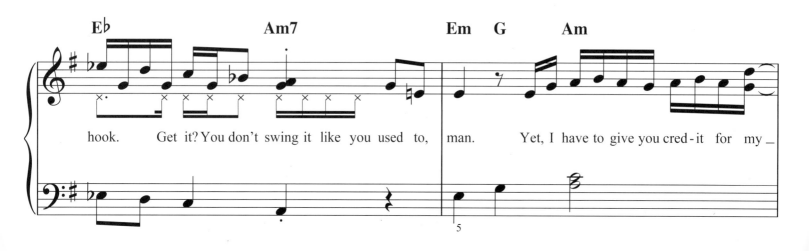

Eb · · · Am7 · · · Em G Am

hook. Get it? You don't swing it like you used to, man. | Yet, I have to give you cred-it for my _

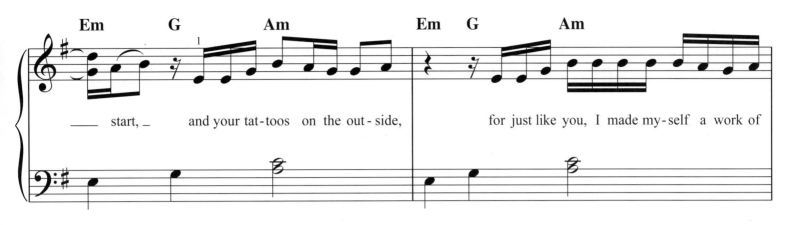

start, ___ and your tat-toos on the out-side, for just like you, I made my-self a work of

art. I'll nev-er hide; I can't; I'm too shin-y! Watch me daz-zle like a dia-mond in the

rough, strut my stuff. My stuff ___ is so shin-y! Send your ar-mies, but they'll nev-er be e-

nough; my shell's too tough, Mau-i, man. Well, you could try, try, try, but you can't ex-pect a

214

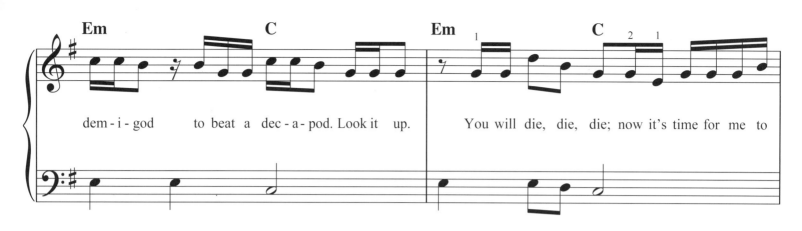

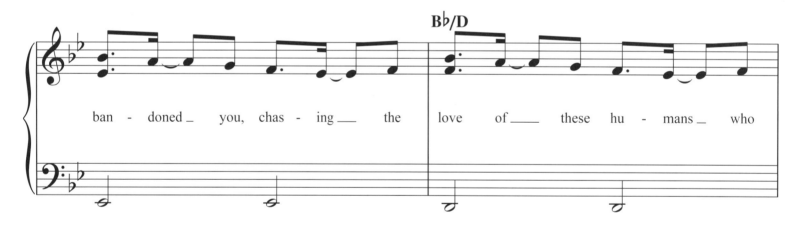

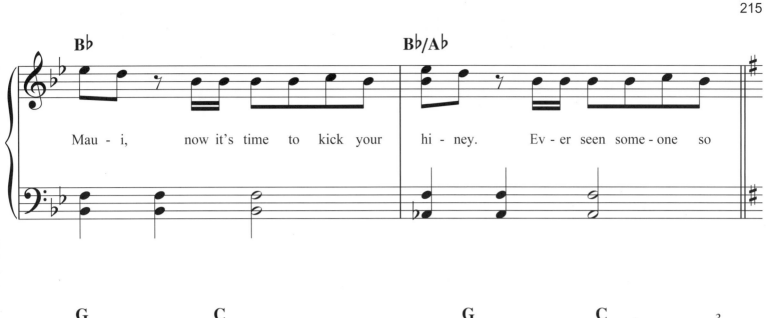

Mau - i, now it's time to kick your hi - ney. Ev - er seen some - one so

shin - y? Soak it in, 'cause it's the last you'll ev - er see. C'est la vie, mon a - mi. I'm so

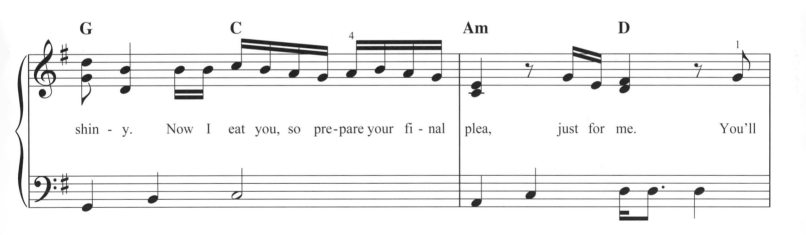

shin - y. Now I eat you, so pre-pare your fi - nal plea, just for me. You'll

nev - er be quite as shin - y; you wish you were nice and shin - y.

STRANGERS LIKE ME®

from TARZAN ™

Words and Music by
PHIL COLLINS

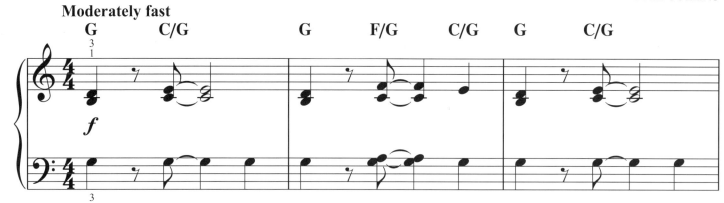

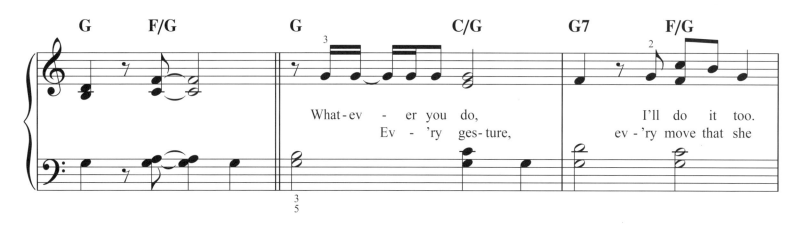

What-ev - er you do,
Ev - 'ry ges-ture,
I'll do it too.
ev -'ry move that she

Show me ev-'ry-thing and
makes makes me feel __ like __
tell me __ how. __
nev - er be - fore. __
It all __ means some-thing
Why __ do I have

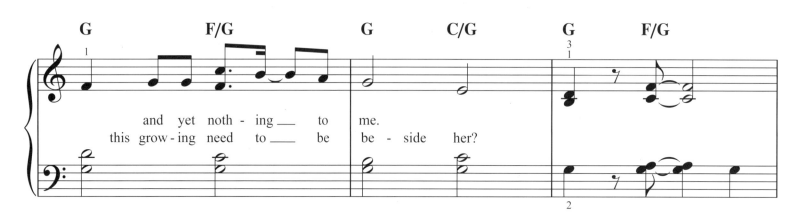

and yet noth-ing __ to
this grow-ing need to __ be
me.
be - side her?

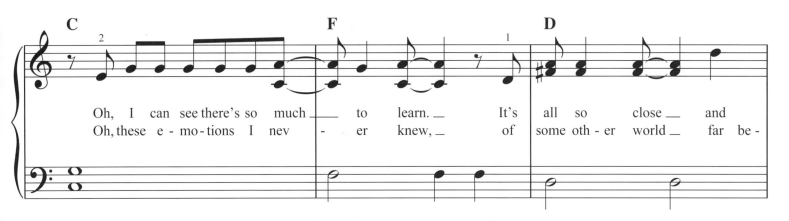

Oh, I can see there's so much to learn. It's all so close and
Oh, these e-mo-tions I nev - er knew, of some oth - er world far be-

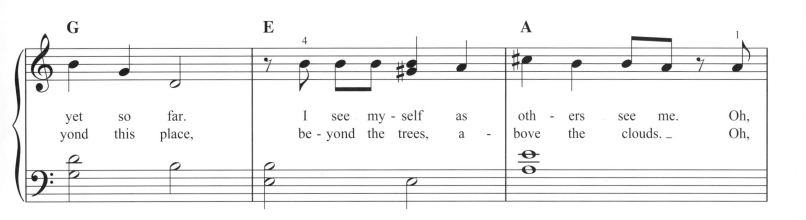

yet so far.
yond this place,

I see my - self as oth - ers see me. Oh,
be - yond the trees, a - bove the clouds. Oh,

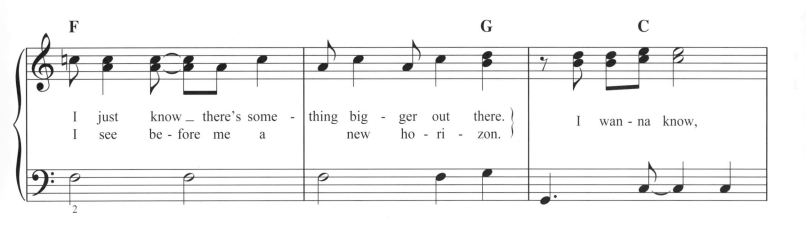

I just know there's some - thing big - ger out there.
I see be - fore me a new ho - ri - zon.
I wan - na know,

can you show me? I wan - na know a - bout these stran - gers like me.

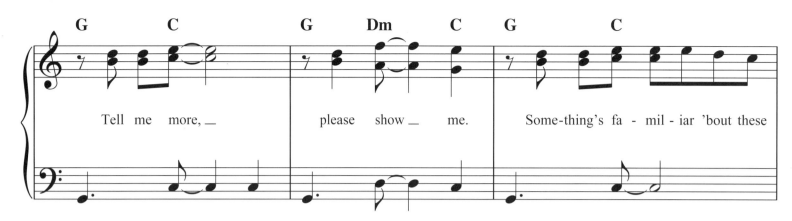

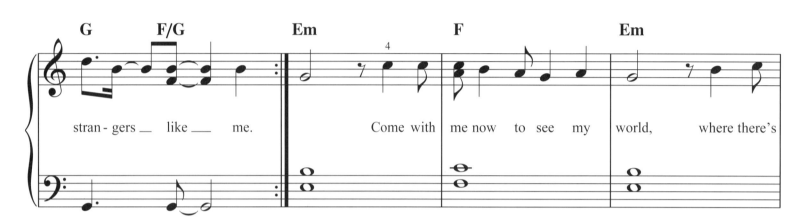

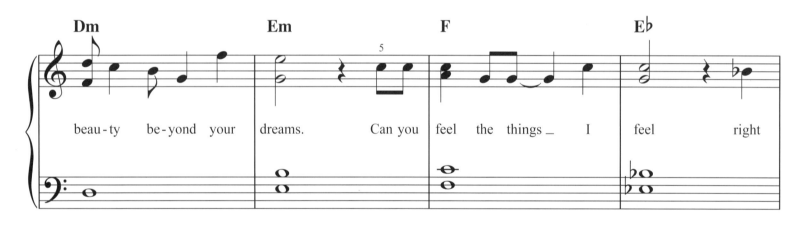

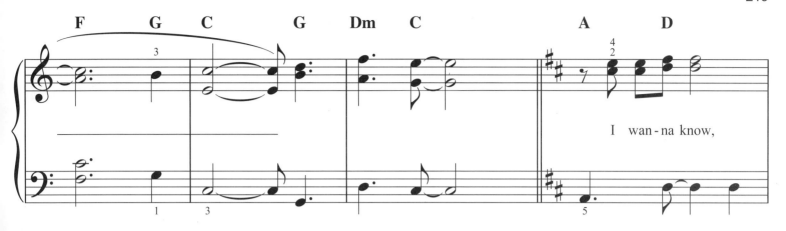

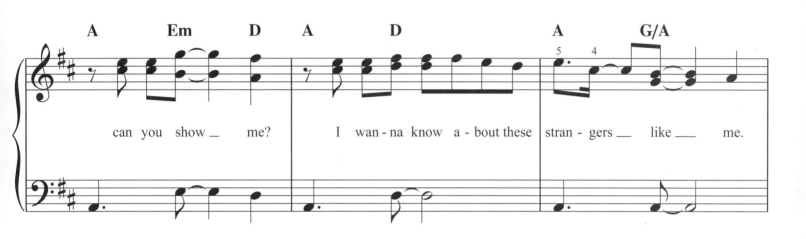

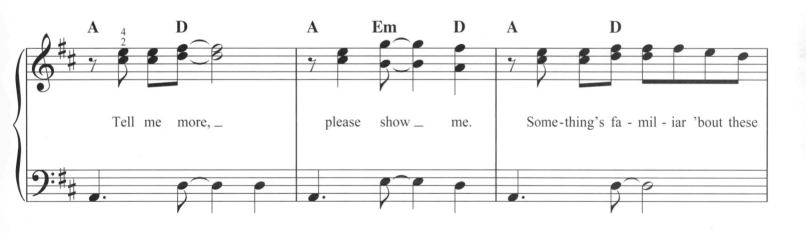

WE KNOW THE WAY

from MOANA

Music by OPETAIA FOA'I
Lyrics by OPETAIA FOA'I
and LIN-MANUEL MIRANDA

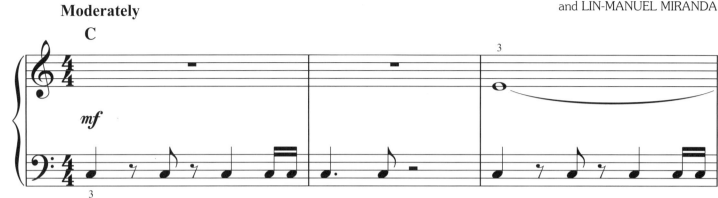

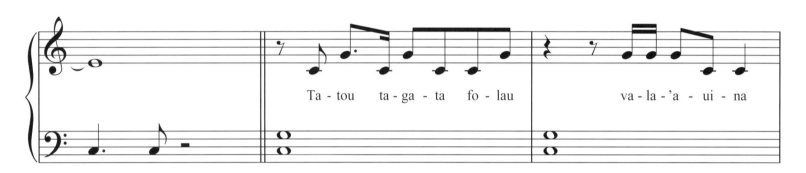

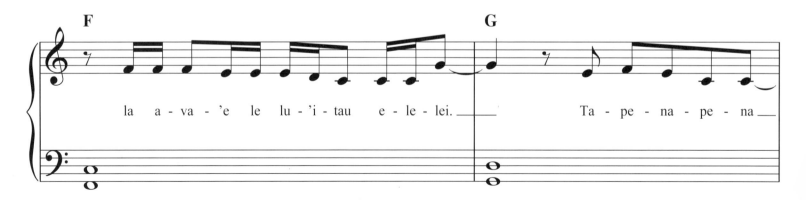

221

We sail the length of the seas ___ on the o - cean breeze. At night we name ev - 'ry star; ___

___ we know where we are. ___ We know who we are, ___ who we are. ___

A - way, a - way, we set a course to find. A brand new is - land ev - 'ry-

where we roam. ___ A - way, a - way, we keep our is - land in our mind;

and when it's time to find home, we know the way. A - way, a - way. We are ex -

plor - ers read - ing ev - 'ry sign. We tell the sto - ries of our eld - ers in a nev - er end - ing

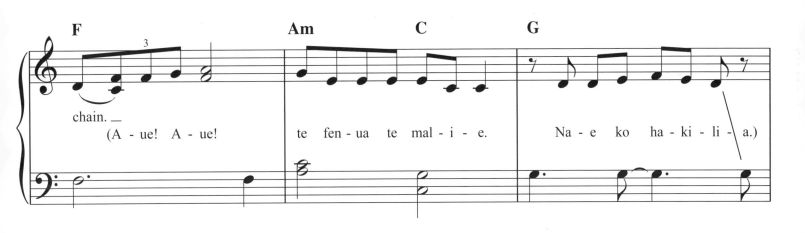

chain. (A - ue! A - ue! te fen - ua te mal - i - e. Na - e ko ha - ki - li - a.)

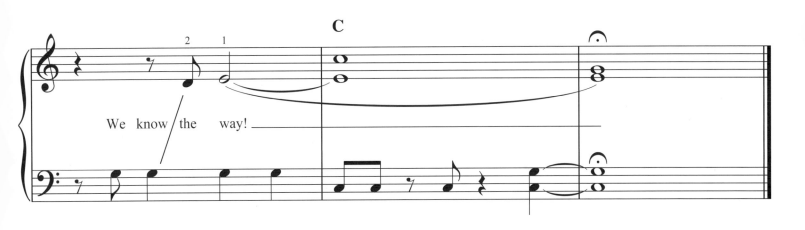

We know the way! _____

WHEN WILL MY LIFE BEGIN?

from TANGLED

Music by ALAN MENKEN
Lyrics by GLENN SLATER

Moderately fast Rock

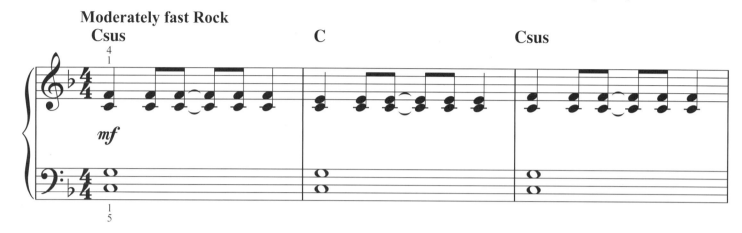

Sev - en a. m., ___ the u - su - al morn - ing
Then af - ter lunch, __ it's puz - zles, and darts and

line - up. _____
bak - ing... _____

Start on the chores, _ and sweep _ 'til the floor's all
pa - per mâ - ché, ___ a bit __ of bal - let and

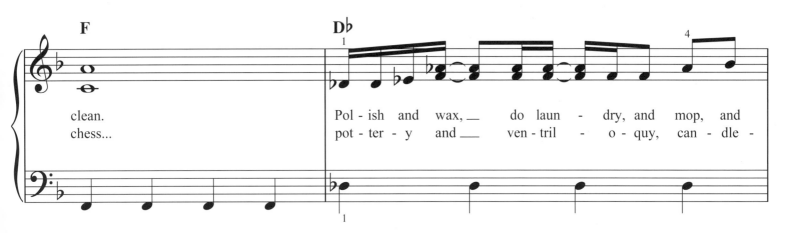

F ... **Db**

clean.
chess...

Pol - ish and wax, __ do laun - dry, and mop, and
pot - ter - y and __ ven - tril - o - quy, can - dle -

Ab ... **C** **C/Bb** **F/A** ... **G/B** ... **C**

shine - up. _____ Sweep a - gain, and by then it's, like, sev - en fif - teen. And so I'll
mak - ing... _____ then I'll stretch, may - be sketch, take a climb, sew a dress. And I'll re -

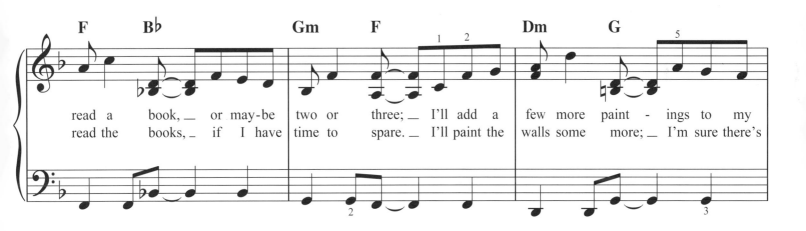

F **Bb** ... **Gm** ... **F** ... **Dm** ... **G**

read a book, __ or may-be two or three; __ I'll add a few more paint - ings to my
read the books, _ if I have time to spare. __ I'll paint the walls some more; __ I'm sure there's

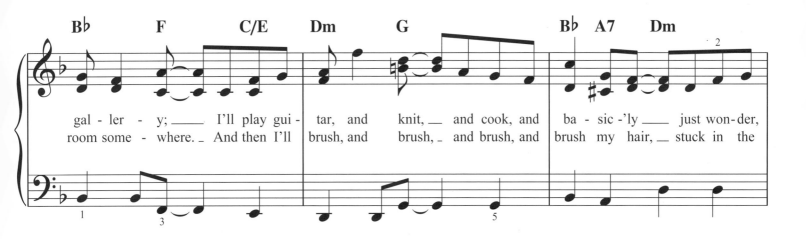

Bb ... **F** **C/E** **Dm** ... **G** ... **Bb** **A7** **Dm**

gal - ler - y; _____ I'll play gui - tar, and knit, __ and cook, and ba - sic -'ly ___ just won-der,
room some - where. _ And then I'll brush, and brush, _ and brush, and brush my hair, __ stuck in the

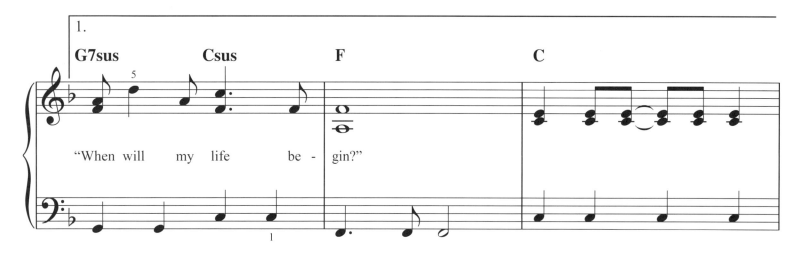

1.

G7sus   Csus   F   C

"When will my life be - gin?"

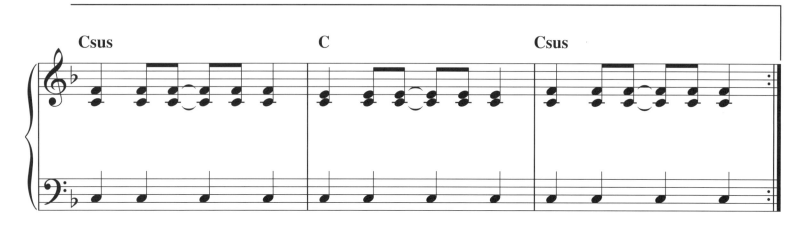

Csus   C   Csus

2.

G7sus   B♭sus2 A   Dm   Gsus   F/A

same place I've al - ways __ been, _____ and I'll keep won-d'ring and won-d'ring and

B♭   Am   D7   Gsus   Csus   F   Fsus

won-d'ring and won - d'ring, "When will my life be - gin?"

Slowly, freely

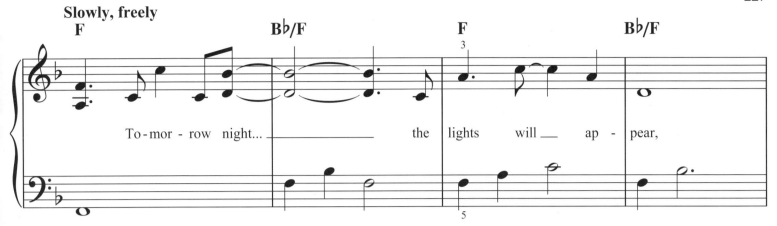

To-mor - row night... _____ the lights will __ ap - pear,

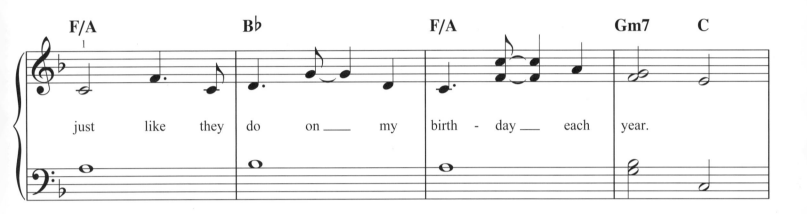

just like they do on __ my birth - day __ each year.

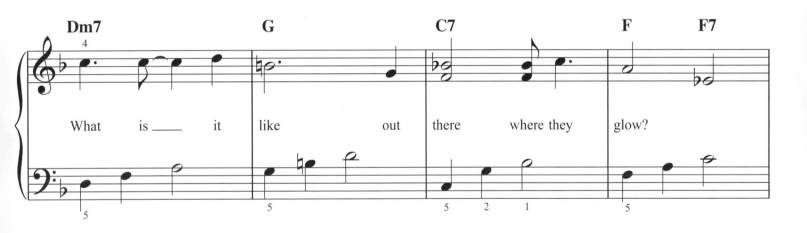

What is __ it like out there where they glow?

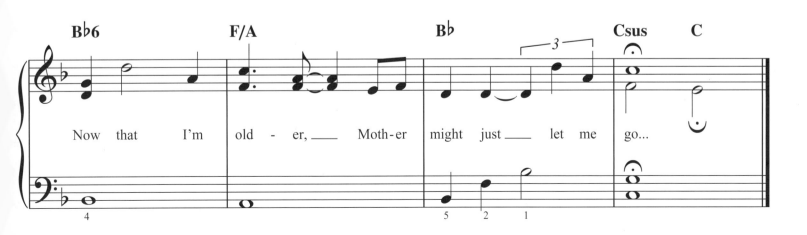

Now that I'm old - er, __ Moth-er might just __ let me go...

A WHOLE NEW WORLD
from ALADDIN (2019)

Music by ALAN MENKEN
Lyrics by TIM RICE

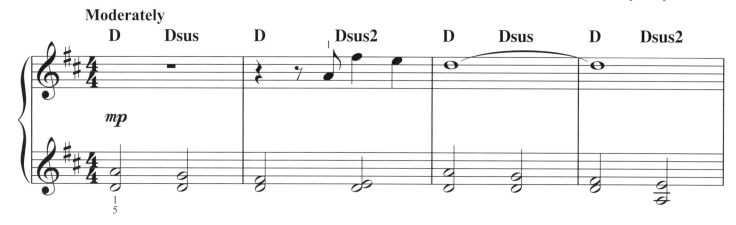

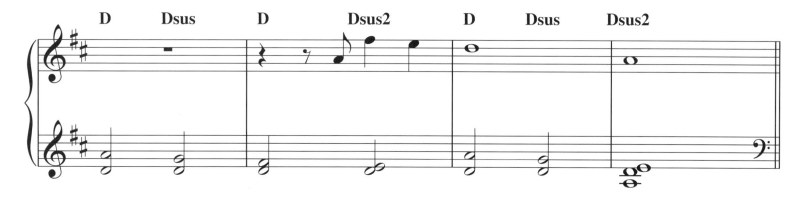

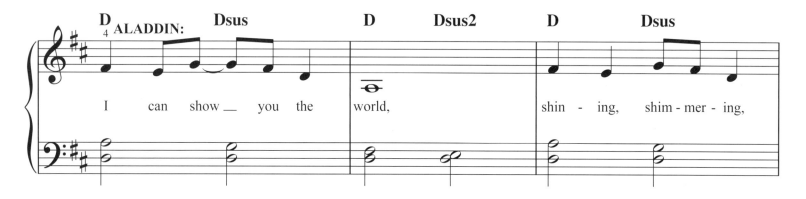

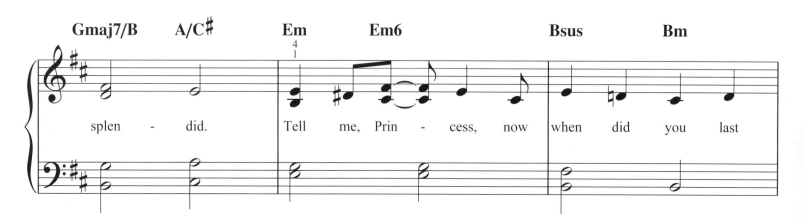

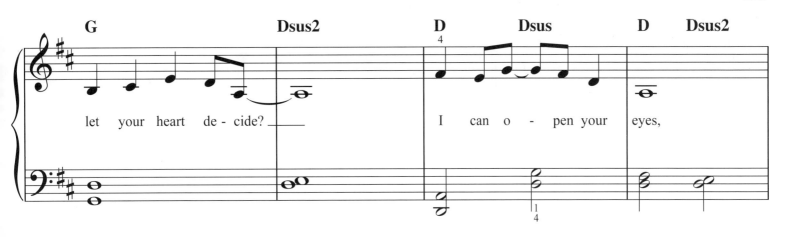

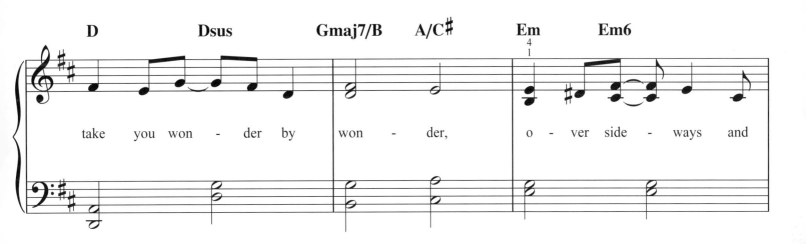

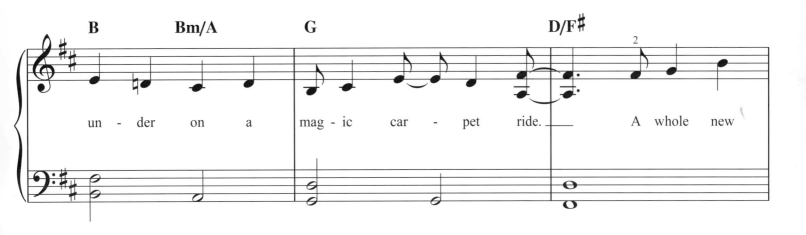

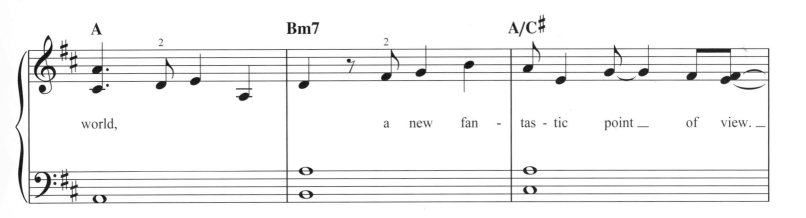

No one to tell us no, ___ or where to go, ___ or

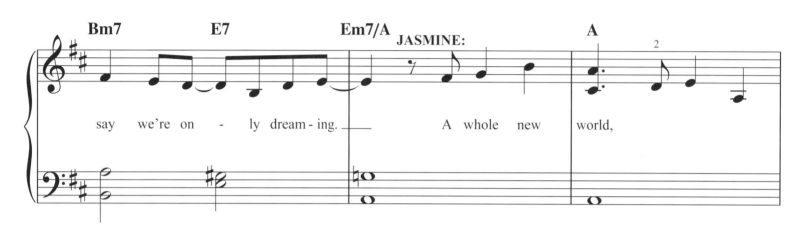

JASMINE:

say we're on - ly dream - ing. ___ A whole new world,

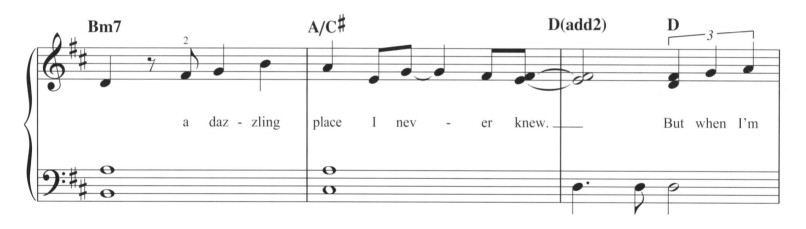

a daz - zling place I nev - er knew. ___ But when I'm

way up here, it's crys - tal clear ___ that now I'm in a

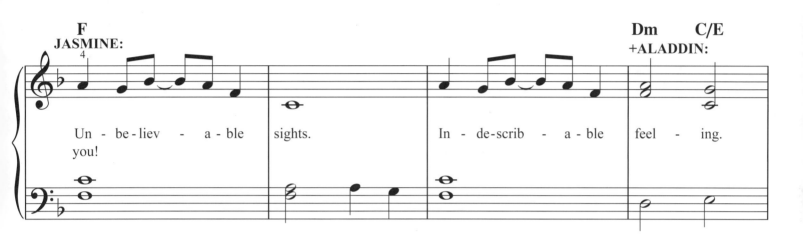

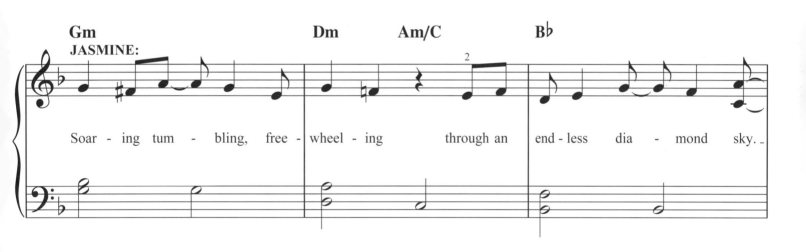

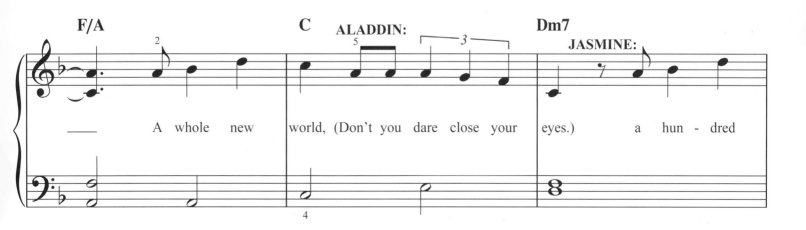

thou - sand things ___ to see. ___ I'm like a shoot - ing star. ___ I've

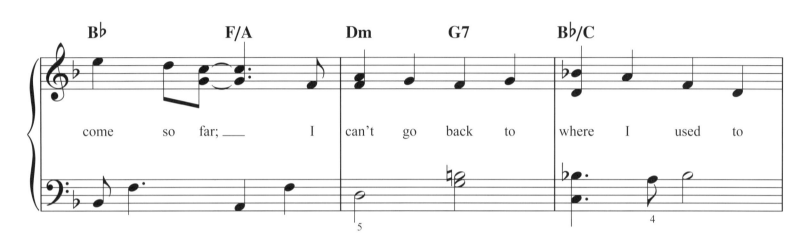

come so far; ___ I can't go back to where I used to

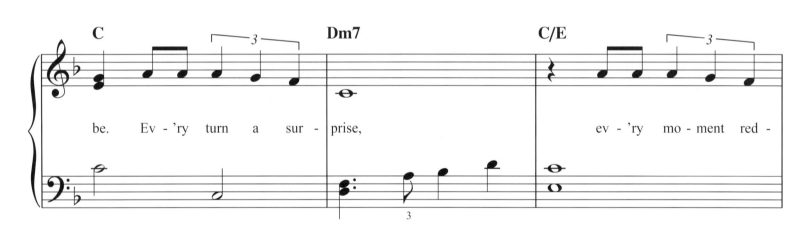

be. Ev - 'ry turn a sur - prise, ev - 'ry mo - ment red -

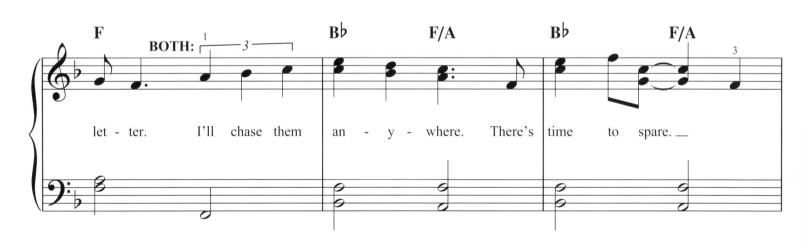

let - ter. I'll chase them an - y - where. There's time to spare. ___

233

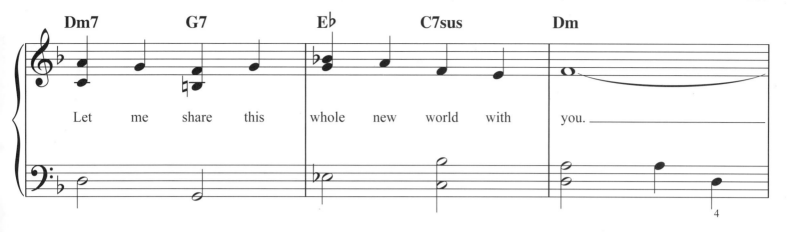

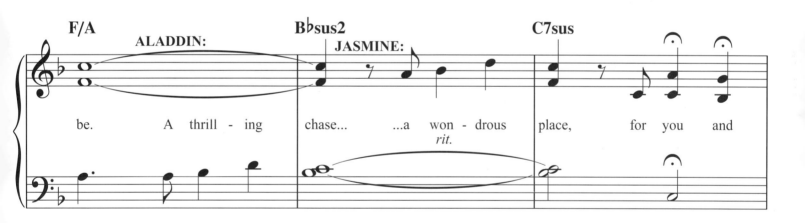

YOU'LL BE IN MY HEART*

(Pop Version)

from TARZAN

Words and Music by
PHIL COLLINS

For one so small, you seem so strong. _ My arms will hold you, keep you
Why can't they un-der-stand the way we feel? _ They just don't trust _ what they

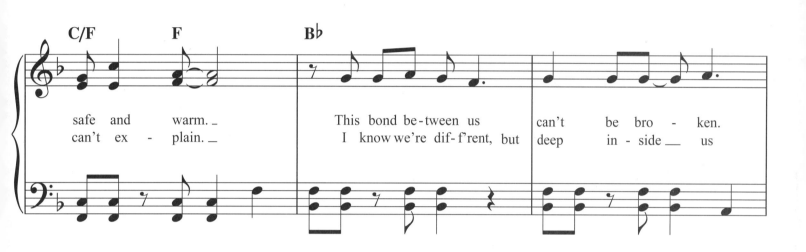

safe and warm. _ This bond be-tween us can't be bro - ken.
can't ex - plain. _ I know we're dif-f'rent, but deep in - side _ us

I will be here; don't you cry. 'Cause } you'll be in my
we're not that dif - f'rent at all. And }

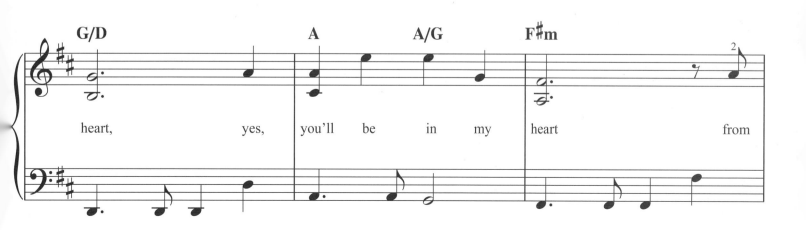

heart, yes, you'll be in my heart from

236

To Coda

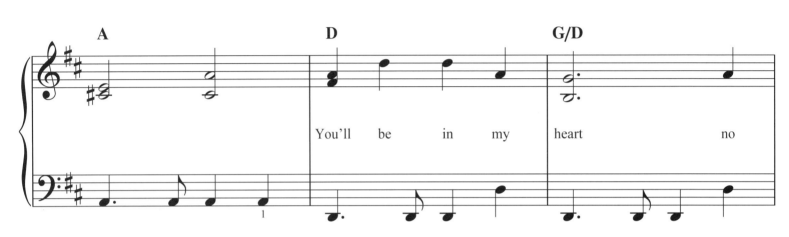

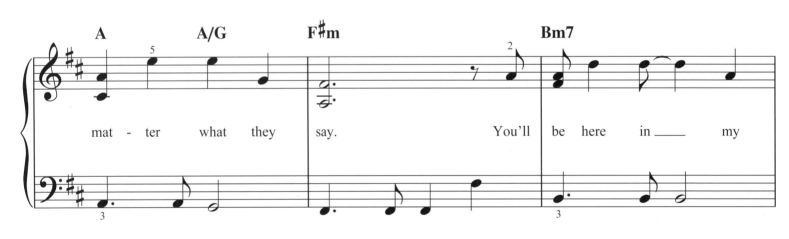

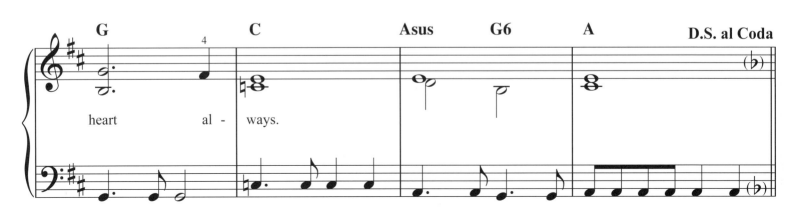

237

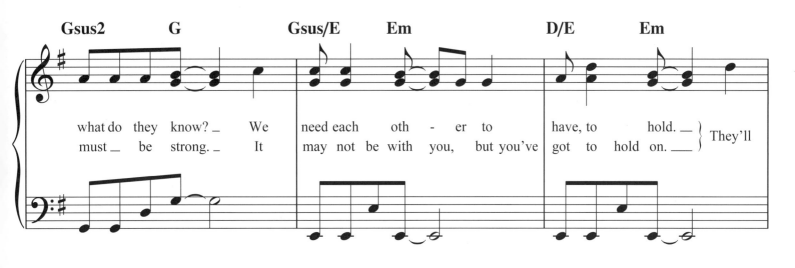

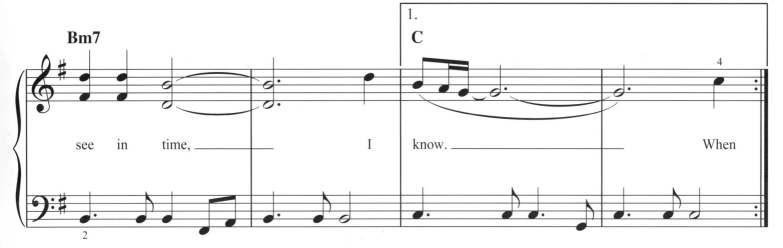

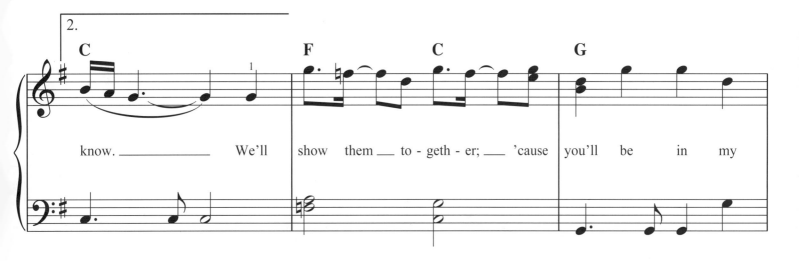

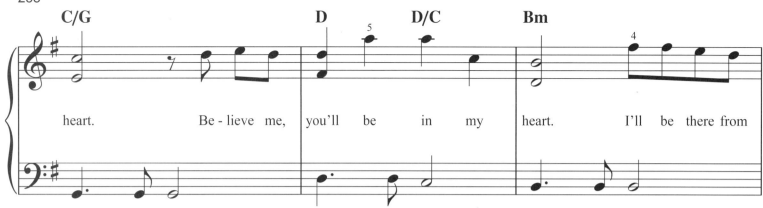

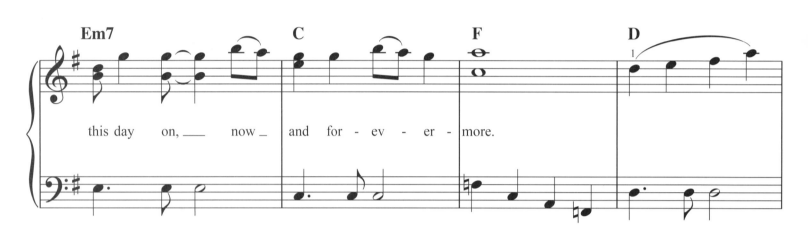

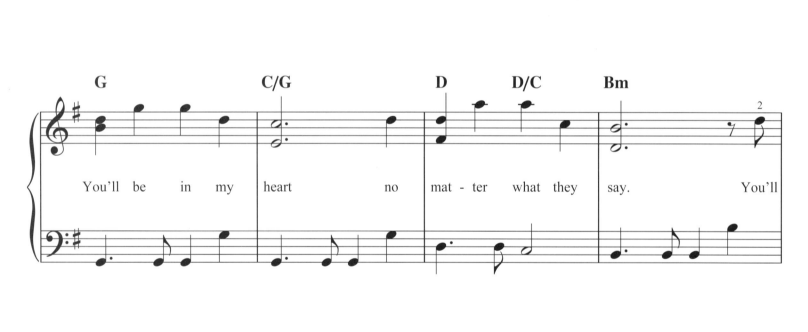

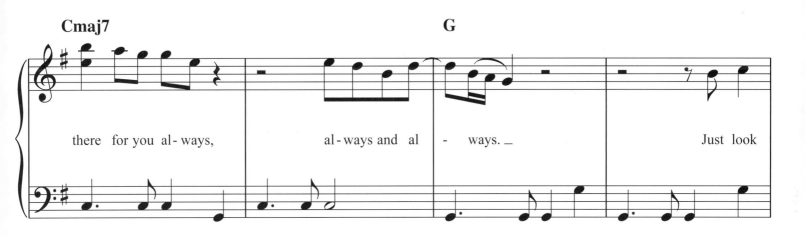

YOU'RE WELCOME

from MOANA

Music and Lyrics by
LIN-MANUEL MIRANDA

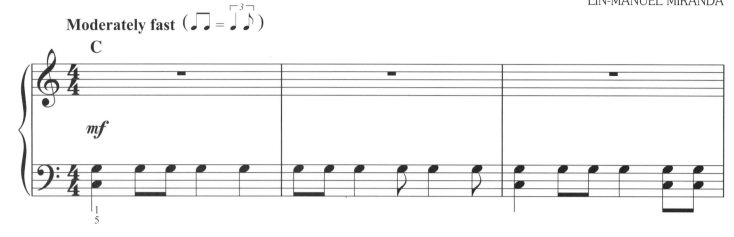

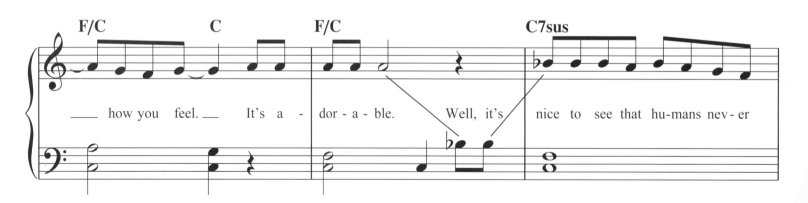

change. O - pen your eyes. Let's be - gin. Yes, it's real - ly

me, it's Mau - i. Breathe it in, I know it's a lot; the hair, the bod,

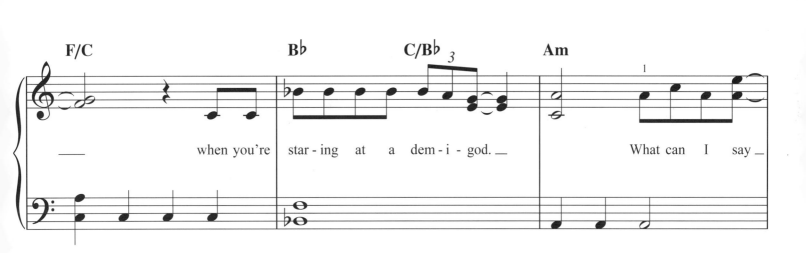

when you're star - ing at a dem - i - god. What can I say

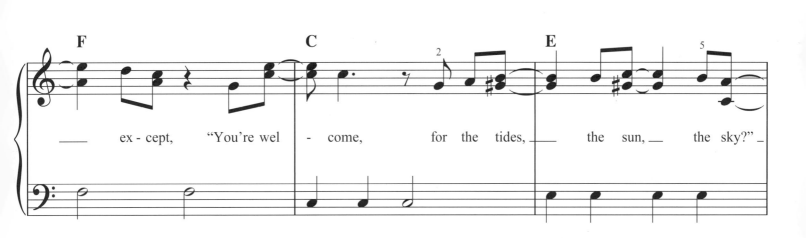

ex - cept, "You're wel - come, for the tides, the sun, the sky?"

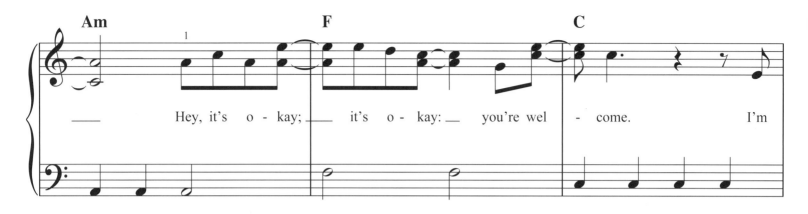

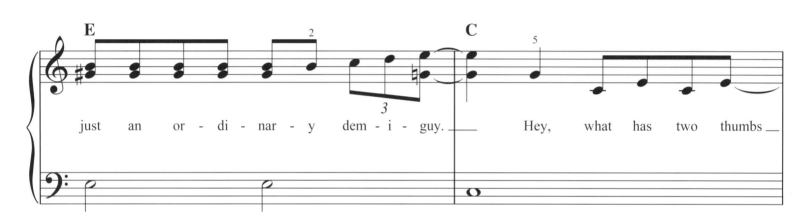

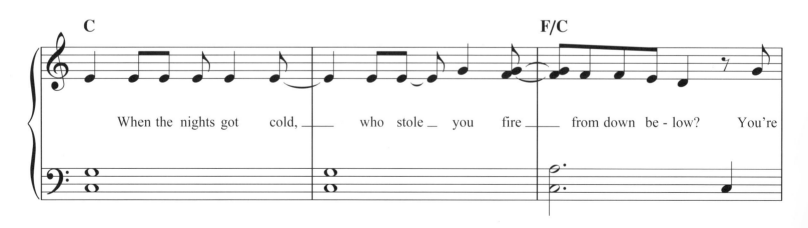

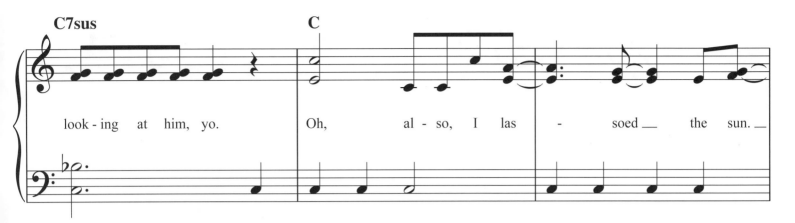

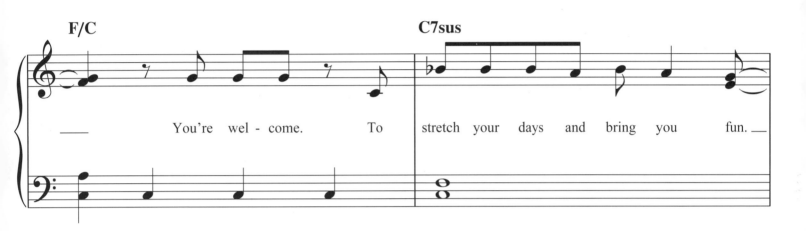

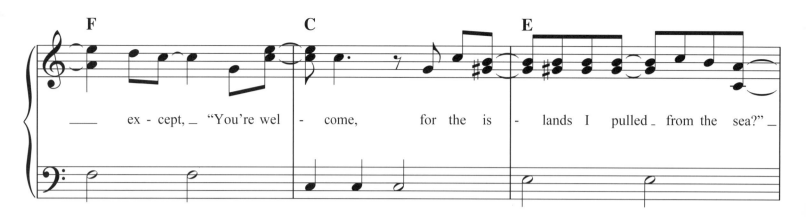

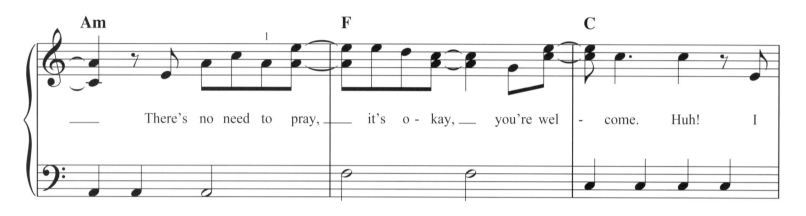

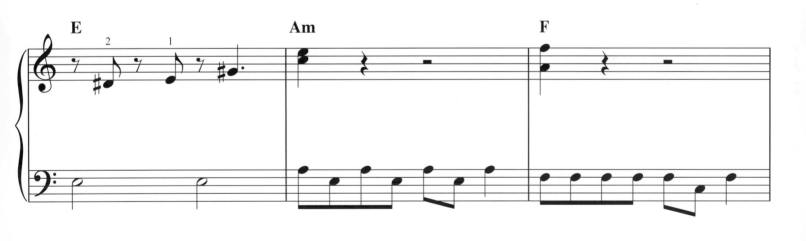

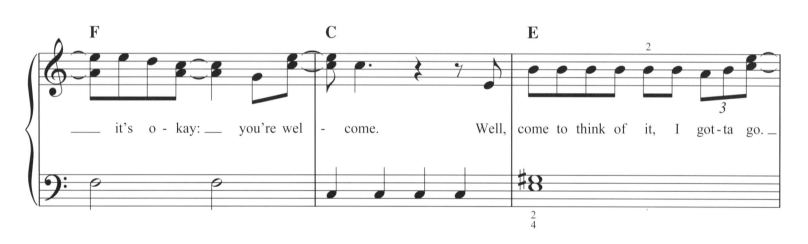

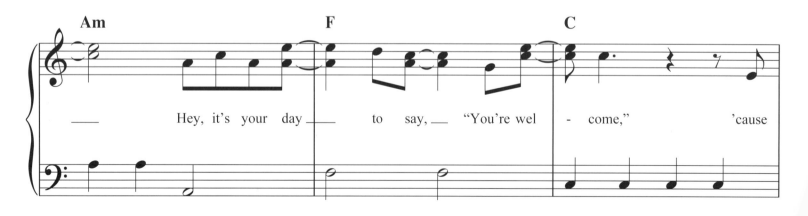

I'm gon-na need that boat. I'm sail-ing a-way, a-way. You're wel-

-come, 'cause Mau-i can do ev-'ry-thing but float! You're wel-

-come! You're wel - come! And thank you.

8vb

Additional Lyrics

Rap: Kid, honestly, I could go on and on.
I could explain ev'ry nat'ral phenomenon.
The tide? The grass? The ground?
Oh, that was Maui, just messing around.

I killed an eel, I buried its guts,
Sprouted a tree: now you got coconuts!
What's the lesson? What is the takeaway?
Don't mess with Maui when he's on a breakaway.

And the tapestry here in my skin
Is a map of the vict'ries I win!
Look where I've been! I make ev'rything happen!
Look at that mean mini Maui, just tickety
Tappin'! Heh, heh, heh,
Heh, heh, heh, hey!

ZERO TO HERO
from HERCULES

Music by ALAN MENKEN
Lyrics by DAVID ZIPPEL

Driving 4

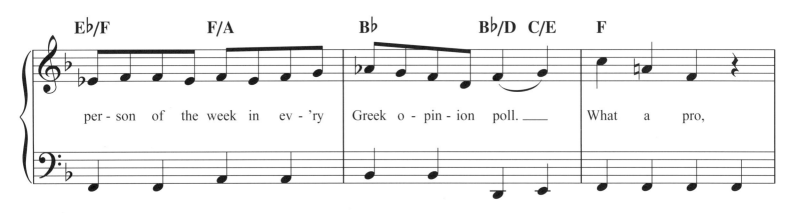

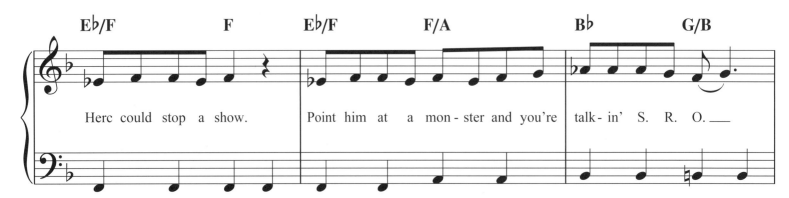

He was a no___ one, a ze - ro, ze - ro. Now he's a hon - cho,

he's a he - ro. Here was a kid___ with his act down pat. From

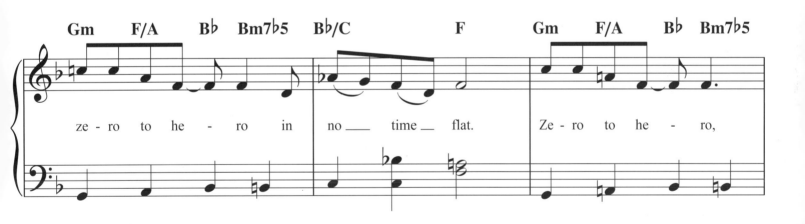

ze - ro to he - ro in no___ time___ flat. Ze - ro to he - ro,

just like that. When he smiled___ the girls went wild___ with

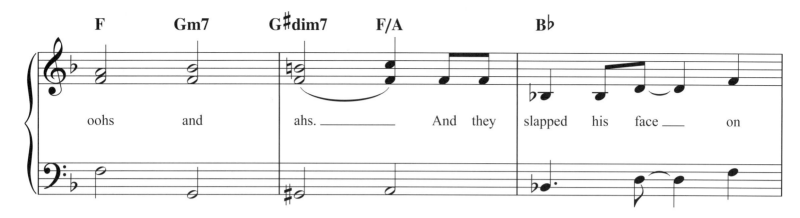

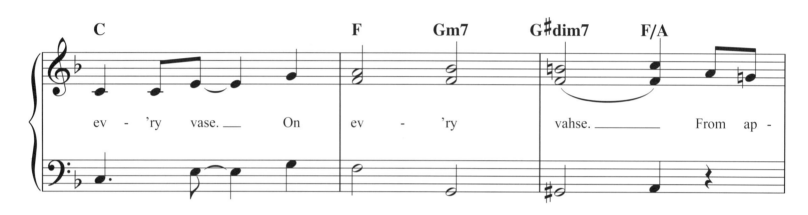

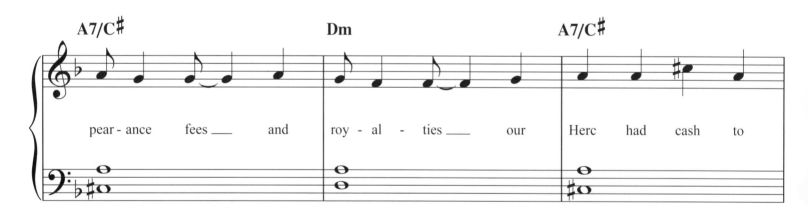

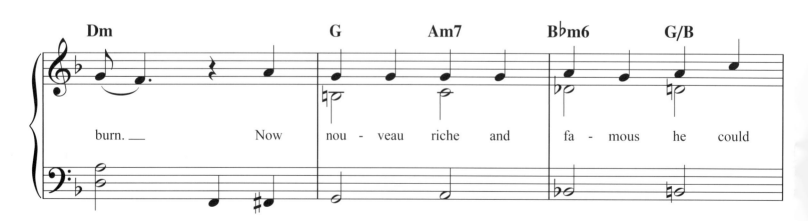

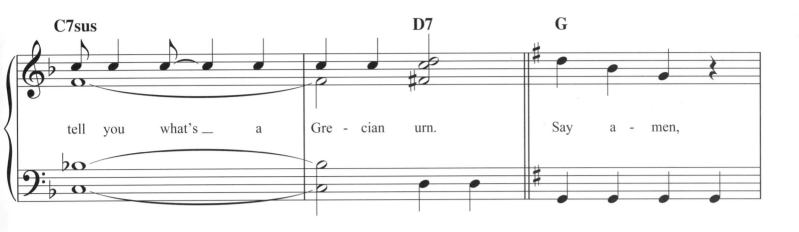

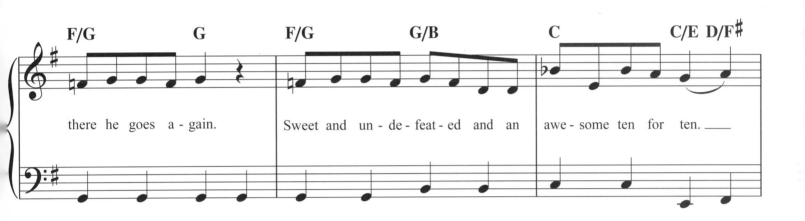

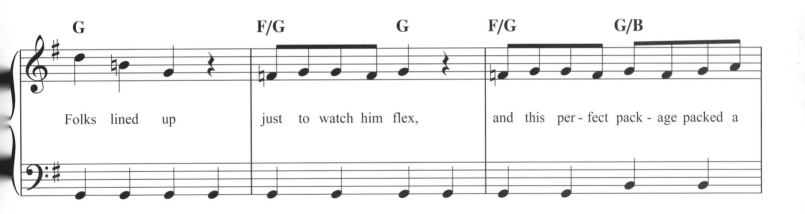

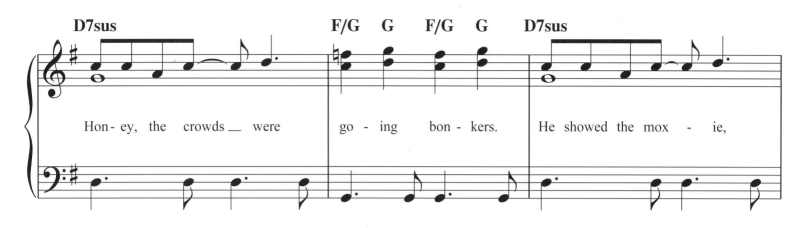

Hon - ey, the crowds __ were go - ing bon - kers. He showed the mox - ie,

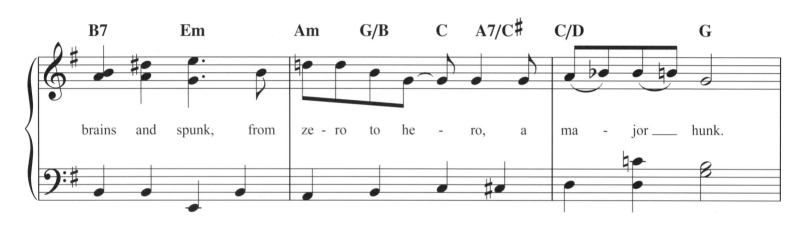

brains and spunk, from ze - ro to he - ro, a ma - jor __ hunk.

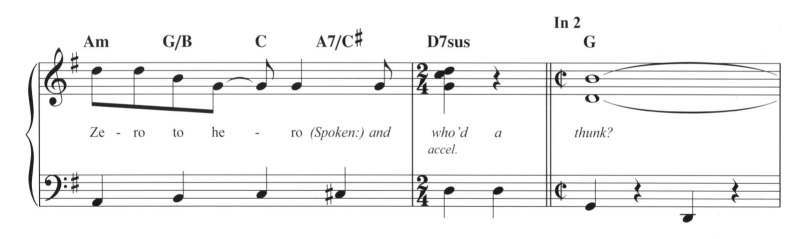

Ze - ro to he - ro *(Spoken:) and* *who'd a* *thunk?*
accel.

In 2

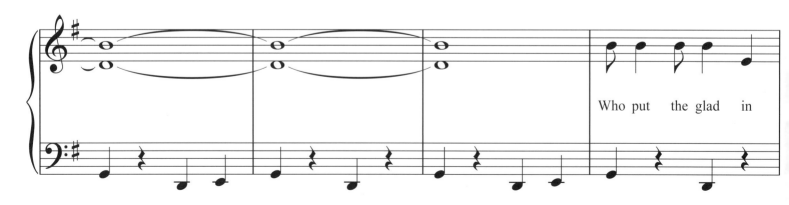

Who put the glad in

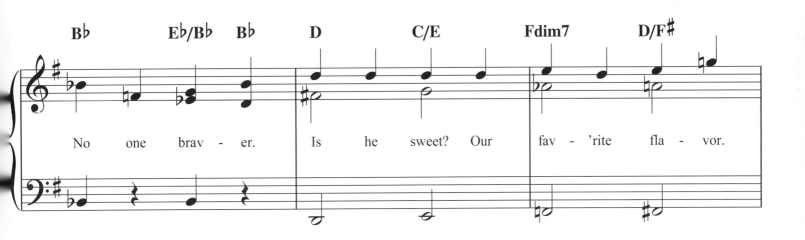

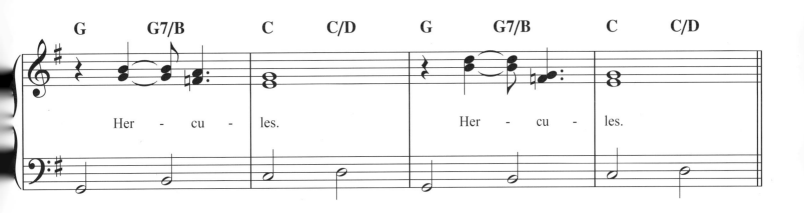

254

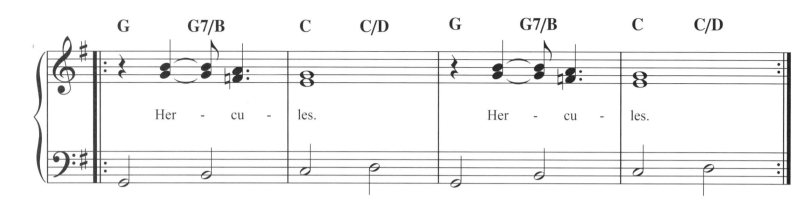

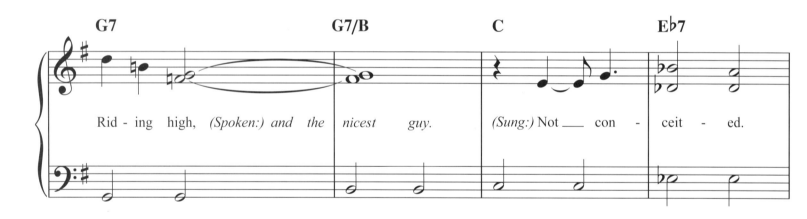

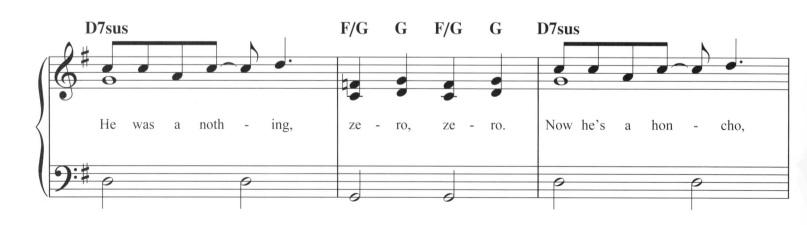

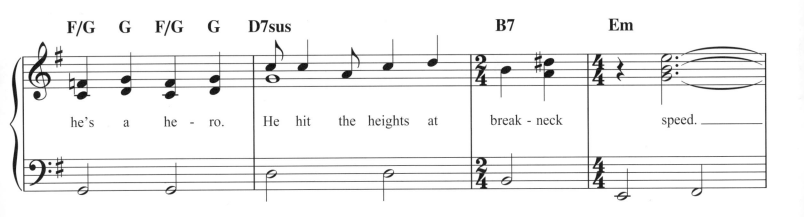

F/G G F/G G   D7sus   B7   Em

he's a he-ro.   He hit the heights at   break-neck   speed. ___

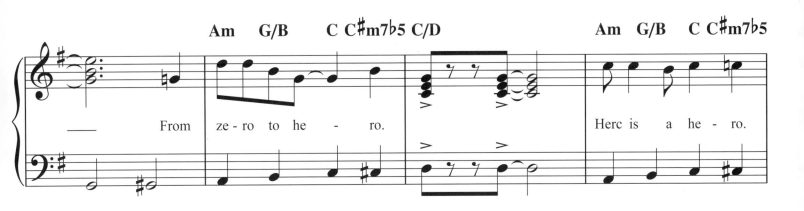

Am G/B   C C♯m7♭5 C/D   Am G/B   C C♯m7♭5

___   From ze-ro to he - ro.   Herc is a he - ro.

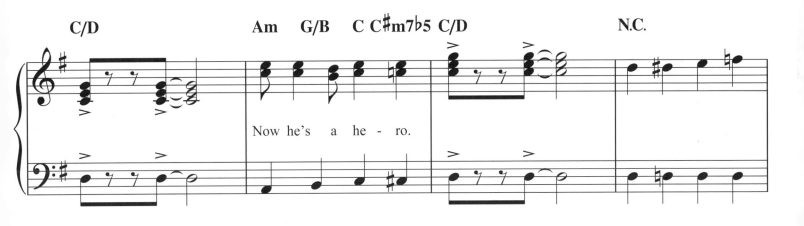

C/D   Am G/B   C C♯m7♭5 C/D   N.C.

                 Now he's a he-ro.

                                          G

UNDER THE SEA

from THE LITTLE MERMAID

Music by ALAN MENKEN
Lyrics by HOWARD ASHMAN

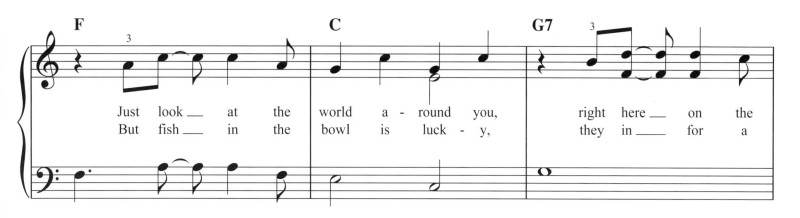

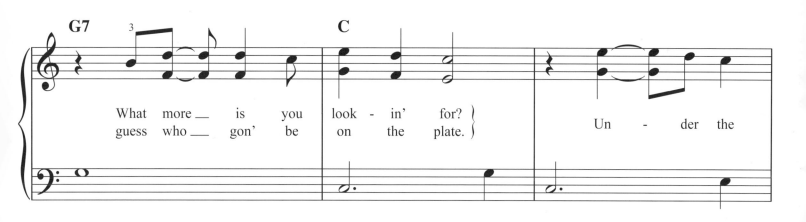

258

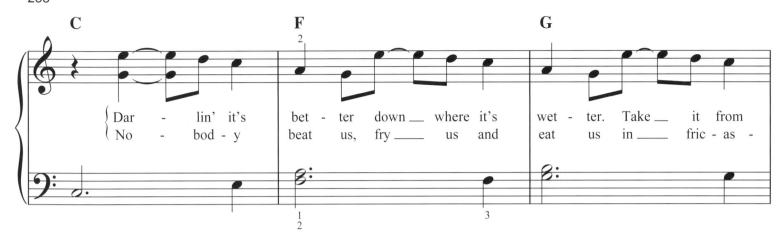

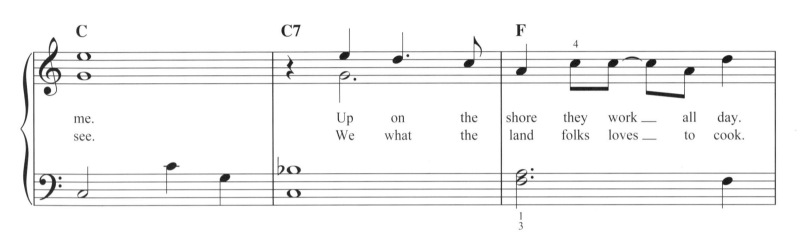

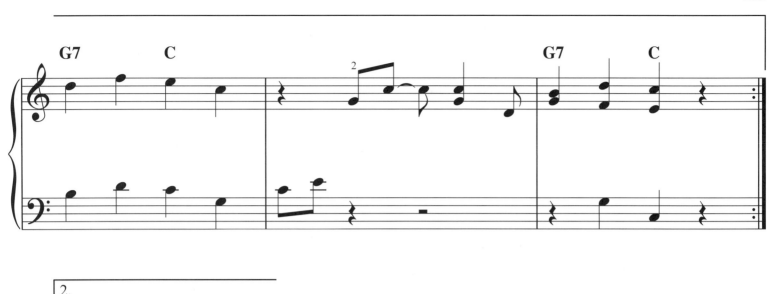

sea.   Un - der the   sea.

Since life is sweet here we ___ got the   beat here nat - u - ral -

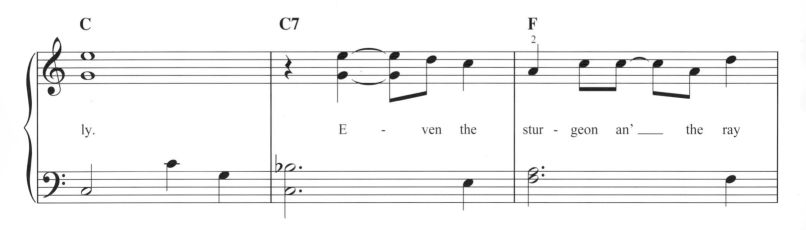

ly.   E - ven the   stur - geon an' ___ the ray

they get the urge 'n' start ___ to play. We got the

spir - it, you ___ got to hear it un - der the sea.

The newt play the flute. The carp play the harp. The

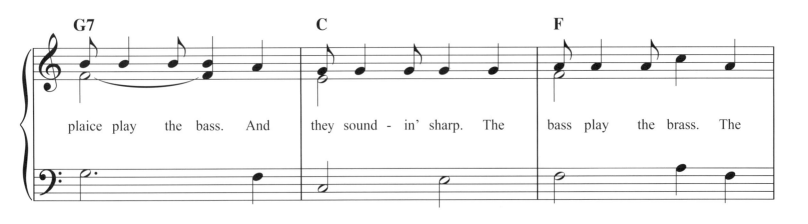

plaice play the bass. And they sound - in' sharp. The bass play the brass. The

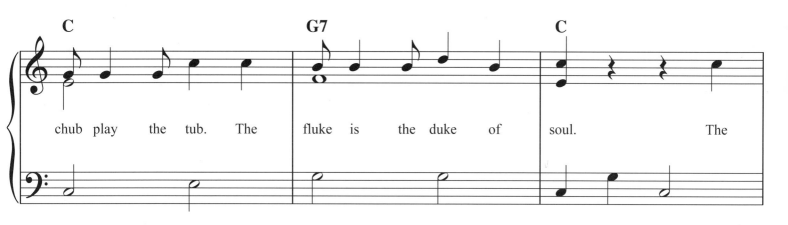

chub play the tub. The fluke is the duke of soul. The

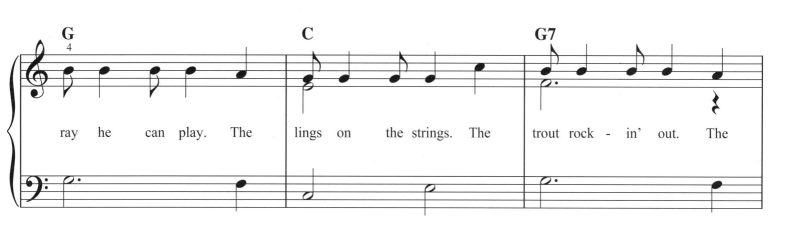

ray he can play. The lings on the strings. The trout rock - in' out. The

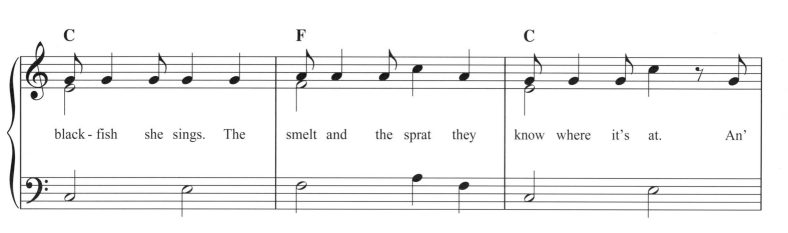

black - fish she sings. The smelt and the sprat they know where it's at. An'

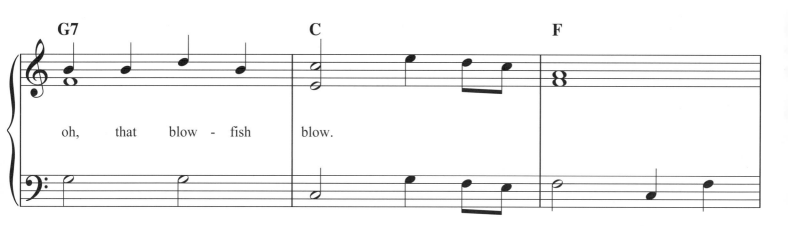

oh, that blow - fish blow.

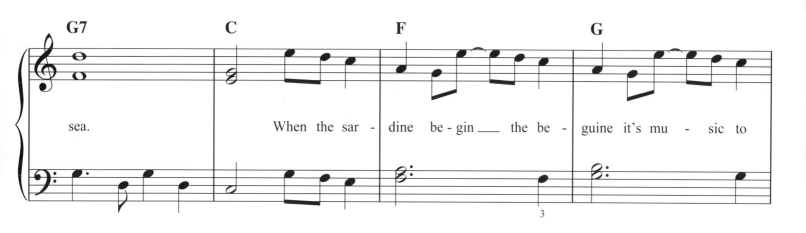

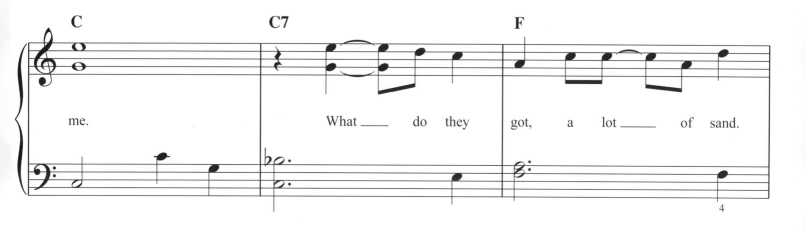

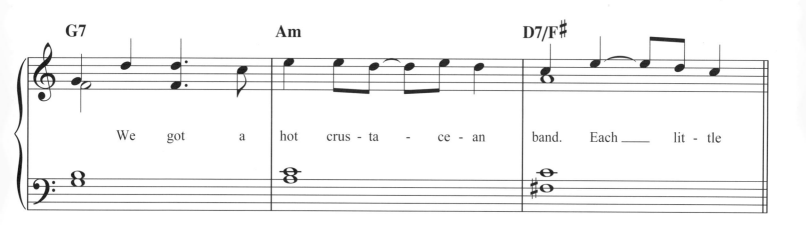

clam here know — how to jam here un - der the sea. Each lit - tle
slug here cut - tin' a rug here un - der the sea. Each lit - tle

snail here know — how to wail here. That's — why it's hot - ter un - der the

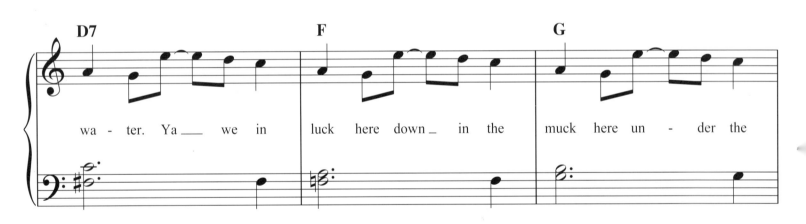

wa - ter. Ya — we in luck here down — in the muck here un - der the

sea.